SUPERLUMINAL
CHANGING THE ARROW OF TIME

L KERR

My son once told me that he would love it if magic were true; if there could be strange creatures and people with superpowers. This book makes me think that maybe there is. John faces inner struggles in an ever-expanding universe. He is propelled through timeless dimensions, meets dark forces, and is confronted with the reality of his own nature. The author made me want to know his story, and she didn't disappoint with her mystical story of darkness battling against the Light. I loved this tale; I think you will too.

Michelle van Rensburg – *Actor, playwright, director*

To Chrissie

May you be
blessed in everything
you do this year

SUPERLUMINAL

CHANGING THE ARROW OF TIME

L . K E R R

ECHAO
MEDIA

This book is dedicated to Maes, a writer in the making. To Elouise and Angus – anything is possible.

Acknowledgments

Many thanks to all the people who supported me through the journey of writing this book. I could not have done it without you. The author does the writing but the team makes the book.

Special thanks to Sandra Massie who read all the early drafts and spent endless hours helping redraft and refine the manuscript.

Thank you Julia Maxfield, you gently but firmly encouraged me through constructive editing and cheering me on to keep writing. I can't wait to read your novel.

Rachel Rennie, for never giving up on me and for pushing when I think I've no more to give.

Jess Kandula, your input has been invaluable.

To Gerry West, thanks for all your advice and practical help.

James Andrews, a talented graphic designer and technical adviser. You have been full of ideas and a great support. And a valued friend.

To all my wonderful family, especially my husband and best friend, Brian. We've had an interesting time exploring and visiting locations in the book. And we know the big secret when things get tough – that love never fails.

Prologue

Superluminal. Changing the Arrow of Time

Time is like an arrow travelling along a predictable forward path along the speed of light. The second law of Thermodynamics demands that time will eventually reach its target, where deterioration will bring everything to the end. The Omega Point.

The prophet Daniel was given clear insight into the nature of time, then told to seal up the scroll until the end of days, when a great mystery will unfold to the people of the earth.

One will arise who seeks to change the laws of time.

And he shall think to change the times and the law; and they shall be given unto his hand until a time and times and the dividing of times. Daniel 7:25 KJV

The law cannot be changed unless something *Superluminal* comes into force. An energy that is faster than the speed of light.

Chapter 1

The brown paper parcel

John watched his wife as she struggled to climb the last few metres to the summit of the Scottish mountain. Over her left shoulder John could see Brodick Castle – now a pinprick, nestling into the trees in the lush green landscape far below.

Sarah loved her homeland. She called it, "A land shaped by glaciers and a people forged in the fires of hardship and many battles." Today though, it looked like the steely determination ingrained in her soul was being challenged to the limit.

Unashamedly, John teased Sarah as she held out her hand for support. "C'mon old girl, let me help you up."

He tried to kiss her.

"Hey! Less of the old – if you don't mind!" Her face shrunk into a scowl, but this soon passed as she stepped onto the familiar rocky outcrop. The stunning peak took her breath away. "No time to waste being grumpy," she said.

"It's great to be first for a change," John stated smugly.

Every year a similar scenario played out: no matter how hard he tried, Sarah was always waiting for him to catch up.

She pulled a face at him. "Okay, I get it. You bagged this one. Perhaps I am losing my grip."

"Never!" John wrapped his arms around her. "I'm just reaching my peak! No pun intended." John lifted her tiny body and swung her around triumphantly.

Most years, as they made their annual pilgrimage, they would reach the top to discover the peak shrouded in mist. On that day, however, it was a clear sunny day, and the panoramic views were spectacular from Goatfell – the highest peak on the island of Arran.

Oh boy, this is a special day, John thought. *Not only have I reached the summit before Sarah – I've got her all to myself.*

It was the first time they had been truly alone together in seventeen years. Their son was away on a school trip, and although he missed Josh and loved him dearly, secretly, he was happy to have Sarah's undivided attention. He wasn't exactly jealous of his son but he looked forward to spending time alone with his wife.

He pulled out a hip flask, nodding his head in her direction. "Tea," he jested, as he poured out a traditional shot of whisky to celebrate another conquest of their mountain. It felt like the old days as they giggled and shared their day of freedom.

"Hey, look! A golden eagle," Sarah shouted excitedly. They watched, hypnotised, as the golden-winged king-of-birds glided on the thermals far above the craggy peak of the mountain. John spread a blanket on the ground, and they sat amongst the dwarf juniper and sweet-smelling heather and passed a few hours chatting about nothing in particular and drinking in the glorious panoramic vistas.

It was one of those super-clear days when the distant isle of Ireland drew magically closer. All in all, it was a perfect day for them – until Sarah cried out.

"Help me; I can't get up. My legs are numb!"

John began to laugh but stopped abruptly as he saw the terror behind her eyes.

For the last two days, he'd set up camp next to the phone in the living room. On Sunday, he'd dragged a duvet from his bed and waited for the hospital to call.

He chided himself again that he hadn't noticed the signs, or more accurately – he'd decided to ignore them. Embarrassingly, the darker side of his nature, and his primal urge to dominate, had surfaced on that climb. It hadn't occurred to him that there was anything wrong with her. He was too busy stroking his fragile ego. Truthfully, he'd been gloating, that for the first time, he'd beaten Sarah to the summit. As he played the scene over in his mind, he recalled that she was unusually short of breath, and her skin normally pink and glowing with health – looked pale and clammy. In hindsight, it was obvious that she had wanted to preserve that day forever – because she knew they would never return.

That day was now etched in his memory as the worst day of his life. Sarah was unable to climb down the steep descent.

Strangely, the Mountain Rescue Team arrived within minutes of his phone-call. Two strong young men appeared behind them, immediately taking charge. The one with the dark hair swept up in a ponytail, bent down to talk to Sarah. She seemed comforted by whatever he said as he carefully strapped her to a stretcher.

"Aren't you going to call a helicopter? This is an emergency!" John yelled.

The light-haired rescuer calmly replied. "Oh, don't worry John we have our own wings – we'll be down before you know it."

Exhausted, Sarah was out of it, as she buried her head

under the blood-red blanket.

There was no explanation for what happened next. Somehow, they were transported down the mountain in a moment. *Has time shifted?* John shook his head. *What just happened?* He put it down to the trauma of their situation, but as Sarah was being transferred into the ambulance, John turned to thank the men – they had disappeared.

The phone rang for some time before John roused from his daydreaming. Steadying himself, he tentatively lifted the receiver.

He was expecting to hear from one of the medical staff at the hospital, but a stranger's voice cut across his concern for Sarah.

"Hello Mr. Kayin, you don't know me, but I would like to meet with you to discuss a business opportunity, and –" John slammed the handset onto the cradle.

"Damn call centres!" he shouted into the empty room.

The caller persisted. "Mr Kayin, please don't hang up. I know that that you are upset because your life is in turmoil just now, so why don't we –"

"What did you say, how do you know that I . . .?" John froze. "This is crazy!"

Thirty seconds later, the caller rang again. John looked at the phone in dismay. "Oh God, the word is out." The university had promised to be discreet. McPherson, the principal, had genuinely sounded apologetic, but he had nevertheless suspended his employment for six months pending the investigation.

Annoyingly, the caller persisted. This time John picked up the receiver and aimed at the wall, screaming, "take that you damn intruder and stop prying into my life!"

The phone slid down the wall crashing into Sarah's

favourite family photograph, landing on the polished oak floor, with the sound of metal and glass grinding.

Although he knew deep down that it was wrong– illogical even – in that moment, he felt elated because he'd needed someone or something to blame. A few minutes later, however, his manic laughter stopped abruptly. Shockingly, he realised, that like the photograph, his family seemed trapped between the shards of glass and twisted metal.

He slumped into his favourite seat, remembering the day he had dragged Sarah around countless shops to find the perfect chair. He recalled how she had chosen the soft beige material, but how he had insisted on the dark green leather Chesterfield; the wing-backed type. He liked the way the buttons held the leather tightly in place. *It makes me feel safe.* He had never officially been diagnosed with OCD but had all the symptoms. They had negotiated for some time, but neither would back down, so eventually, they had come to a compromise. He got his chair, and Sarah cleverly managed to arrange the furniture to accommodate it. It was the anomaly in the room, but it gave Sarah great pleasure from time to time to tease him about his *manly chair,* sitting proudly amongst the pastel cushions and soft fabric couches.

Looking down at the blasted chair now, he saw a prison holding him hostage as he watched daytime TV. Something unfamiliar to him. Today, however, he found himself mesmerised by the strange characters on the screen. And the overly dramatic plots were beginning to make sense. He felt increasingly compelled to watch. *Somehow it's good to know that someone else is in a worse state than me,* he admitted, as he sobbed into one of Sarah's cushions.

He couldn't understand.

I just want my life back again to the way it was. Why is this happening to me?

Throughout the day, he found himself experiencing strange little episodes. Moments where he felt he was losing consciousness. Maybe he was going insane?

Is this what it feels like to have a breakdown? Who even cares? He just couldn't bear to be awake with the monsters in his mind.

He closed his eyes, trying to think of something good. An image of Sarah formed before him. She was radiant – it was the day she told him that she was pregnant with their son, Josh.

The following sixteen years of their marriage had been blissful. They were in love.

It was at the end of the seventeenth year when everything changed. Some curse had been released over his family, altering their lives forever.

His thoughts turned again to Sarah's plight. Not long after they entered the doctor's office, John knew that malevolent forces were at work – crashing through the gates of his soul. He couldn't think straight. A score of voices bombarded him. *How could this happen to Sarah? Isn't she strong and healthy? Why her? It should have been you! God! She is a health fanatic. She runs every day; watches her diet.*

John was unaware that he had once again descended into a dark pit. He looked up and realised that the consultant and Sarah were staring at him.

". . . what?" He shook his head violently as if somehow this would stop his swirling thoughts. He had no memory of how they got to the hospital.

It took him a few moments to find his way back. Looking towards the doctor and back towards Sarah, he paused.

Predictably she seemed unruffled, receiving the news

with a resigned nod of her head.

Sarah had known for some time that something was very wrong. Muscle weakness and little episodes of numbness with temporary paralysis had warned her that her body was in a crisis. Strangely, she was relieved to discover that her conclusion was correct. The doctor was merely confirming the diagnosis. After doing extensive research, she was pretty sure that she had all the symptoms of ALS. A disease that would slowly rob her of all that made her human until it finally terminated her life.

She looked at her husband and saw him crumple – only on the inside though, she knew the signs.

John's mind was darting about again. After receiving news that Sarah was involved in a car crash, he rushed to the incident, imagined her dead and his world collapsing. Relief flooded over him when he reached the scene of the accident, and Sarah ran towards him shaken but unhurt. They fell into each other's arms, relieved, and Sarah had given him a beautiful night of love after her near miss.

John now wondered if that day was a premonition of what was to come?

Back in the room, still bound to his chair by some invisible cords, he could feel dark forces pull him towards oblivion. There was no way to resist. For the second time in his life – John wept. His whole life was fragmenting. Sarah was dying, and his son was missing. He could feel sharp splinters breaking his mind and ripping his internal flesh. *Thank God. The day is almost over,* he thought. Relieved that he could pull the world off his weary body and collapse into the cradle of darkness again.

As an unwelcome first light appeared, he knew that he would have to start all over again.

Oh, how he wished his heart would give up the mechanical beat after beat.

Then something surreal crept into him unaware. His mind stopped racing. At last, silence! That deep place where he withdrew from the world. He'd struggled with anxiety and a tendency towards depression for most of his life.

Where is Sarah now? She is the only one who can work the magic and pull me out.

A single word floated into his mind. *Suicide*? *No*! Surely that was for the weak. The ungrateful. It was a crime against humanity! Still, he gave himself permission to contemplate the possibility. Curiously, it was a relief to have something different to occupy his thoughts. A little distraction.

As he played with the idea, he felt the sickening dread that had tied knots in his stomach begin to unfurl. For the first time, he could empathise with those who cut themselves to relieve the pressure. *Strange*, he thought. *Is it possible that allowing the pain to bleed can bring relief to the tortured soul?*

John allowed himself to ponder the choices before him. Each one presented as the *easy way out*, yet as he did with everything, he meticulously analysed every scenario and concluded that they were all flawed. Thoughts of Sarah and Josh weeping over his dead body gave him the chills.

As he dozed off in the winged chair dreaming of escape, his mobile began to buzz relentlessly.

A text message lit up the screen. "Please don't be disturbed, Mr. Kayin. I genuinely have good news for you. Meet me tomorrow at 10am." John read the message over and over, looking for some clues. He looked at the clock with a slight upward shift in mood.

Maybe?

Fourteen hours!

At least the message served as a temporary respite from the many ways to commit suicide. Perhaps it was a genuine call? Or more likely some kind of entrapment. Some dodgy newspaper reporter looking for a juicy story about a predatory college lecturer.

The doorbell rang. Interrupting his thoughts about the murky waters of the gutter press.

Peering through the wooden blind slats, he could see the outline of a delivery driver holding a package. Relieved: he cautiously opened the door to face an older distinguished-looking gentleman. Intrigued, he took the parcel from the driver, who nodded before walking back to the car – leaving John speechless.

For the first time in many months, John allowed himself a few moments of excitement. He surveyed the parcel carefully as he placed it on the coffee table. It was meticulously wrapped in thick brown paper; the string tied in a carefully crafted knot.

He knew that he was procrastinating. Was he the brunt of a very cruel joke?

Inhaling deeply, he could wait no longer and frantically tore open the parcel. As the crisp brown paper released its contents, John fell to his knees, eyes staring in disbelief as he tentatively picked up a new bundle of money. A great deal of money, fresh from the bank. Like a trained bank teller, he deliberately counted the notes. *Unbelievable! Fifty thousand pounds*! After several confusing moments of trying to digest what had just happened, he feverishly ransacked the brown paper and found a note. He stared at it for some moments before unfolding the paper.

Meet me tomorrow at the Alpha Towers. My driver will pick you up at 9am. By now, I hope you are aware that this a genuine business deal, and I guarantee that it is all above board. If you decide not to keep this appointment, simply return the package to the driver tomorrow.

Reading the note repeatedly, John searched for a reason to turn down this extravagant offer.

Thirteen hours!

For the next two hours, he paced the room. Recently, his chaotic mind had ruled over him like a separate entity. Now, he knew what he had to do. Moments later, exhausted, he fell into bed.

Chapter 2

The Proposal

After a strangely peaceful night – although he hadn't slept much – John arose early.

He pondered whether to wear a suit or casual clothes, deciding, in the end, to go smart. Pulling out his sombre grey suit from the back of the closet, he carefully appraised himself in the mirror. *Not too bad*, he whispered under his breath, *considering the state you were in yesterday!*

Feeling more confident and looking a bit more respectable, he began to focus on the events of the day. Pausing to consider his options – he knew deep down that he'd nothing to lose. *Who knows, maybe it's time for my lucky break?*

Frowning, he glanced in the mirror once more, aware that he was falling into the trap of superstition – with irrational thoughts of fate, dark powers, and luck – but quickly swept these concerns aside.

The driver arrived promptly to pick him up. After George formally introduced himself, he remained silent as he whisked John onwards to the Alpha Towers through the busy London traffic.

John became aware of the heavy thudding in his chest. A cocktail of stress hormones was coursing through his veins. Fear and excitement were battling for his attention. His neurons were firing signals alerting him. *I should run?*

Ignoring the advice, he decided it was too late. Turning to look out of the window, he felt compelled to lift his head to feel the warmth of the sun, forcing himself to switch off his negative thoughts.

Just then, George turned on the radio, filling the air with the beat of optimism. A small grin lifted one corner of his mouth as he listened to the Beach Boys sing out his answer: *"Good, good, good, good vibrations!"*

Five minutes later, they parked off-street in a large office campus, surrounded by three high-rises and a long low building, encompassing a central grassy park and a small parking lot.

George led him to one of the tall buildings, silently indicating that they should enter a glass lift.

John looked at the skyscraper and the glass structure looming precariously over him. The thought of riding the glass box made him feel nauseous; sweat began to run down the back of his neck. *How can this glass structure be fixed onto this wall?* He knew this time that the adrenaline coursing through his body was due to sheer panic. He'd suffered from an intense fear of tight spaces since childhood. This was a mystery to him as he had no recollection of any traumatic experience that could trigger his irrational response. *Damn it, I can climb mountains*!

Today, he resolved that he was going to conquer this childish behaviour. At the top of the tower, he forced himself to look down with steely determination.

Tentacles of death wrapped around his body, compelling him to fall.

"This way, sir." George's voice shook him from his morbid thoughts. He turned to look at George then paused for a moment to face his tormentor while silently making a vow to defeat his foe.

Refocussing, he turned his attention to the two intricately sculpted wooden doors that beckoned him to enter. What future was waiting for him behind the grand doorway carved with fierce looking lions and strange mythological beasts? He could not imagine but allowed himself to hope that his run of bad luck was over.

A mature woman opened the door then guided John into the grand sitting room.

He gasped, unable to find the right words to describe the apartment. *Beautiful, luxurious, palatial? or 'way out of my league?'* Whatever! It made him feel extremely uncomfortable.

The woman introduced herself: "Gloria . . . my name is Gloria. Would you like a drink?"

Not quite sure who this woman was, he hesitated momentarily, then knew instinctively that she was not his benefactor. Although smartly dressed, neither her clothes nor her demeanour spoke of wealth. Whoever owned the Penthouse, he reckoned, was loaded. Filthy rich!

"Why don't you have a look around the apartment while I make a fresh pot of coffee?" the woman said.

John complied with her offer, aware that she also felt uncomfortable. Reluctantly, he began to explore the huge internal hallway with its many doorways and beautiful works of art adorning every wall.

Cautiously opening a few of the doors, he was greeted with several exquisitely dressed bedrooms, a well-stocked library and a gymnasium. Although he had permission, he was reluctant to enter any of them. It was like he had been given the keys to an expensive art gallery.

What if I'm being watched? He looked around slowly, feeling uncomfortable and strangely guilty, so returned to the lounge before someone caught him prying.

After finding Gloria in the kitchen again, he felt a sense of relief and began to relax a little.

She encouraged him to step onto the small balcony. "Have a look through the telescope. On a clear day, you can see all the way up the Thames. It's spectacular!"

"Thanks, but I need to know who . . .", he was about to ask who he was there to meet when the door burst open, and a voice called out his name.

"John Kayin. It's a pleasure to meet you. Thanks Gloria, you won't be needed until later. Just leave the coffee in the lounge." Gloria replied, "Would you like me to arrange lunch or make a booking Mr. Kayin?"

John's mouth gaped open, but no words came out. The man smiled broadly as he shook John's hand.

"Yes, John, I see you are surprised that we share the same name. You are probably wondering if we are related. Well, indeed, we are." The stranger seemed excited to disclose this information.

John stared at the man, looking for some familiar traits. Something that would reassure him of their common ancestry; he found nothing. This man was of a different breed; aristocracy perhaps? He was well educated; spoke with the tongue of an academic, probably Oxford or Cambridge? He'd certainly not graduated from a local comprehensive school.

"Let's just say, we are distant relatives. We have so much to talk about. Let me reassure you, my friend, this is a day you will never forget. Why don't you pour yourself a coffee next door and I'll make some arrangements with Gloria!"

Flummoxed, John was unsure what he should do. He decided to obey, so he made his way towards a large sofa and sat down. Left alone for a few moments, John had some time to ground himself. Who was this man who shared the same surname? *Maybe he's a distant uncle come to give me some good news.*

His father had always been secretive about his family. In fact, John couldn't remember ever meeting anyone from his father's side. He only knew his mother's relatives. *Could it be news of a family inheritance? That would be too good to be true, surely not?* he pondered.

The mysterious man came into the room with such an air of confidence and certainty that John felt himself relax a little. It was good to have someone else in charge.

"Ah, John, let's start again. I intended to be here to meet you but there was a slight delay with my flight. Let me introduce myself properly. My name is Peter Kayin. I'm sure you are wondering why I asked you here." Without waiting for an answer, he continued "I see you have brought a briefcase with you, so I assume it contains the down-payment I sent you?"

John nodded. "I wasn't sure what to do with it." Glancing suspiciously at the briefcase, he realised that he hadn't left the money at his house in case he was being scammed. Perhaps this was a set-up and, they were planning to rob him and, then he would be in deeper trouble. His brief involvement with moneylenders gave him cause to be suspicious.

Sadly, he knew at that moment that he had lost his trust in people. Looking at the man presenting in front of him, he just hoped that Peter Kayin was a genuine relative, and hopefully, he would bail him out of his financial problems.

Peter sat across from him, poured himself a coffee, then turned his attention to the younger man. He was ready to offer an explanation. "Firstly, John, I admit that I enticed you here with the offer of a business deal. That is only part of the reason you are here."

John felt his hands begin to sweat, and his mouth dry

up. *Please let this be good news*!

Peter continued: "We have much to discuss, but first, let me explain some important conditions to you."

He paused to make sure John was paying full attention.

"My proposition to you is that you will remain here in the apartment for three days. I expect you to listen to everything I have to say. Then I will ask you to make a decision to join me by accepting my offer on Saturday at 3pm.

If you are in agreement, then we shall proceed to the next level. However, if you decide to walk away, you can keep the money with no strings attached. You will never hear from me again.

The last but very important condition is that if you leave any time before Saturday, you will forfeit the money. Is that clear, John?"

Anxious to please his benefactor, John nodded. "Yes. I understand. I'm ... just a bit ... surprised," he stammered. "I had no idea that I had a relative living in London." He was curious to find out more but felt way out of his depth.

"John," Peter addressed him in a serious tone, "there is no way I can begin this meeting without warning you!" Leaning forward, he continued, "everything you are about to hear will rock the very core of your being, changing all that you know or believe! I very much hope that you will stay and that we will have a great deal to celebrate. If, however, you decide to leave after hearing me out, you will be fifty thousand pounds richer. Whatever way you choose; you are a winner."

John attempted a smile, but this man intimidated him at every level. *What does he want with me? He's way out of my league – from a completely different social stream – we're miles apart. What could I possibly have to offer?*

"Now, John, I want to give you the opportunity to leave – minus the cash, of course. Or you can spend a pleasant few days listening to an old man. I believe this journey will change your life irreversibly. What I'm about to tell you will affect the whole of mankind. You need to confirm to me if you understand my conditions. Do you want a little time to think it over?"

"No!" John blurted out. "I just need to know that . . . I don't want to get into anything illegal. It's not some Mafia scam or . . ."

Peter laughed. "Oh John, this is way beyond the trivial pursuits of petty criminals. This is about powers in high places."

John gasped.

"I'd like to be completely honest with you from the outset because we know your current situation is unsustainable."

John looked at his hands in dismay, embarrassed that the man knew the story about his rapid descent into the murky world of loan sharks.

He had needed the money to pay for Sarah's expensive private healthcare. Sighing, he considered her prognosis by mainstream medical experts. *Terminal.*

His mind wandered back to the terrible day she was diagnosed. He thought that was the second worst day of his life but that happened a few days later when his only son Josh disappeared within 24 hours of being tested for the genetic disorder.

He was aware that he was descending down a familiar spiral staircase into despair. God! He'd just about secured a second mortgage on his house when the accusation came – out of nowhere. The girl in question was a peculiar, disturbed female who pleaded with him to upgrade her exam results. His refusal led to accusations of inappropriate behaviour towards her.

The ongoing journey took him through police visits, an impending court-case, and being forced to leave his job. The second mortgage was cancelled. John leaned forward, his head feeling weighty in his cupped hands.

Despair overtook him as he uttered: "What the hell have I done to deserve this?" John stood up to leave. At least he would still have his dignity; after all, he tried his best for his family. *Life is totally unfair*.

Peter read his thoughts.

"I can fix it for you, John. All the fragments of your life, every piece! And put them all back together. Not only that, but everything will be much better than before.

You see, John, you don't know much about how the world operates. The unseen forces. The powers that make or break you."

John felt queasy.

"What do you mean – you're not talking about good and evil, are you? Surely you are not asking me to believe in God?"

Peter surveyed the man in front of him, staring hard as if he were looking through him. He stood up and somehow took on the posture of an old sage, replying, "And so the story begins, John!"

"You are not going to spin me a yarn about being a messenger of a God – are you?"

John's accusation caused Peter to reply with a wry smile: "Not exactly, but we are getting a little closer to the truth, my friend. You see, John, I want us to take a brief journey through time – metaphorically, of course – to examine where we are now, and just how we got here." He added in an upbeat tone, "I'm talking about the human race, of course."

As Peter tried to lighten the mood, he could see that although John was restless, he was intrigued.

Picking up his coffee, Peter slowly sipped it, allowing John some time to absorb his words.

After a few minutes, he continued: "Let's be honest. Most people go through three score years and ten without too much concern about the greater truths. They go about their days living like ants, just looking for food and shelter and perhaps a little hedonistic activity to break the monotony. Some even manage to do good deeds for others, with a sprinkling of religion thrown in for good measure.

And then! We have *The Exceptionals* – like Einstein. What a beautiful brain, don't you think? Consider Leonardo or Michelangelo, both highly creative people – but what good are masterpieces to you when you are dead? My friend, the truth is, at best, humans procreate in the hope that their children will find a better way. They never do, and so the story goes on in the endless cycle of despair.

Don't you think it's time for change?"

John caught sight of himself in the mirror over Peter's shoulder. He looked ashen. This was not going at all the way he expected.

He couldn't think straight. This conversation was scaring him. "Do you believe in God?" he cried out.

The reply was emphatic. "Of course I do!"

"Right, that's enough; you really want me to believe that you are some kind of angelic being or a prophet sent from God to deliver a special message." John stood up. He looked at the briefcase and back to Peter. It was at times like this he wished he smoked.

Peter spoke in a calm, controlled voice. "Okay, I'll come clean, John. I was trying to break it gently, but I can see that you are finding it difficult to trust me. Let me start again. We will take the time to talk about everything. Just remember, you have nothing to lose. You just have to listen. That's all. Then you're free to walk away if you disagree. I give you my word; I will not force you into a corner.

It's important that you chose your own path."

John took his seat, seemingly reassured by Peter's honesty. He just had to keep his mind from over-reacting. *Keep your core together, don't let these crazy thoughts control you*, he repeated to himself.

It wasn't long before he came to a conclusion: *Anyway, I need the money!*

"As I said, I want to be totally upfront with you John. I want you to understand that not only do I believe in God, I also know that he exists.

However, I have chosen not to follow his ways. To put it simply, my *Proposal* is that there is another way for us to exist without God, and I want you to join me in that new world."

"What!"

John's head was spinning in confusion. Until today he had been a confirmed atheist, so if what Peter said was true, it upset his whole philosophical approach to life. Firstly, he would have to ditch everything he had believed for the past thirty-odd years. Then he would be expected to take part in some bizarre scheme to outwit a supreme being that he did not believe existed. That just made his head hurt!

Observing John for a few moments, Peter knew that the young man was wrestling with his last statement. "I can see that you are having difficulty wrapping your head around that, so let me put it another way. I am planning a new way for mankind to exist. A way that will bring you unimaginable wealth and power. Believe me, if you choose this way, you will have access to unlimited knowledge. Great as these rewards will be John, there is something far more exciting."

Peter hesitated for a few moments before he continued.

"You will never die, John, think about that. Not you, your wife, nor your son, Josh. You see, my dear friend, I possess the sacred key. We are about to open the door to *Immortality*!"

John couldn't decide whether to laugh or cry at this outlandish statement. What kind of proposal was this mysterious man offering him? None of it made sense. *Time for a reality check. Surely this must be pure fantasy. But why would this stranger arrange this meeting, then offer me money to go into battle against an unknown god?'* His thoughts were caught in the updraft of a whirlwind, feeling giddy; he couldn't find a place to land.

They sat in silence.

Eventually, John spoke. "I don't know how to respond, Peter."

"That's fine dear boy, take your time. It's a lot to take in."

John paced the floor for a while then sat down as he became acutely aware of reaching deep inside himself. Conversations were taking place inside his chest. It was different from the familiar fearful arguments in his head. This felt more like a mature debate. Like being in a courtroom where the future was being debated by a prosecutor and a defender, he had the unlikely role of the judge. Was this his soul he was listening to? He had no idea, but he liked the feeling of being in control.

What if I go along with this religious zealot for a few days? I'll have enough money to bale us out of debt. Three days and I'll be out of here. What other options do I have anyway? he reasoned. But still, he was hesitant. He looked steadily at Peter but could not read him. Could he trust this man? He seemed sane enough but his story was bizarre.

Peter interrupted his thoughts. "Look, John, I understand how this must sound. I hadn't planned to do this, but I am giving you the opportunity to leave now before we go much deeper. Perhaps I underestimated how difficult this would be for you. Go on, walk away now and look – you should just take the money. I know you need it, and I've got more than enough. Take it as a gift from a deeply concerned relative. There will be no repercussions, I promise you."

John closed his eyes, aware of the incredible gesture Peter had just made. He decided to end the debate in his internal courtroom. For the first time in two years, he felt that he was in charge of his own destiny. *The money is in the bag now. All I have to do is listen, and maybe some of this is true! What have I got to lose?* He sat down, committed to the next three days.

Peter smiled warmly at his new student. "Ah dear friend, I can see that you have made your decision. Are you with me?"

John agreed: "I'm with you, Peter, what do we do next?"

"All in good time, we have a busy schedule, but let me encourage you about where we are going with this. What you will learn in the next few days will be invaluable. Many people have been searching for this holy grail for thousands of years. Let me reassure you, what you are about to experience is for an elite group of people. I will be your mentor, and I'm going to teach you about how the world really works. I will introduce you to the powers that run this little planet, earth. You will learn about technological advances that are way beyond the reach of the masses. We have real science to guide us. Physical certainties. We now have the knowledge to create a new breed of humans."

Peter waited for the revelation to sink in.

"We are truly on the cusp of the next evolution of man.

Immortal man!"

John stood up again, hardly able to contain himself. Every cell in his body was firing with energy. He was elated. What did Peter say? This path was for the elite. Never in his entire life had he believed that he was special. In fact, until recently, everything he did was comfortable, predictable, and pretty much boring. He couldn't remember doing anything remotely risky – ever!

They talked for another few hours about the existence of God. John was fascinated by Peter's depth of knowledge. He shared information about powerful people in just about every nation in the world: from presidents to royalty. He talked about knowing members of clubs and societies that John had no idea existed.

John concluded that this man did indeed belong to some kind of elite group. Peter was obviously wealthy and powerful, so he couldn't fathom why this sophisticated, well-educated man was interested in him? They came from different worlds. Poles apart. The idea that John could be of any use to him seemed ridiculous.

Chapter 3

The Cure

Peter put his arm around the younger man's shoulders. "This has been a lot for you to take in, so let's have a break. I hope you've worked up an appetite. Come, let's eat." Peter directed John towards the dining room.

The room was exquisite, housing a huge table capable of seating at least thirty people.

Strangely, John felt intimidated again as he entered this room. Somehow the vastness of the space made his world feel small as if he could never really belong in this luxurious setting. He felt ashamed at his lack of achievement.

Peter sensed John's mood deflate. Encouraging him, he stated: "All of this could be yours one day!"

"What did you just –" John turned to look at Peter only to notice a copy of his favourite painting on the opposite wall. He inhaled deeply! Shrugging off an eerie feeling of deja-vu, he quickly gathered his thoughts as he expressed his surprise. "Wow! I'm feeling quite – I don't know what to say!

Peter turned to look at the painting.

". . . This is great a copy of the *Execution of Lady Jane Grey*. I can't believe it. The original hangs in the National Portrait Gallery. What am I saying! Of course, you know this." John exhaled with a long breath.

Peter responded with a hint of a smile. His face slightly distorted, turned to one side.

Lost in wonder, John felt quite overcome in the presence of this incredible painting. *Well, surely it is a very good copy*, he surmised. He was only vaguely aware of the food arriving and a feast being set up before them.

Spellbound, he continued to gaze at the painting, remembering the dozens of visits to the gallery, to stand and stare at the image of this youthful innocent woman.

"She reigned for six days as queen, barely eighteen years old. Her beauty was enthralling, her vulnerability tangible. Totally composed. She had accepted her fate," John whispered reverently.

Although a self-confessed atheist, spending endless hours with the painting was the closest encounter that he could ever describe as a spiritual experience.

There was something about the image that captivated him. What essence had the artist captured? It was more than a painting, deeper than a portrait. The golden frame held the secrets of an unseen world. A moment in time, frozen, and yet it was much more than that. Delaroche, the artist, had somehow caught a glimpse into the dying girl's soul.

"You know, Peter, this is the most viewed painting in the National Gallery. They can tell because they have to re-varnish the floor there more often. The wood gets worn down because people have to stop and look. They are transfixed."

Peter nodded as if this was the first time he had heard the story. He needed to help John feel special.

Breaking the spell, Peter asked, "Are you hungry?"

John realised he was ravenous as he hadn't eaten much for days.

"Try the meat; it's delicious Wagyu beef. Chef tells

me the cows are hand-reared in the best conditions. Indeed, they are treated like gods. Given the best food, comfortable quarters, and every day they are hand massaged to improve the tenderness of the meat."

Something flashed through John's mind. He glanced at *Lady Jane* but quickly dismissed the comparison.

The unlikely pair continued to discuss art, food, and world events as if this was an ordinary business lunch.

Slightly frustrated, Peter was aware not to overwhelm his protégé with too much too soon. He needed him on board and so allowed him this time to assimilate the morning's revelations.

Meanwhile, John was relieved to have some time to breathe. He had to get a handle on what was happening. It felt like he was living in another world, unfamiliar; alien.

Peter stood up, indicating that it was time to move, but John's legs would not allow him. He was desperate to know more but was aware that fear was beginning to engulf him once more. Aware that the story unravelling before him was surreal, he wondered if Peter was a crazy eccentric; even so, he felt compelled to find out more.

As they relocated from the dining room, Peter reflected on John's initial response to his plan. He knew that he was interested but nervous about the challenge before him. John wasn't going to be a pushover; indeed, he would have to draw on all his skills to convince this young man to join him. It was imperative that John made the decision without any major coercion; he would have to carefully lay out his plan without scaring him off. Peter reminded him that he could walk away at any time but pointed out the grand prize that awaited him.

He poured John a small brandy.

"I know it's early, but I suspect this has all been a nerve-wracking experience for you; I mean listening to my story. It's not for the faint-hearted. Only those with true vision and perception will understand."

John corrected his posture, sitting up straight and paying attention to his mentor.

Peter opened up the conversation again. "Let me ask you a question, John. I have explained that I believe in *The Maker*, but tell me why you do not recognise a Creator?"

Taken aback by this direct question, John had difficulty articulating his reply. Surprised, he discovered that he had no concrete answer to explain his atheistic philosophy but made a somewhat feeble attempt by offering *Darwin's theory of evolution*.

"Yes, it's the stock answer, but how does that prove anything?" Peter responded sharply.

John scrambled about in his brain for answers but his only explanation was that scientists had proven Darwin's theory and it was being taught in schools.

Peter persisted, "Yes, but tell me how you know that Darwin's hypothesis is true. What makes you live your life based on the premise that Darwin got it right?"

"It's science, isn't it? I don't know, I guess . . ." John's voice trailed off. "

Perhaps I can help you out, my friend; you believe Darwin because it's what you've been told. You've heard of the term *social control*. The school system is an excellent way of programming children. You know the drill. Repeat after me . . ."

Feeling ashamed by his lack of knowledge, John announced: "Well, I haven't seen any signs of a Creator."

"Haven't you?" Peter laughed heartily, "Well" he said in a superior manner, "we shall have to re-educate you, and that, my dear friend, we shall do tomorrow." He was aware that his pupil had reached a saturation point and looked a little dejected.

Peter changed the subject. He congratulated his student on his perseverance, indeed that he hadn't taken the money and run when he had the chance. They both laughed and John visibly began to relax for the first time that day. Looking John squarely in the eye, Peter shook his hand and spoke in a serious tone: "You are one of the luckiest men alive. So few have been chosen!"

No further explanation was given, but these words caused a ripple of excitement to surge through John's body. He almost cried.

"I have a little homework for you to read up on in preparation for tomorrow, but first, I would like you to go visit your wife. I think you need to see her today. You are going to be making major decisions that will affect your family. She needs to know."

Peter broached the next subject with some caution but tried to sound casual; he didn't want to alarm him. "While we are at the hospital, I would like you to see a specialist in genetics. He is a good friend of mine and will be working closely with us to treat your family. I guarantee that you are going to be very pleasantly surprised today.

We have excellent new treatments to help your wife – cutting edge technology. I hope you don't mind, but I've taken the liberty of making an appointment with him at five pm."

John wasn't really sure what Peter meant by that but decided not to ask just yet. He was having difficulty grasping Peter's *Proposal*, so he decided to let everything unfold as the older man saw fit.

He was relieved that he was going to see Sarah. The guilt was mounting as he hadn't seen her for three days. She would be worried. *How can I tell her that I was unable to pay last week's hospital bills?* He had been delaying the inevitable. If he wasn't able to pay, she would have to go back to the public healthcare system.

All he had to do was get through the next three days because he needed the money – the fifty thousand – tentatively waiting for him in that briefcase.

As for an appointment with a geneticist, he guessed it would make sense to find out more about the new treatment for Sarah and Josh that Peter was suggesting would help them.

Thirty minutes later, George dropped them off at the Galton building. A private hospital set behind an ornate brick wall, of whose existence most people would have been totally unaware. A modest but contemporary building, hidden behind a dense hedge of trees. The doorway was serviced by a controlled entry system. John pressed the impersonal buzzer, briefly looking at the security camera above his head. The door opened electronically.

Once inside, John was always welcomed personally by the receptionist and nurses. Staff nurse Joan Graham – one of his favourites – greeted him with a cheery smile while guiding him into Sarah's room. Peter discreetly stepped aside then made arrangements to meet with him later.

"How is she today, Joan?" John whispered as they entered the darkened room.

"She is exhausted now; I'm not sure if we should wake her just yet. She has just fallen asleep but you can sit with her for a while."

Lately, John felt a sense of dread when he visited his wife. It was difficult to see her deteriorate week by week, but recently every day brought bad news.

John sat down next to his wife. His mind ruminating on Peter's *Proposal*.

He wasn't sure what it was all about, but it wasn't

long before he concluded: "There's no other way!"

Guilt squeezed his heart once more. He could hardly bring himself to look at her. She looked so small and fragile lying on the bed surrounded by various wires and an array of fearfully invasive instruments. At least she was sleeping.

What would he say to her about his absence? Another contraction of guilt made his chest heave. He hoped she wouldn't wake up before the appointment as he needed to buy some time. Sitting quietly so that he wouldn't disturb her, he gazed at the woman in the bed; the only woman he had ever loved. *If there is anything I could do – anything!*

"God! If only I could swap places. Why don't you take this bloody awful disease away from her? She doesn't deserve it?" He spoke quietly under his breath. It seemed like hours before Joan returned and whispered, "Time to leave."

Relief swept over him, but still, he felt ashamed as he asked the nurse to tell Sarah that he had visited.

"Ah, John, how is Sarah today?" Peter asked with grave concern as they met in the corridor.

John looking forlorn, answered, "Deteriorating. She sleeps most of the time now."

As they walked together through a glass-walled corridor, John looked out into the central courtyard to the small garden where Sarah spent time enjoying the fresh air and sunshine.

He remembered the last time they were there together. She loved the outdoors, so this little space had become her sanctuary.

The architects had named it *The Garden of Hope*. It was set out in a minimalistic Japanese style. In the centre, facing her favourite seat, a small meticulously pruned

Acer tree welcomed them. They talked about looking forward to seeing the delicate, greenish-gold leaves change to put on their dramatic autumn show of vibrant shades of russet browns, reds, and orange.

Sarah loved this little tree because it reminded her of the one they had at home. It was always the highlight of the gardening year. A short but brilliant burst of colour, before the leaves suddenly fall, heralding in the colourless days of winter.

John looked at the tree and saw that autumn was calling. He could almost feel the leaves trembling. He hated winter, the dead season. He looked at the gravel beds, combed to perfection with ripples of undulating grooves forming patterns that somehow seemed to calm his soul. *There it is again. That word – soul!* He shivered as he realised he was beginning to use that word too often.

Peter introduced him to Dr. Savage: "An unfortunate name for a doctor." He laughed reassuringly as he ushered John towards an empty chair.

Peter sat next to him, pulling his chair nearer to John as a sign of support. They both looked expectantly at the doctor to explain what he could do for Sarah.

The sparrow-like man with a tiny body and a small beak-like nose looked anything but savage, John noted.

"Mr. Kayin, or may I call you John?" Not waiting for an answer, the specialist continued with a clinical aloofness practiced by many doctors. "Peter will have told you that I am a genetic researcher, and I also practice genetic medicine, so I am well qualified to discuss your wife's case. I have looked at her medical notes and see that she has been given the best treatment possible here at the Galton Hospital, but we know that her prognosis is not good. In fact, she is now in the terminal stage of life expectancy. John gasped.

All the hospital can do now is offer palliative care."

The colour drained from John's face as he was brought face to face with that word again. The only thing *terminal* meant was that the end was creeping up on them. He closed his eyes and tried to breathe.

"That's bad news, John, but let me tell you that there is hope. I am conducting a study with a small group of patients. We have had very positive results with a new treatment. It is not yet available to the general public but I believe your wife would make an excellent candidate for this study."

John swallowed hard. Could this be what he'd been hoping for?

"The treatment requires state-of-the-art technology and precise testing. We don't have all of the equipment at this hospital; however, we can start the treatment here to stabilise her, but she will have to be transferred to another facility where I have my laboratory.

We need very careful testing and strict monitoring of your wife's progress. She will receive 24-hour care from a dedicated medical and nursing team. Would you like me to explain in laymen's terms what we are planning to do?"

"It sounds expensive," John replied, aware that he couldn't afford last week's medical bill."

"No-one could afford this treatment, John – well, very few, but don't worry about that now, it has all been taken care of. Let me briefly explain the procedures to you.

We are going to treat the patient in two ways. Firstly, by genetic manipulation. You will be aware that Sarah's *DNA* is flawed."

John answered, "Yes, she has a genetic disorder and it's irreversible."

Dr. Savage continued: "We have perfected a method of editing genes. To put it simply, it is like an old-fashioned reel of film where the editor cuts and splices unwanted information in a movie. We intend to substitute her flawed genetic material with *Recombinant DNA* using *CRISPR Cas9 technology* to replace what is damaged. The new *DNA* gives the cells instructions to make healthy material.

The second treatment is more about restorative work that involves *Nanotechnology*. The best way to describe this is to think of micro robots targeting damaged parts of the body and repairing them, one cell at a time.

Dr. Savage continued to explain the intricacies of *CRISPR editing* and *Nano-medicine* but soon John was overwhelmed by science.

He didn't care. *I just want her back.*

He knew he should ask more questions, like where do they get the *Recombinant DNA,* or how does a person cope with tiny robots crawling about their body?

He looked at Peter for help about making such a decision because the whole idea sounded like science fiction.

Peter interjected. "This is cutting edge science, John. Mainstream laboratories up and down the country are experimenting with this technology. Students, from all over are ordering *DNA samples* online to find solutions for every disease known to man."

John looked perplexed.

"The truth is, John, we have been using these methods for a long time, so we are no longer in the experimental stages. Sadly, most labs are still focusing on animal experiments. We are way ahead of the game."

Feeling a great surge of excitement course through his body, John asked: "You mean that you can stop the disease?"

Peter's facial expression confirmed his answer.

"Let me put it this way. Sarah has nothing to lose now.

She is in the last stages of her illness. This is your only option to save her. It will not only stop the disease process, but more importantly, we can reverse the damage."

"You can stop the disease?"

"I have to make you aware of something. This treatment doesn't have government approval. Even so, we need you to sign an agreement. The medical team are risking their careers to do this. Your signature will confirm that you are complicit in this process. You asked me earlier if we were about to do anything illegal. Well, its not technically illegal, but some may say it is unethical. Do you understand that we have to keep this treatment top-secret? If it gets out, we will all be in trouble. Is that acceptable to you, John?"

Ignoring the ethical implications, John hastily signed the consent forms giving his permission to Dr. Savage to start Sarah's treatment. She would be dead within a few months anyway, or maybe sooner. *I can't live without her.*

The consultant spoke for another fifteen minutes explaining the procedures, but John just wanted to escape. He felt troubled by the decision he had just made but couldn't work out why. Surely he should feel relieved? He had just signed a document that would allow the medical staff to breathe life back into his wife's withering body!

Peter noticed John's restlessness.

"Come, my friend, I think we need to put your mind at rest. This has been a difficult decision for you. I know just the person you need to talk to."

The three men walked out towards another wing of the hospital. John was surprised when they entered a doorway into a small private apartment.

Peter went first into the sitting-room where a young couple was watching TV. The girl seemed genuinely happy to see them, greeting Peter then Dr. Savage with a hug and a kiss on the cheek. Peter introduced them. "Greta, David, this is the gentleman I told you about. I thought perhaps you could share your story and explain why you are here. Would that be alright?"

Greta motioned to John to come sit beside her, responding, "Of course it would be a pleasure. I haven't been outside this room for weeks or seen any new faces so it will be great to tell someone my story. I know it's for my benefit to be quarantined just now, but I'm feeling a bit stir-crazy." The girl said this in good humour, with no hint of complaint – just stating a fact.

Greta began to relate her story to John, explaining that she had arrived at the clinic six months before. She stopped for a moment, her eyes filled with tears as she turned sideways to look directly into John's eyes. "I was very ill and had to be carried in by the ambulance crew. My vitals were all shutting down. There were no more treatments and no more medicines; I had come to an end and had entered the hazy world of palliative care. I was twenty-five years old and I hadn't even lived!

There was so much I wanted to do, but fate had stolen my future. My family helped me prepare for death. I wasn't really afraid, but it hit me hard when they started talking about what kind of funeral I would want. I wasn't ready for that." Tears were streaming down Greta's face now.

John knew he had to do something, but she was a perfect stranger. Although he wanted to put his arm around her, he felt restrained. Instead, he offered her a surrogate handkerchief as the only means of comfort to hand.

She managed a smile saying, "It's okay . . . honestly,

I'm fine, I'm really happy. I can't thank these two lovely men enough. Six months ago, I was preparing for my funeral, but today I am seventy percent clear of the effects of ALS and improving every day."

John swayed backwards.

"What!" he exclaimed. "Did you tell me that your symptoms of ALS are being reversed? How can that be? My wife has just been offered treatment, but I thought it would only give her a few more years. You are telling me . . ." He stopped mid-sentence. It was beginning to sink in. This is what Peter had been trying to tell him. He hadn't really understood the extent of the new therapies. Here, in front of him, was the physical evidence. This was beyond theoretical physics. This was something, or rather someone solid, he could see and touch. No reservations now, he took Greta into his arms, and they both held on to each other. "I . . . I'm, . . . I don't know what to say", he stuttered between sobs.

"It's a miracle." Greta laughed.

"No! It's science," both Peter and Dr. Savage said in unison.

They all laughed, and a few minutes later, he and Peter were on their way to dine at a small exclusive London restaurant after making promises to return to see Greta in the next few weeks.

Chapter 4

Sarah's story

Sarah counted time as before and after D Day. D standing for diagnosis. Before D, she was one of those people for whom life seemed to go swimmingly. She loved working in advertising. Her dream job as a graphic designer just didn't seem like work, more like play. John was the sweetest man – they worked well together and he adored her.

She was the decision-maker and John the cautious one. She didn't mind.

When Josh came along, it felt like their family was complete; there was room for one more, but it just didn't happen. She never felt cheated, though.

After D, it felt like the beginning of an apocalypse as chaos came crashing into their lives. True to form, as a pragmatist, she accepted the news with quiet stoicism. No point in creating a fuss, she reckoned. No melodramatic display of overworked emotions. It wasn't her style. She couldn't change her diagnosis, so she believed it was more sensible to accept and deal with it. She pretty much had known that there was something seriously wrong for some time, so she had resigned herself to accept the reality of the situation.

What upset her most was that potentially, she could

have passed the faulty gene onto her son, Josh. *No! No! No! that can't happen. Please!* Everything changed the day that Josh left home. It never occurred to her that Josh would run away after he took the test. If only she had been able to go to the hospital with him, but she'd had a fall the day before and was laid up in bed with a fractured femur.

Before Josh left home that fateful day, she'd tried to maintain an optimistic mood for all their sakes. She hated being with gloomy people as they drained the life out of you, but the day after Josh left, she cried – all day. Feeling hysterical at one point, uncharacteristically, she screamed in frustration. That was the last time she had shed a tear. She marked the day with an imaginary black veil. It felt like something inside her had already died. Never in her life had she experienced the endless darkness of mourning. Not even when her parents had passed away.

A week later, she resigned herself to the fact that Josh wasn't coming home any time soon.

Of course, he was running away, but it grieved her that he didn't speak to her about it. Maybe just as well because it hurt her to admit that she had no answers.

Two weeks passed, and life carried on – although nothing was the same. Days were full of loss of one thing or another. It seemed like her losses were incremental and brutal. Somehow it seemed frivolous to focus on mundane things like her appearance. Always a smart dresser, it pained her to revert to flat shoes. She loved her heels, but they had to go because she couldn't risk another fall.

She had a mental tick list. Before long, the smart suits would give way to trousers with elasticated waists, and somewhere down the line, it would be worse. There was no up-side to her condition. Never one to feel sorry for herself, she dutifully soldiered on for John's sake because she knew that it was all too much for him.

With all the negativity surrounding her condition, at least she still had a roof over her head. Thankfully, her employers were sympathetic and allowed her to work from home. They were still repaying their mortgage, and her medical bills were piling up, so thankfully, her income kept them afloat.

Daily she checked the mail for word from her son. Sometimes a postcard popped through the letterbox bringing her updates on his travels. At least she knew that he was alive, but that was cold comfort to her. She knew that he would come home one day, but she hoped that it wouldn't be too late for her. More importantly, Josh would be devastated if he didn't get to say goodbye. She knew her son! He was avoiding his future by staying as far away from home as possible.

Around a year after her diagnosis, the world came crashing down. Her health was deteriorating rapidly, and her strength seemed to be seeping out of her body day by day.

Her employer had been great, but it was decided that it was time to let her go. Her disability pension would help pay the mortgage so they would be able to survive financially. At least they didn't have to worry about paying the bills or moving house.

Days were spent attending appointments at the hospital and coping with a steady stream of carers. Her dignity was slipping away daily.

John wouldn't give up though, he spent his evenings searching for the latest research papers looking for the *elusive cure*.

It was on the eighteenth month, post D when John rushed into to bedroom/cum living room – she'd had to move downstairs. Although she could still walk, the stairs had become her *Mount Everest*. Eventually, she struggled to use the stair-lift, submitting to the inevitable; another day of defeat had arrived. There was no point in denying it; her prognosis was poor. *It's time to face reality, girl!* She chided herself.

"Sarah, look at this! There's a private clinic in London that claims to be doing intensive research into ALS and having some success. I'm going to call them in the morning and see if we can get you an appointment." John spoke with great enthusiasm.

Sarah was getting used to her husband's *favourite research paper of the week*. She had been patient with him until now, but truthfully, she was weary. It was time to stop this madness. She let him try to explain why this latest research was the right one for her but interrupted his last statement. "It has been found to extend life –"

She interrupted. "Come sit here next to me, John. I need to say something, and I need you to listen. Tenderly she stroked his hand as she gazed into his misty eyes. "You have to understand, John. I don't want my life extended. Not like this!"

John sighed deeply but continued, "Okay, I hear you, but I want you to do this for me. I have such a good feeling about this. Just let me make an appointment."

Sarah had noticed that John had been acting strangely for the last few months. He seemed really stressed, and even his appearance had deteriorated. Although she was worried about him, she didn't have the energy or the will to keep doing this – even for his sake. She had come to terms with her destiny, and she had to help John accept it too.

But he pleaded once more. "I promise that this will be the last time, Sarah."

Reluctantly, she acquiesced to his pleading but

adamantly stated.

"Okay, but this is the last time – and I mean it!"

The next few weeks were a blur; she seemed to be living in a dream-like state. Her last cognisant conversation was a few days ago. It was in one of her waking moments, which seemed to be depleting every day. Sarah had resigned herself to quietly sleeping away her last days. It was easier, and the medication made her very drowsy. Today, however, she was alert.

John was hovering restlessly by her bed. She picked up on his nervousness; aware that he had something to tell her. *It must be bad news*, she thought, because he was beginning to stammer again. John had to go for speech therapy after his dad left. The stammering usually resurfaced when he was feeling insecure. She would have to ask him outright what was wrong.

Chapter 5

The Arrow of Time

The meal was pleasant enough, but John was anxious to know more. He tried to pump Peter for information; however, he soon realised that his mentor would not mix business with pleasure. An hour later, he was relieved when Peter paid the bill, and they got on their way.

Once back at the penthouse suite, Peter gave John some scientific papers to browse over; he explained that he didn't want him to be ignorant of what he was getting into.

"Let me explain, John. We are entering a completely *New Age.*

In ten years, time, life as you know it will be unrecognisable and in twenty years, well . . . nothing will be the same."

John stiffened as a wave of existential fear overtook him. He tried to speak; swallowed hard, but the words were trapped in his throat.

Peter continued. "You live in a world of troubles, like a bird trapped in a cage."

John's eyes narrowed. He felt cloistered.

"Is that the way you want to live for the rest of your time on earth, John?"

John shook his head. "No . . . I mean . . . I just get

freaked out when you talk about new types of humans and everything being unrecognisable. I can't imagine what that kind of world would look like. "I'm not sure what I'm signing up for, Peter. It all seems –"

"Far-fetched. Like science fiction?"

"I guess."

"These changes will happen whether you like it or not. Consider this, dear friend; wouldn't it be better to be in on the game? I want you to understand that most people are oblivious about advances in technology and how they are accelerating at such a rate that would explode your mind if you could see it all at once."

"I'm really a bit of a technophobe. It's difficult for me to take this in, Peter."

"Then let me be your mentor. I'll guide you into the truth that will give you wings."

John nodded in submission.

"Good. Let's make a start then. I'd like you to have a read through these papers to familiarise yourself with the science. They are all fairly easy to read, so don't think I'm expecting you to become an expert overnight." Peter smiled sympathetically. "Also, if you like, you can do some research online. Check out some of the links I've given you. It's ironic; everything I'm talking about is already in the public domain. It's like an open secret that nobody wants to acknowledge. Humans don't really like change."

Before Peter excused himself for the evening, he encouraged his student to read the five scientific reviews about emerging technology.

John glanced over the subjects: *DNA* and *CRISPR Cas9* editing, *Nano-medicine*, *CERN* technology, Quantum computers, and trans-humanism.

"Woo! This is a bit heavy for bedtime reading," John balked.

"This is the future for all of us," Peter responded excitedly. "This is the new path for humankind – every man, woman, and child!" John looked perplexed. His mentor walked over and stood over him, carefully measuring his words as if unveiling a great mystery. "Together, we will create a race of *super-humans*."

Feeling bewildered, John asked for clarification. "But how can that be? I don't understand. Surely, we would have to give permission before you change anything on this kind of scale? Don't governments monitor that stuff all the time through ethics committees and legislation?

John noted that Peter responded rather smugly with a wide grin.

"The public is naive, my friend. Think about *DNA*, discovered in 1953 by Watson and Crick, arguably the biggest scientific discovery ever! Within just 50 years Watson was the director of the *Human Genome Project*, an organisation that mapped every single gene in the human body. Do you understand the implications of that achievement?"

John shook his head, not willing to say the wrong thing.

"Precisely! And most are oblivious. What incredible knowledge we have gained. I want you to listen carefully."

John sat forward.

"This project has given us access to the forbidden keys of life."

John hesitated before lamely responding. "What do you mean. What keys . . .?"

Peter paced in front of John's seat before responding "Don't you see, *The Maker* may have created all of this, but now we know His secrets. Indeed, what a beautiful feat of painstaking detective work. Don't you think?"

John could feel the pounding in his chest again as he

tried to grasp this new mountain of information. His mind was frantically trying to work out the implications for humanity's future, but was having trouble assimilating everything Peter was saying.

Surely, it will take someone with the mantle of a prophet to predict the outcome, he decided.

Peter's voice continued to boast of his achievements, but John was lost in his thoughts.

"Are you listening to me? I asked you, who do you think funded this work?"

John slowly snapped back into reality, shrugging his shoulders.

"You did! Along with the rest of the naive population." Peter, enjoying himself immensely, laughed with a caustic hint of sarcasm.

"More about this tomorrow. Today we are covering the basics.

Dr. Savage has already explained about *Nano-medicine,* so I will leave you to study that one later." He paused, making sure that his student was paying attention. He could see that John's mind had wandered again.

Oblivious to Peter's demand for his attention, John was thinking about how Sarah was doing. Had they begun the treatment? Questions swirled about his head about the long-term effects on her mind and body.

"Are you okay, John? Would you like me to continue?"

"Oh, sorry . . . it's all just a bit much to take in. Please continue."

Under the pressure of time, Peter forged on to explain: "Now, let's talk about the largest machine ever built on planet earth. It's 27 kilometres long and situated at Geneva on the Swiss-French border. They started building in the same year that Watson and Crick discovered *DNA*. 1953 was a very important year for us. The project was so colossal and expensive that it just went live properly ten years ago. Who do you think funded it? Peter seemed to find it highly amusing when John answered reluctantly.

"I guess *I* did!"

"You did indeed, together with every other European taxpayer." Continuing, Peter asked: "Do you know what they do at *CERN*?"

John looked perplexed, but he tried to explain his minimal understanding of the *Large Hadron Collider's* working. "I think it has something to do with particle acceleration. Don't they want to create the effects of the *Big Bang*? They smash particles together at near the speed of light to see what happens. Something like that?"

"Well done. You know more than most, but let me ask you. Why John? Ask yourself, why spend trillions of dollars to take images of colliding particles? Do you really believe that they would build the world's largest machine to take photographs of what the *Big Bang* might have looked like?"

"A bit of overkill, I should say!" John offered.

Peter laughed at his response. "I encourage you to dig a bit deeper, my friend. I'll give you a clue. Think about what we could do with unlimited energy from other dimensions."

It was obvious that Peter was enjoying sharing this information.

"Did you know that the *World-Wide-Web* was invented by a computer software scientist at *CERN*."

"No, I had no idea."

"Soon, it will become clear just how important that little nugget of gold is. This technology has greatly propelled us forward on our quest."

John decided to admit his ignorance about *Quantum*

Computers before Peter had the chance to put him on the spot. "I guess it's something to do with quantum physics and about how matter can exist in two states simultaneously. Something to do with being either a wave or a particle, but I have no idea how that translates to computers!"

Again, Peter spoke enthusiastically, "You have a basic grasp, but I suggest you look online at the introduction to *Quantum Computers* by the inventor. He will explain the difference between using the current binary system to the massive potential of a cubit system, now accessing information at breakneck speed. It's like we now have the ability to open the padlocks to other dimensions. Very enlightening! Even I struggle with this one, though! Peter laughed heartily again, enjoying his time teaching his student about new world-changing technologies.

Peter grinned gleefully as he proudly announced to his student.

"The Arrow of Time is changing!"

Perplexed by this statement, John let that one fly over his head.

Boasting that he knew a little more about *trans-humanism*, John spoke more confidently. "I have read about a group of crazy, wealthy individuals who think they can become immortal. I've seen the *2045 website*. They are funding research into ways of surviving . . . what! You mean you are . . . is this what you have been talking about?

Peter smiled broadly. He was enjoying himself immensely as he answered: "Anything is possible if you have the blueprint. Knowledge plus money equals power!"

"You are beginning to understand where we are going

with this. I have had so many years to plan this. You have no idea, my friend. As I said before, there have been trials and setbacks, but now we have arrived at the last battle. We have the knowledge and the technology to fulfil our plans." Peter could hardly contain himself as he laid out the next bombshell!

"All we need now – is to win over the minds and hearts of mankind!"

Peter knew that these words had penetrated John's psyche. He could see the jigsaw coming together piece by piece. It wouldn't take long before he would be able to see the complete picture.

It was 9pm when Peter became aware that John would need time to process the vast amount of information he had bombarded him with. His student was smart enough, though; he had given him enough details but had left obvious gaps for John to find out for himself. He'd made sure that the scientific papers were basic enough for the average layman to understand. Peter had faith that John would do his own detective work to discover the missing pieces.

True to form, John spent the next five hours trawling the internet for information. Only brain fog stopped him from staying up all night. Exhaustion sent him to bed at 2am. Curiosity would have to wait until the morning.

As he lay on his bed, John realised that he had learned more about the world in the previous 18 hours than he had in the last 40 years. He needed time to think about the workings of the universe. "*But not tonight,*" he said out loud.

Everything Peter had told him was beginning to take shape. As he spread himself out on the oversized bed he felt an overwhelming sense of pride rise up. He could hardly believe his luck being chosen by Peter for the assignment. It was so good to feel special.

This distant relative, whoever he was, had given him something he had never known before – a sense of belonging. His mother was a good woman but she hadn't really achieved much. He had the sense that she had projected some of her dreams onto her only son. His father, well . . . that was another story; he'd waited all these years for him to return. Today he made the decision; his father was as good as dead to him!

His body ached with tiredness, his mind too. Excited about the promise of tomorrow, he relaxed into his pillow. Everything felt like it was falling into place, but things like this just didn't happen to a regular guy like him. *Do they?*

The overload of information collapsed on him like a mountain of mud. The landslide of ideas swept his consciousness away. For the first time in years, he slept like a baby.

Chapter 6

The Maker

The alarm clock gently purred by John's bed. For the first time in years, he woke up feeling refreshed and optimistic. He could see the city stirring into life and the sun beginning to rise over the horizon as he walked onto the small balcony off his bedroom.

This morning it felt good to be alive and curious about the world again.

Peter had painted a fantastic picture of a world without sickness or disease. A world where the unthinkable was achievable. Living forever seemed an incredible idea, but it did seem more than a bit far fetched!

He laughed and looked at the clock again.

Yeah, time for a quick shower before breakfast.

Clearing the mist from the mirror to shave, he looked at his forty-year-old face. *Not too bad,* he thought. A few more wrinkles were beginning to appear, but he reckoned they added to his craggy good looks. A few months ago, he had exercised and kept a healthy weight, but now he looked down at his expanding waistline and groaned.

Peter arrived at precisely 8am. As if observing him for the first time, John noted that he was extremely distinguished, and classy. Yesterday had been so traumatic that he hardly noticed how spectacularly tall and handsome this man was. A full head of thick wavy silver-white hair added to his stature. John guessed he was around sixty-five to seventy years old and in excellent shape.

"Come, John, let's have coffee outside, it's such a beautiful day to be cooped up inside." John hadn't noticed the huge balcony hidden behind a wall of curtains. It was massive, almost as large as the sitting room. Canvas sailcloth covered half of the area providing shelter from the elements. They sat down on comfortable sofas. Huge overstuffed cushions padded out the China-blue rattan furniture.

The men sat opposite one another, poised to begin their journey together.

Wasting no time, Peter set out his rigorous plan. Anxious to have the day mapped out, he explained: "Time is short, and we have a lot to cover." The older man took charge as he described details of the morning sessions.

He instructed John to take a notepad and jot down anything he didn't understand but directed him to listen and reserve any questions for later. "By the time we need a break we can go for a walk or a jog, whichever you prefer. After lunch, we shall resume session two, and you can ask whatever questions you wish. I assure you, I will, of course, answer honestly and as fully as I can. Is that okay with you?"

"Yeah, that's fine by me, fire away," John replied, although he wasn't sure if he felt safe or thoroughly intimidated by this strange man.

Peter responded enthusiastically to this cue.

"John, I want you to be aware of my long history with the one you would call *The Creator*. However, I prefer to call him *The Maker* because I decided not to follow his plan for creation. I have chosen not to give him the status of being called *my* God.

For a very long time, John, there has been a battle raging between *The Maker* and a group of beings who – although acknowledge *The Maker* – do not believe in his ways, or more precisely, the way he runs the world."

John frowned.

Trying to find a way to explain his idea better, Peter thought it over for a few moments. "Let me put it in business terms that you will easily understand. They don't like his style of management. Do you understand me?"

Baffled, John replied: "You mean that they want to overthrow His government?"

Peter responded curtly. "*Precisely.*"

"*The Elohim* is another name for *The Maker*. They are a dictatorship that doesn't take into account our needs or desires. To tell the truth, they really don't understand us. Hence, we have had many wars for thousands of years. Sometimes we have victories, and sometimes we are defeated, but we *never* give up. But now, my friend, we have everything we need to win. This will be the last battle."

Remaining silent as instructed, John dared not say exactly what he was thinking.

Peter continued, undeterred by his student's anxious body language or his raised eyebrows. "Let me make this clear. *The Elohim* created an impossible world. They gave us life and immortality, but none of us could keep their unfathomable laws. Break one law, and you are an outcast! It's like a parent leaving a small child alone with the cookie jar. How many times did you put your hand in the cookie jar when no-one was looking?"

John squirmed in his seat, silently responding. *I wouldn't like to answer that question!*

"Ah! My dear friend, we would have defeated the

Elohim a long time ago, but there will always be timid little sheep who try to follow the rules. They want to keep us safely herded into the sheep-pens, but throughout history, there have been rebellions. History makers, men, and women of renown have been the pioneers pushing back the boundaries. They don't want to be sheep!" They talked for some time as the morning sun rose and cast a deep shadow under the canopy.

Peter stood up. "Perhaps now is the time to show you what has been going on behind the scenes. This is where the real fun begins. There is a whole realm of existence that you are unaware of. What I am about to show you will probably terrorise you, and then it will greatly disturb you, and then you will be truly amazed."

John flinched at the prospect but said nothing.

"I'm going to take you on a journey that will make this real for you. He continued with his instructions: "You have to listen to everything I tell you to do. Don't move more than a foot from my side. You have to stay within my frequency. When we start moving, you will hear a high-pitched sound. That is my sound, and it is unique to me." Peter added with a wry smile: "If you move away, it might take a while to find you, and we certainly don't want you to get lost in space?"

Instinctively, John grabbed a nearby cushion. He wasn't sure why, but he needed something physical to hold on to.

"What we are about to do might be called time-travel, but technically we are simply moving between dimensions. It will only be for a few minutes for observation purposes, but it will feel much longer. As Einstein so eloquently put it – time is relative." John swallowed hard; his body began to shake uncontrollably. It was time to run, he reckoned! He had nothing in common with this superior being and doubted that they could even be related. He looked towards the door.

Skilful at understanding human psychology, Peter observed the young man's reactions. He knew that this man was not much of a risk-taker. His ultra-anxious body language was screaming out that he wanted to run for his life. Hiding behind a cushion was a bit of a giveaway.

Although Peter knew this experience would speak louder than a thousand words, wisdom prevailed – John wasn't ready yet. This was frustrating because he was keen to introduce his student to the greater realities of the universe, so with great reluctance, he decided to delay their journey.

It was important to allay the young man's fears: "Oh John, forgive me. I can see that I've greatly disturbed your equilibrium. Perhaps I'm rushing you. Don't be alarmed. Inter-dimensional space travel can wait! Why don't we take another approach? We'll come back to this subject later."

John wished that he had taken the money and run when it was on the table. "Oh, God!" He exclaimed as he remembered that he had signed the forms. "Sarah will have started her treatment, and I don't have enough money to pay the hospital bill."

Every cell in his body was firing on adrenaline alert, ready to sprint out the door at the first opportunity. He had read stories about alien abductions and people with horrendous stories, describing probes and painful experimentations. This story was definitely going off-world. John cautiously turned and looked at Peter again, with an alarming thought: *What if he is an alien?*

Unfazed by John's obvious discomfort, Peter persisted: "So, dear friend, let me answer that burning question you are desperate to ask me. Who am I, and what could we possibly have in common? Well, I guess that is two questions" Peter laughed.

John stayed silent, his mouth like sandpaper, but he nodded to Peter to continue. "I want to put your mind at rest. I am not an alien. Neither am I John the Baptist or Elijah for that matter." His sonorous booming laugh resounded over the balcony into the hazy London sky. A few seconds later, an eerie echo returned to surprise them. Both men laughed this time. The situation was just so bizarre. Then Peter continued soberly, "However, what I am about to tell you is equally strange."

Leaning towards John, Peter stared into John's startled eyes.

"I am an Immortal. An ancient one."

John stood up and walked towards the edge of the balcony. Holding onto the rails until his finger turned white, he shuddered. It was difficult to accept Peter's shocking revelation as he looked down at the busy London street where people were busily going about their daily lives. He turned to face Peter, exclaiming, "How can I believe you! This makes no sense. You mean that you cannot die – ever?"

Peter joined him on the balcony rail. They both looked down at the small specks, a multitude of black figures walking towards the daily grind. "Tell me what you see, John? What do they all have in common? What keeps them going?"

John knit his brows together as he responded, "They are just trying to make a living. Commuting to work. That's what people do. Isn't it?"

Without hesitation, Peter replied, "Slaves. That's what they are. They are giving their lives to the system. I'm giving you the chance to escape."

The younger man conceded: "So, how . . . that would

make you thousands of years . . ."

"Yes, I am from times past." Peter declared.

Unable to contain himself, John replied, "But how could that be. Are you saying that you are eternal, that you've always existed?"

Peter reminded him. "I asked you here to listen to my story. Three days is all I have to tell you everything. In the end you will decide if you believe me, so please hear me out."

The two men sat in silence as John tried to absorb Peter's fantastic story.

Chapter 7

The Revealing

"This might come as something of a shock to you, but I have to tell you that my real name is *Cain*.

We might spell it differently in this modern era, but here is the truth: I was the first baby ever born on this earth and infamously have the rather unfortunate label of being the first murderer!"

John recoiled, shaken by Peter's confession. "No. No. This is crazy. I can't be part of this." He got up, ready to leave.

"Don't be alarmed, my boy, come, sit back down and let me explain. It's not as bad as it sounds. There was a good reason to kill my brother, Abel. He turned the *Maker* against me and said that I wasn't his real brother. He was a trickster and plotted and schemed to grab the best land because he wanted me banished from Eden. We had a fight, and I accidentally killed him."

John tentatively sat down on the edge of his seat.

"It's still a bit of a mystery about the identity of my father. All I know is that I wasn't included in Adam's genealogy. Come inside, and I'll show you."

John was now operating in obedience mode because he couldn't fathom what to make of this story. Sheepishly, he followed Peter into the lounge.

When Peter touched a hand-held device, a ghostly blue holographic screen illuminated the *Book of Genesis* in mid-air. He read through the list of Adam's children scanning for Cain's name but found a gaping void. *And Adam brought forth Seth. . . what!* He had never noticed that before. *How could that possibly* . . . he repeated silently.

Surely Adam was Cain's father, and his bloodline would continue through every child. John looked back at Peter as an idea started to form in his mind.

"Yes, John, you have worked it out. We have the same bloodline. Of course, mine is pure, but your *immortal DNA* is considerably diluted!"

John gasped. "Even if we are related in some way, what could you possibly want with me?"

"Don't worry about that for now, I'll explain later."

John felt giddy. It was all too much to take in, hardy registering any of Peter's words.

"It's okay, we've checked you out, and there are still enough genetic receptors for our purposes." This last remark went totally over John's head. He had no idea what this crazy man was talking about.

"I guess you want to know how I could possibly still be alive." Peter flicked the light screen over a few pages and proudly declared. "Look. There it is, you see *The Elohim* put a marker in my body.

As we discussed earlier, *DNA* is like an instruction book for creating new cells. Well! I have to tell you that my unique *DNA* is indestructible! Every day of my thousands of years of existence, I have emitted a signal that prevents anyone or anything from killing me. It's just a fact. I cannot die! My genetic code is immortal. It's like having a personal force-field. Can you imagine how that scenario plays out?"

John nodded his head to confirm that he had heard –

not that he had understood.

Peter added, "I will explain how that works, but obviously it's something to do with our family genetics."

No, it's not obvious to me, John thought but agreed with a feigned smile. The day had started well but was quickly descending into a dark shadowy world.

Now on a roll, Peter no longer noticed John's body language as he continued to relate his story.

"At first, it was great; I travelled eastwards and found that I had a gift for creating fantastic structures. I built many cities, but I have to say that my first city is still my favourite. I named it after my offspring, Enoch, son of Cain.

Don't be confused with his namesake, who kowtowed to *The Elohim.* He is also an *Immortal,* but he is most definitely on the other side. He is known as Enoch, son of Jared. We have to watch out for him. That man is my nemesis! I'll tell you more about that later. I don't want to get side-tracked."

Interesting, he's losing his cool. That man, Enoch, must have some hold over him. John noted.

"To continue – my family were craftsmen, skilled at making and building. All of us were creative. *The Watchers* helped us to invent musical instruments, metalwork, and weapons of war. We proved that we could live without *The Elohim*. Life was good. Let me explain; you see, there are two types of *Watchers*. Some on the side of *The Elohim* and the others, let's just say – they are with us!

John tried to grasp the concept of two groups of beings called *Watchers* involved in some mighty cosmic battle. It was difficult to wrap his thinking around the idea. He sighed audibly, but Peter was oblivious to his discomfort now, too caught up in relating his own history. Lost in his private world, he continued.

"It might be difficult for you to understand, but the air was much cleaner then. Everything was crystal clear. You could see the stars and the planets shining like fantastic light structures. The colours were much richer, and the sky seemed to be continually filled with incredible formations of energy and light. The luminaries were much closer to earth, so it was easy to track the constellations movements with the naked eye.

It's difficult to imagine nowadays how we knew and understood the names of the constellations. Although they are barely recognisable now, at that time, we could see them clearly mapped out in shapes like the Bull of Taurus, or Aquarius, the Water Bearer. There was no need for telescopes then."

The world that Peter was describing sounded amazing to John. He wanted it to be true.

"People lived for a thousand years and had incredible bodies. They looked different – more transparent."

John noticed Peter's mood change again; at that moment, he looked visibly disturbed.

"In the beginning, everything was amazing. Then things started to change. The planets started to move away, and it was as if a fine dust spread over the earth. It wasn't enough to obscure the sky, but everything began to look duller. The deterioration had begun."

Peter's voice raised to an angry tone as he described what happened next.

"Then, humans began to change, and their bodies altered dramatically as people started to age rapidly. Before long, they began to get sick and die. No-one expected that! We were all in shock! It's not as if people hadn't died before but it was extremely rare and only due to severe injury. It was a different world then, John. It was beautiful beyond description because everything vibrated with energy.

Scientists have an explanation for what happened and is still happening today – they call it the *Law of Entropy,* which basically means that everything in the universe is deteriorating. *"*

There was something about this story that seemed to be true to John, although he couldn't quite explain to himself. It was just that the truth sounds true when you hear it. He looked at Peter's face and saw such deep sadness that he felt it pull on his own heart.

In that moment – somewhere deep in his subconscious – he became aware that he shared genetic emotions with Peter.

"Strange things happened in those days. The winged creatures came and changed everything. Things went from bad to worse. They made huge mistakes when they started mating with humans. They produced chimeras, a kind of half-human, half-angelic being. At first, their children were like super-beings, but before long, the mixed genes produced mutants: giants!"

John puckered his eyebrows.

"Oh, dear friend, I see skepticism written all over your face. You were fine sitting here talking to an immortal relative and contemplating a bit of space-time-travel, but giants? Really! You think that is a step too far."

John shrugged.

Peter touched the screen again. The words began to swirl around as if each letter held some kind of mysterious energy. They looked at the illuminated words in awe – as if each one contained secret information from an ancient text within a hidden world.

Surprisingly, Genesis six confirmed the story that Peter had just related to him.

They called the offspring of the illegal union between *The Immortals* and earthly women *Nephilim.* Eventually, they mutated into a race of giant hybrids. John scrolled back to his youth when his mother dragged him to church each Sunday morning. He had no memories of this story but scratched his head as if he should have known about this.

Determined to finish his story, Peter pressed on, "Things got pretty wild then. *The Nephilim* degraded with each generation into uncontrollable beasts. Their offspring were called *The Elioud.* I will spare you the gruesome details, but can you imagine how many calories a fifteen-foot being would require in a day?"

John shook his head, but nevertheless answered, "I don't know, perhaps five thousand?"

"More like twenty thousand. They had huge appetites, in more ways than one. Soon most of the human race had contaminated genes."

John looked at the ancient man in disbelief. He had always thought stories of giants and beasts were myths and legends.

Peter once again turned to the screen showing him numerous stories about giants. Similar stories unfolded in every culture around the globe. Megalithic structures, artwork, ruined cities, and folklore repeated the same story when giants were treated as gods.

A familiar image of the Egyptian pyramids flashed across the screen. "You know about the pyramids in Egypt, but let me show you that there are pyramids all over the world. Do you know where the largest one is?"

John stated the obvious, "That would be at Giza?"

"Well, that's where most people would say but it's actually in Mexico."

This surprised John.

"Do you have any idea who built them or how they were built?"

John dug deep. "The ancients," he offered lamely. "I

have no idea, though."

Peter shook his head. "No one knows John. Experts have provided many hypotheses but no one would be able to build a pyramid today, not with all the state-of-the-art technology, computer analysis or even heavy lifting gear. And that is a fact!"

John was scratching his head now.

"There are megalithic buildings scattered all over the world. I'm suggesting the possibility that these buildings were constructed by a different type of being. I know that it's hard to take in but do some research. It will surprise you. If we can't work out how primitive cultures build the pyramids, check out the mysterious *Baalbek Stones* in Lebanon," Peter said. He knew this would perplex his student.

"Changing direction," Peter said, "I guess you are wondering what happened to the giants?"

"It had crossed my mind."

Peter responded with a surprising but plausible answer.

"The genetic mutations had spread to almost every family at that time. It was a time of madness. Even I have to admit that their behaviour was so out of control that the only way to stop the bloodbath was by the intervention of *The Elohim*. They had to destroy the beasts. You know the next part of the story."

"I do?" John responded.

"Haven't you always wondered about the flood? Well, even I have to admit that it was necessary." There was only one family left with a pure human bloodline.

For the first time in his life, John understood the reason for the flood. The story from *Genesis* was starting to make sense to him!

"It is a strange story, John. I know it all sounds far-fetched." Peter continued in a weary voice. "The giants had such power over people. They were *gods* to them.

Why do you think every ancient culture had temples where humans were sacrificed? People were so terrified of them that, in the end, they gave them their children to appease them.

Closing his eyes to blot out the image, John shuddered.

"Why don't you do some research while I attend to some business. Check out the history of ancient cultures. Look at the archaeological sites, artefacts, and artworks. They all point to the same story. It's a worldwide phenomenon.

I'll be back in a couple of hours. We can go for some exercise and then lunch. Then you can fire questions at me all afternoon."

John poured himself a strong black coffee then wasted no time before he began his research.

Astonishingly, he discovered that all of the ancient cultures had similar stories. The Sumerians spoke of *The epic story of Gilgamesh*. The Mayans and the Greek gods were all portrayed as giants. The Egyptian world was full of strange hybrids of man and animals. The story went on like weaving a tapestry of the history of the giant-hybrid world. It was astounding to find out that there were literally thousands of similar stories worldwide. The Dead Sea Scrolls included *The Book of the Giants*. Even the bible was full of stories of giants.

When he discovered an image of the Baalbek stones, he was astounded yet again. This was part of the megalithic structure at the Temple of Jupiter – previously the Baal Temple – in Lebanon, 75 kilometres north of Damascus. He learned that there are three monster stones at the site weighing over a thousand tons each.

It would have been impossible for ancient people to use primitive methods to move such massive stones from distant quarries. One of the stones was identified as the largest stone block from antiquity ever moved in pre-modern times. It weighs 1650 tons.

It baffled him to learn that estimates recorded it would take forty thousand men to move it. *Surely, logistically this would be impossible to co-ordinate.* He reasoned. It was challenging to get his head around the scale of this stone. He looked up the weight of a Giza pyramid stone – a mere 2.5 tons. A jumbo jet? Its 400 tons of metal paled into insignificance against this monster. *How could these primitive people move an object at the combined weight of four jumbo jets?* This was an enigma.

He sat for a while, trying to find a reasonable explanation. John scratched his head again, concluding: *This is simply impossible! No-one can explain who built these structures.* It remains a mystery to this day, he read, but ancient stories recounted stories of *Nephilim* builders.

It felt like a little bit of his life drained away as he read: *Legend says that the original temple of Baal was built by Cain to hide from the wrath of God!* He felt his stomach lurch, so he quickly turned the page. Historical buildings in Peru provided further evidence of unexplained structures. Again, demonstrating precision engineering that would be difficult to replicate in modern times. It seemed impossible to believe that ancient man could have constructed them with primitive tools – sites such as Sacsayhuman and Tenochtitlan – the second largest city in the ancient world. Curiously, John considered how the name of Cain's son, Enoch, was hidden in this city's name. *Didn't Peter say that he'd named the city after his son?* He pondered. *There just seem to be so many coincidences.*

The door burst open, interrupting John's intense studies. Peter was wearing his running shoes. "Come on, let's go out and get some fresh air to clear our heads."

Although John was fascinated by his research, he was grateful to have a break as his head was packed with information. He needed time to think.

They ran in unison without exchanging a word. Until recently, John had been a keen runner, but ironically he was having difficulty keeping up with this ancient man.

Oh boy! I'm definitely going crazy. I think I'm beginning to believe this outrageous story! He mumbled.

They lunched at a riverside cafe. Both aware that this was not the place to discuss *The Proposal*. They passed a pleasant half-hour talking about the pros and cons of bicycle hire and agreeing that frustratingly, it was becoming impossible to drive in London as cyclists were taking over the city. They talked about the feasibility of driverless cars and the general progression towards a new technological era. Peter's knowledge was so vast that he could talk about any subject with great authority.

John could have spent all day listening to him; he was so interesting, and his knowledge was compelling. Curiosity however, spurred him on to walk smartly back to the apartment. The men were comfortable in their own thoughts, so there was no need to talk on the way back. John had many questions he was anxious to ask; he just hoped he asked the right ones.

Chapter 8

The Nephilim

Peter made himself comfortable once again, sitting opposite John in the palatial lounge. It was obvious that the younger man still had doubts. However, he sensed that John was coming to a few steps closer and was sure he would not leave before the entire story was revealed. Humans are naturally curious.

Gazing intently at his mentor, John tried to glean every piece of information from the superior being. He had too much to lose, now that he had committed to Sarah's treatment, and he also needed the money.

Just one day ago, he had been an atheist with no thoughts of a spiritual world or belief in a creator. Stories of giant *Nephilim* creatures who virtually caused *The Maker* to flood the Earth seemed ridiculous, but all the historical evidence he had checked out supported this view. It was his turn to ask questions, and he knew what the first one would be.

"What about the giants after the flood? If God . . . I mean *The Maker*, made a clean sweep of all the –"

Peter interrupted, "Hybrids, chimeras, beasts, whatever you like to call them."

John nodded, then added, "Yes, I mean, they were no longer human. They were a crossbreed of humans and angels, and dare I say . . . animals. Wasn't the flood supposed to be a new start because all of creation had been polluted, but my research suggests that it wasn't long before they reappeared?

Did the angels, you know . . . have relations with women again?" He didn't wait for an answer before expressing something he found out in his research.

"Do you know that Jesus was crucified at the place where David buried the head of the giant Goliath after he slew him! Strangely, that's why they call the site *The Place of the Scull* or Golgotha named after Goliath of Gath!"

Immediately, John felt uneasy about this declaration. It seemed like an eerie coincidence to him. He felt his core begin to shake.

Peter sidestepped the last statement, but nonetheless he was pleased that his student was well and truly hooked into the story. He had begun to use his intellect to work out the evidence. Encouraged by this, Peter praised his student. "I'm so glad you are pursuing the truth, my friend. It's time to put the pieces of the jigsaw together. History is like a map waiting to lead you to the buried treasure hidden within. It lies dormant, sometimes for centuries, just waiting to be discovered at the appointed time. Excellent detective work, my boy."

Satisfied that John was tracking with him, Peter was ready to answer the question.

"Let us examine the events from the time of the great flood. There was one family who remained genetically untainted by the *Nephilim* bloodline. You know them as Noah and his three sons. However, one of their wives carried the mixed gene. We can follow this line through Noah's son Ham to his descendant Nimrod.

This man, Nimrod, had great potential. He was known

as a mighty hunter, and like me, he was a builder of great cities. He was different from the other hybrids who had degenerated into beasts." Peter added sarcastically, "You could say he had less animal content.

The previous generation of beasts had uncontrollable appetites for food, women, and animals, and this became their downfall because there simply wasn't enough food to sustain their cannibalistic tendencies."

John squirmed. The idea of cannibalistic giants sounded like some gruesome scene from a horror movie.

Undeterred by John's discomfort, Peter carried on with his story. "Nimrod was different. He was a great man, less animalistic than his predecessors. He had mutated into a hybrid with superior abilities. Let's just say – he was more refined than the pre-flood beasts."

It was at the time of Nimrod we discovered the secret of gene manipulation. Ways had been found to reign them in through selective breeding of women with *The Immortals*. And so Nimrod became the chief warrior; indeed, he was the arch-enemy of *The Maker*."

John listened carefully to Peter as he continued to explain how the hybrids had made excellent soldiers as they followed the ways of *The Watchers* and learned how to fashion weapons of war.

Nimrod had incredible strength and power, but it was his intellect that made him great. In fact, he so threatened the dominion of *The Maker* that they had to destroy his masterpiece.

"What masterpiece?" John asked, intrigued.

"Ah, I see I have your full attention. You remember the story of the *Tower of Babel*, of course."

Determined to preach his message, Peter continued with unabated zeal – despite John's startled look.

"It's ironic: we had such advanced civilisations then. We were not at all primitive; as modern historians would say. They would have you believe that we were on all fours or living in caves, eh?

We were so near to the overthrow at that time, but *The Tower* was destroyed by *The Maker*. This was when we had to scatter all over the earth, and everyone began to speak in different languages.

Communication was lost, and it was a time of great confusion. They thought that they had defeated us, but we never give up!" Peter thumped his fist on the table, seemingly oblivious to any pain.

Oh my God! John shrank back, afraid to say anything in case he angered this man any further. Now and again, John noticed something in Peter that unnerved him: did this apparently benevolent man have a more sinister streak, or was it passion he was detecting?

Although he wasn't sure of what this *Immortal* was capable of, he decided to give him the benefit of the doubt, so sat silently waiting for him to continue. He had no other option.

"We lost a lot of knowledge then. *The Tower* was gone, and our capability to reach the other dimensions was blocked. But now, my friend – listen carefully. We have regained a lot of ground – and more!" Peter grinned, satisfied that his plan was taking shape.

"Nimrod was the right man for the job, but it was just the wrong time. Fortunately, our knowledge is growing exponentially every day. Quantum computers work at breakneck speed, so now we are good to go! This is our time!"

John started to speak but the words dried up in his mouth.

"We know how everything works, from the vastness of the cosmos, right down to the fine-tuning of the human body. We will never give up. We are in this war for however long it takes." Peter enthused.

John tried to assimilate this information before moving on to his next question. Everything that Peter had told him seemed to be at least feasible. *History can be read through another lens,* he imagined.

Growing in confidence a little, John asked the next burning question.

"Why do you want to change humans, Peter? I mean, I get that you are planning to make us *Immortals* like you, but why?"

The response: "Ah, good question, we are heading in the right direction. We will explore this more fully tomorrow. However, I will give you some insight into this." Peter was in his element, enjoying every moment of this discussion; after all, it wasn't every day that he got to tell anyone about the events of his unique sojourn on earth for thousands of years. John was indeed special and would be one of a handful of people who would get to know his story. Well! Not all of it, but enough to get him on-board with his great plan for planet earth.

He answered John frankly. "Humans will be vital for the continuation of this world. Of course, we want to provide a way for all humanity to exchange their meagre lives and become immortal like me. Why should you get sick? Why should you grow old and die when we can change all of that with technology?

You have no idea how difficult it has been to bring us to this place. We have been waiting and planning for this event for such a long time. Scientists already know about this and they have a beautiful name for it. They call this great moment of the recalibration of all things, *The Singularity.* Some call it the *Omega Point*. It is the time where civilization, as you know, it will advance to such a degree that previous generations would not recognise it. Technology will deliver us to the point-of-no return."

"This Omega you speak of. It sounds like the end of the world. Isn't this what the bible talks about in *The Book of Revelation*?" John wasn't sure if he had spoken that question out loud until Peter answered him.

"Precisely! the world as you know it will be finished. Then our time will come."

Meditating on this response for a while, John tried to envisage this new world – without *The Maker*.

Did the temperature just drop? John shivered as ice-cold thoughts travelled down his spine.

Will Peter's new style of management usher in a better world?

It seemed the rational thing to do – he had to find out more before deciding to join with *The Immortal*. Perhaps it was too late?

With another pressing question on his mind, John asked his tutor. "Why are your people interested in this world? Why not go to some other planet?"

Peter shook his head. "That is a tough question, but let me try to explain. *The Maker* had a purpose for this planet. The simple answer is that there is no other place in the universe quite like Earth. He made a world of incredible precision, with an environment that could sustain life, including humans. Everything is set to work like clockwork. It is so finely-tuned that even minute changes could result in extinction. Changing the oxygen level by just one percent could result in total annihilation. Move one planet out of alignment, and gravity would pull the earth apart."

John nodded.

"Remember, John, everything works in systems, and each one facilitates the other. You will remember from schooldays that the sea, plants, and trees work together to create the necessary gases for life to exist. Science has a name for this; it is called the Anthropic Principle. In other words, it seems like this planet has the perfect physical and chemical properties necessary to maintain life and indeed qualifies as the optimum place for all life. So, dear friend, to answer your – there is no other planet suitable for us at this time.

You have to hand it to *The Maker*; he is a scientist of great precision."

Each time Peter answered his questions, John felt like he was beginning to see Peter's vision, but he had plenty more questions on his list.

"Can I ask you why you want to alter man so drastically? I get that the genetic changes would be necessary to defeat sickness and death, but why move beyond *immortal DNA* into the realms of *Transhumanism*? It sounds like that is nothing new – but it didn't work too well before?"

Peter quickly responded. "Yes, I agree; the *Nephilim Initiative* was primitive, but this time everything will be regulated and monitored. There will be no giants!"

Quickly posing his next question, John asked, "Why stretch this to a post-human society? Isn't that a step too far? Once you start merging humans with machines, well! … I guess they will no longer be –"

Let me finish that statement for you, Peter interjected: "They will no longer be made in *The Maker's* image. We will have completely destroyed the image of God!

That is our goal. You must understand that we cannot completely destroy *The Maker*; we can only disempower him. That way, he will no longer have control of the way we live or, more importantly, how long we live. We have to obliterate everything that is linked to him."

We will have a *New Genesis*!" Peter declared proudly.

John's reaction to this statement was tangible. This latest revelation struck a chord of fear inside him. The glass in his hand shattered, and a trickle of blood flowed out of the palm of his hand. Peter calmly handed him a freshly laundered handkerchief to mop up the steady stream of blood, shockingly red against the stark white cloth.

It was as if time slowed down, and everything shifted into low gear. Ridiculous thoughts surged through John's mind. It felt like his life-force was flowing out of the tiny cut on his hand. *What the hell am I getting myself into? Is this man a psychopath just like Hitler? Does he really possess the capability of turning us into immortal half-man, half-machine beings, like Cyborgs? Maybe it's time to walk away!* He lacked the courage, though, and he knew it.

"Are you alright John, would you like a glass of water, perhaps?"

"I'm fine . . . I'll survive."

Just then, Peter's phone rang, allowing John a much needed moment to pause and time to gather himself together.

He overheard Peter's conversation. "Oh, thanks, that's wonderful news, just great. When will he arrive? Yes, that's perfect!"

Feeling like he was suffocating, John wandered off onto the balcony to catch his breath.

"Here you are," the older man looked excited as he explained, "I have some great news for you, my friend. We have located your son, Josh! He is okay, and my people are arranging for him to come back to London on the first available flight from India. I'm happy to tell you that you will soon be reunited with him. He should be here the day after tomorrow."

John staggered forward and fell into Peter's arms. Uncontrollable weeping sprung up from the depth of his being.

Peter reached out to comfort him. "It's going to be alright, I know this must feel like a roller coaster ride for you. Don't worry, my boy, soon it will all make sense.

Chapter 9

Systems within systems

Peter stood at the bar and opened a fresh bottle of whisky. Handing a glass to John, he said, "Let's have a stiff drink to celebrate the return of the prodigal."

Breaking with tradition, John quaffed the amber liquid in one gulp then held out his glass, indicating his need for a refill. Drinking whisky of that calibre is meant to be done slowly, in a ritualistic way. Swirl the amber liquid around the glass, smell, taste, then linger.

Not today, though, all traditions seemed to be obsolete because the world was changing – and his son was on his way home.

John began to relax as the warm liquid spread throughout his body, pleasantly anaesthetising him. He could feel his resolve strengthening. *I don't really have a choice; I have to go with Peter for the sake of my family.*

Pressing forward, he asked.

"If there is a *Creator* who controls the world, what about Darwin?"

With a glint in his eye and grinning cheek to cheek, Peter responded.

"Ah, dear Darwin and his pet monkey science.

"Yeah, but what about the chimpanzee?" John contended.

"Yes, it's a good argument – we share similar *DNA*.

John answered, "We have a lot in common."

"My dear boy, if you base your beliefs on physical structures alone, do you believe that your genesis was from a banana or an Abyssinian cat?

"I, . . . no, what do you mean?

A human and a banana share sixty percent *DNA*. – ninety percent for the cat, in case you are wondering.

John stroked his chin, trying to follow Peter's line of thinking.

"So, what you are saying is that all living things are made out of similar substances, but that doesn't mean they share the same genesis."

"Exactly.

From the dust of the ground were you all made!" Peter exclaimed.

They sat in silence for some time. The mentor could see that the student needed to reprocess his thoughts.

"I want you to stop and listen to Darwin's idea. Pay attention, John! Before we even discuss the scientific method – or lack of it!"

"Do you know that the word science simply means *knowledge,* and most knowledge is accumulated through observation? Your eyes are scientists, John. Trust what you see."

"Really?"

Peter continued, "Darwin wanted you to believe in the *Accidental Universe*. He says that every structure in the physical world is the result of random interactions over time.

John was sitting attentively as Peter duly challenged everything he believed to be true.

"He wants you to believe that every galaxy, star systems, mountains, trees, and people are maintained in perfect harmony by chance. When you look at the cosmos. What do you see?"

Peter poured another drink. He needed to give John time to understand. It was part of the deal! He had to tell John about *The Creation*.

"What's the chance of thirty-seven trillion cells organising themselves into a multitude of complex systems that make up a human body?

John shook his head. "I've never thought about it, but it sounds improbable."

"If you think that is improbable, multiply that by innumerable systems in the universe!"

"Dear Darwin, he was one of our great successes. Unfortunately, all good things come to an end. He gave the world an idea that could provide no real evidence and no scientific method to prove his theory." Peter roared with laughter. "We managed to fool the world for a while by providing some fake bones as evidence of the missing link between man and ape. Science needed some hard evidence, so we gave them the Piltdown Man – and for good measure – the Nebraska man. Unfortunately, both were discovered to be forgeries – after many years – by some savvy scientists.

You would have thought that would be the end of Darwin, but no, the scientific method continued to be ignored." Peter shook his head in disbelief.

John struggled to give up his faith in an idea that had fuelled his beliefs for over thirty years.

"But it's taught in every education system in the world as scientific fact?" John argued.

"Evolutionary theory is a great marketing tool to give people what they want – a world without *The Maker*. Don't you find that people believe what they want to be the truth? It suited the scientists, and it suited the masses."

"Does that mean that all scientists are on your side?" John asked.

"Good grief, no!" Peter gasped. "If only that were the case. Most scientists are unaware that we exist. They have no idea we are directing them!

Darwin is now defunct. He has served his purpose.

"I know that you need to grasp this, so let's consider another model: we'll call it the *Mathematical universe*. This universe is a single structure – made up of an incalculable number of exchanges of information. Still in this model, there is pre-programmed order.

Think of a universal contract where all the parts cooperate. Now think of everything within that structure in terms of systems, and it is easier to understand. For example – a human, a dog, or a tree system. Each one highly complex and has its own design."

"Think about the self-conscious human. Your species has a noble position in this world."

John felt slightly on edge with that remark. Was there a hint of sarcasm – he wasn't sure?

Peter continued, unaware of John's discomfort.

"The male and the female are designed to operate differently. The woman's reproductive system is unique. Some would call the womb a sacred temple.

John closed his eyes momentarily as he remembered his own son's entry into the world after being cocooned in Sarah's body for months. He remembered how protective he felt towards both of them.

He could hear Peter's voice drone on, so he had to shake himself to keep listening.

". . . and for example, the human body is made up of a multitude of processes and all of them have to work in harmony. Part systems don't work. This is the downfall of Darwin that says man evolved over time."

John shook his head, trying to shift his thinking.

Peter forged on. He was almost glowing with energy as he explained. "Many scientists are now shunning Darwin due to the unfolding secrets of *DNA*. The complexity of a single cell makes Darwin's idea unbelievable.

Everything is possible now; the *Human Genome Project* has given us incredibly detailed information about how humans are made. It's almost too good to be true.

Peter stood up to make his next announcement.

"It's taken millennia, but now – we've cracked the code. *DNA* is an ancient alphabetical language from the beginning of time. In fact, it's like a computer programme, containing pure information."

Now hanging on every word coming out of Peter's mouth. John needed to know.

"What do you mean?"

Peter sighed and shook his head. It's an instruction code." It is your bodybuilding machine.

John took a few moments to absorb what he had just heard. He remembered the letters of the code – *ATCG*.

"You mean that this is the language of *The Maker*. It's the God code?"

Peter's eyes were sparkling. "Yes indeed, this is the blueprint for every living thing, imbedded in the tiny strands of *DNA*."

An idea was beginning to form in John's head. He just couldn't make up his mind if it was a good thing. Tentatively, he asked Peter: "Do you mean that you possess the book of instructions to build a human?"

Peter could hardly contain his enthusiasm.

"It's not quite that simple! However, we are currently working on changing the human genome, but we can alter and rebuild humans.

Ask any scientist this question. What is the *Energy*

that gives life to the *Stardust*? Science can tell you in great detail about the constructs of living matter, but they can't explain – what is this thing called *life* that can make a pile of dust live?"

John's face scrunched up as he shook his head. "I've never thought about this. Is … this what you call *Spirit*?"

"Ah, my friend, now you are beginning to understand. Spirit is the life-force, and it is eternal. Energy never ceases to be – it merely changes. And therein lies the secret to our plan.

If we can preserve the physical body through gene editing – using my *immortal DNA* –we will keep the *Spirit Energy* centred in this universe."

"Wow. Wow! Yes! . . . I get it." John enthused.

"We are at the forefront of significant change. This is the most exciting time to be alive. Everything that exists will be changed because we now possess the very keys of life. We are about to enter a new world that will be guided by you and me, John.

Now we can control our own destiny, and the *Elohim* will not be able to stop us. We've found the holy grail. There are no restrictions now; we can be anything we want to be."

Holding up his glass, Peter announced: "Let's have a drink to our dear friend Darwin. He served us well, but it's time to put him to rest. Soon we will discuss the details of our plans for the future, but that is not for today." They raised their glasses.

John, slightly inebriated, interrupted him. "That is for the third day!"

They laughed in unison. Just then, the door opened; Gloria entered the room and asked if they would like a hot drink. Both men howled in laughter as Peter shouted: "Yes, dear boy, we had better sober up. Make us some strong coffee, Gloria."

They took a ten-minute break before Peter continued his lesson. "Even without any further evidence, John. When you look at the universe – tell me now, what do you see?

John spoke quietly, almost whispering to himself. "An *Accidental Universe*. Random and without method or conscious decision. Undirected, unplanned. A total fluke. I don't think so! That means pretty much everything is pointless. He laughed at the incredulity of the idea.

"Whereas, a *Mathematical Universe* is planned, purposeful, and ordered. Every living thing is encoded with instruction. Programmed! This requires *A Maker*."

John shook his head for several moments before looking again at Peter.

My God! I've been blinded by science for all these years! I simply wasn't trusting my own observations."

"*DNA* is a message system, giving instructions for *Living Matter* to behave in a certain way. It cannot be random!"

Chapter 10

Free will

Peter turned to the younger man. "Two more questions before lunch, then you must have free time to absorb everything we have talked about. Is that agreeable to you?"

"Of course. That's good, I think . . . I just need to ask you a couple of things that I'm struggling with." *I need to pluck up the courage to ask the all-important questions.* Peter was a formidable character. It was obvious by his posh accent and vast wealth of knowledge that he was intellectually superior. Feeling way out of his depth, nevertheless, he pressed on.

"I get that you don't want to follow *The Maker* but, I don't understand . . . why do you want to destroy him? What is the real reason?" he asked hesitantly.

"Ah, that is a good question." Peter's looked at his student with his piercing brown eyes. "A good professor should always encourage his student to pursue his natural curiosity and teach them how to discover truth for himself."

John wasn't prepared for what Peter would reveal next.

"The simple answer is that if we don't destroy *The Maker* – he will destroy us!"

Outraged, John stood up and held on to the back of his chair.

"What do you mean? How could he do that?"

Peter put his hand on John's arm. "Don't worry about that now. I know that you are angry, but I want to show rather than tell you about his plans. We shall do that later. Trust me, when I take you into the fourth dimension, you will fully understand."

It was frustrating to leave this question only partly answered, but John acquiesced for the time being. He guessed that he would have to trust his mentor to unravel this mystery at the right time.

"I've left the most important question until now. I am baffled about this, so I want you to tell me why . . . are you specifically telling me your story? What's this got to do with me? I know that we are related in some way, but why don't you just take what you need?" John sat rigid in his chair. He felt that the answer to this question would either open or close the deal for him. He watched Peter's body language carefully. It was one of those moments where both men seemed to be standing on an equal playing field.

John observed that for the first time, he looked vulnerable and reluctant to speak. It seemed like time was held in suspended animation as Peter carefully considered his answer. Looking gravely at the young man, he swallowed hard before disclosing.

"Yes, John, that is the *big* question. Although there is a fairly simple answer, and it is this – it boils down to free will. It displeases me that I have to tell you this, but I have certain restrictions in my dealings with mankind. The deal is that I cannot force this upon you, and I have only three days to tell you my story – all of it. Therefore, the revelation of my plan to realign everything is necessary. This will maintain the law of free will, and you will be able to choose your own destiny."

Peter looked annoyed and uncomfortable. Instinctively John knew that he had touched a raw nerve but pressed for an answer.

With great reluctance, Peter admitted: "I had to make a petition for you. As I told you before, most of mankind are oblivious about the workings of the universe. There are rulers and powers and all classes of beings who make decisions about your life in the unseen realms. There are court systems and judges who know all about you!"

John was struggling with this revelation. His leg began to swing like a pendulum.

Peter closed his eyes before revealing, "I went to court and asked for you, based on the premise that you are from my bloodline and that you bear no allegiance to *The Maker*."

Furious, John jumped out of his seat, bumping into the nearby table and knocking the half-full cups flying in all directions. He watched as the liquid created a dark brown stain on the cream shag-pile rug. Ignoring this, he shouted angrily: "So, what did this judge have to say about me?"

Peter responded as if it was an admission of guilt. "It has been judged that if I can turn you to my way – I can have you."

"No way!" John walked towards the window. "That's enough! I need to get out of here!" His internal landscape was crumbling. "Who do you think you are? I don't belong to anyone!"

Peter shook his head. "Oh, my dear boy, don't you know that independence is an illusion. We have all been slaves to some system or other, but I want you to see what I see. There is something quite wonderful unfolding before us. You now have the power to choose your future. How marvellous is that? Look closely, John. I am the face of free will. I have come to set you free!"

John protested again. "But you said we have to stop *The Maker* from destroying the world. Surely altering mankind will bring this reality closer. Surely he will destroy all of us!"

Peter came face to face with John, his dark brown eyes shining, ablaze with fire. "Ah. That's the beauty of free will, son. We will choose immortality. What can he do with the billions of *Immortals* that we create? We will have to live somewhere. I have a wonderful plan. Be assured – he will leave us alone."

The two men stood one foot apart, neither able to move; an invisible line existed between them. Could Peter persuade John to cross over? He wasn't sure but continued relentlessly; he had too much to lose.

"Do you know that he has plans to make a new universe? There will be a new earth for those who want to be ruled by him. For those who don't want to be with him – we will remain here. We will be our own masters. Don't you see, the possibilities are endless?"

Peter patted the young man on the back. "Come, my friend, take a couple of hours to relax. We have been invited to dinner tonight. Many people want to meet with you. It's a black-tie affair. Cheer up, my friend, we will be mingling with the members, and they are coming from all over the world for this special occasion. They all want to meet their saviour."

John gasped audibly, "Me. *A Saviour.* What do you mean?"

"Let's just say that your body will become like a temple, capable of saving all of mankind."

Chapter 11

Sarah's answer

It was time to go back to see Sarah and tell her everything. When John mentioned this to Peter, he was surprised to note the silvery haired savant's reluctance, but he was determined to tell her the good news of Josh's homecoming. There was no way he could make his final decision without her; he needed her input.

Peter suggested they should go later as the car was not available. Gloria had gone to pick up his dinner suit.

Come on, John, think of something, you have to see Sarah, now! John searched for a reason.

He lied; "Today is our anniversary, I've never missed one yet."

Peter conceded, aware that it would be unwise to stop him.

On returning to his room to fetch his jacket, John noticed a dinner jacket in the wardrobe. *Strange!* he thought. He was about to shout out but instinct kicked in. He left the property quickly before Peter could find a way to stop him.

Street-side, John hailed a black cab straight away. It was only a short journey to the hospital, so they approached the tree-lined avenue within minutes.

As they turned into the car park, John spotted a familiar black Bentley parked at the side of the building.

His stomach cramped when he saw Gloria emerge from a side door accompanied by Dr. Savage. They both laughed at some inaudible joke then enthusiastically shook hands. Clearly, they knew each other very well. Why was the maid so intimately involved with the consultant? He lingered in the taxi, pretending that he had dropped his wallet. Intuitively he knew that he was not meant to witness this scene.

As he approached the reception, Sarah's nurse welcomed him with a huge smile. "Great news for you today. Sarah is responding well to the new treatment. She is sitting up and eating for the first time in days.

He didn't wait for an explanation, pushing past the nurse in expectation to see his wife's miraculous recovery. He was not disappointed. For the first time in months, she was sitting unaided. Her eyes brightened as he approached. Then tears flowed down her cheeks as she held onto him.

They both laughed and cried for a few minutes before Sarah spoke. "It's a miracle, John. I feel like I've been in a drug-induced sleep and have come back from the dead. My prince has come, and I am alive again." She held him close.

Although relieved and stunned by this incredible turnaround – something was gnawing in his gut. He wasn't ungrateful, but the timing of events over the past few days just seemed contrived. The treatment couldn't have worked that fast – surely? *God. Lighten up, man*, he muttered. *Just enjoy.*

"I've got more good news for you, my love," John whispered softly as he held Sarah in his arms. He'd slipped off his shoes and climbed onto the bed beside her. "They have found Josh," he hesitated to watch for her reaction, "and he'll be here the day after tomorrow."

Sarah squealed. "Oh John, I knew it. Everything is turning around. Can't you feel it?

Who . . . who found Josh?"

Lost for words, he gazed upon his wife for some time, struggling to know where to begin with the strange events he had been sucked into over the past two days. He decided to come clean and tell her everything. *Let her make up her own mind*, he reckoned.

He explained about the ground-breaking treatment she was receiving and how he had met another patient who had almost made a full recovery. Relief surged through his body as he realised that he was no longer a helpless bystander watching his wife die a little every day. He told her that she was currently the recipient of a costly medical treatment not yet available to the general public. Explaining as best he could, John described how the combination of *Nano-medicine* and *CRISPR gene editing* would quickly improve her condition.

The transformation was dramatic. He immediately witnessed hope return, filling her frame as she pulled herself up to a sitting position, unaided.

"There is more honey – so much more."

As John related his experience over the last 30 hours, Sarah's initial enthusiasm began to wane. When he finished telling his story, he looked apprehensively at her.

"It sounds like you will have to sell your soul to this man, John. This just doesn't feel right. Why would Peter and his people want to help us?"

She had just spoken out John's fears. He swallowed hard.

Sarah bowed her head, holding her face between her cupped hands.

It seemed like hours passed as John gazed intently through her fingers, trying to guess her innermost thoughts. He knew that she would come to the same conclusion as him. She had to – the alternative was not an option! He breathed in sharply as Sarah raised her head.

Looking directly into his eyes, she simply stated: "We have to go ahead for Josh's sake. This is our only hope!"

John breathed deeply. Now cradling his wife in his arms, he silently confessed his motive to accept the proposal was not altogether as altruistic as Sarah's. At least now, both his wife and son had a way out of many years of certain deterioration and the prospect of having to face a slow, painful death. However, he was acutely aware of the amazing power and wealth opening up to him.

He had spent the last night summarising everything that had been offered to him.

His immortal ancient relative had given him fifty thousand pounds to consider a covenant with *The Watchers*, a group of beings who understood and manipulated the workings of the universe. They had been waging war on The Elohim, and it was their intention to overthrow this government of the heavens. They would crush the tyrant system that allowed the world to exist in chaos and kept mankind weak and powerless, and forever under the shadow of death. He didn't pretend to understand all of the science, but he had grasped enough to know that mankind was on the threshold of the most significant transformation of life ever known since the beginning of time.

Gazing out through the window to the courtyard, he could see the Acer tree ablaze with colour. John closed his eyes and felt the heat of the sun on his face.

A few hours later, John was back in the apartment and dressed for dinner. In some ways, he felt excited about his new life, but at the same time, he was anxious about what he was getting into. *Hell,* he thought, *I still don't know what that is!* It all seemed to hinge on the next day. The third day. Briefly, he journeyed back through events and discussions he had shared with Peter. Crazy discussions about creation, bloodlines, history, gods, and giants, even reinventing humanity. It all paled into a meaningless tangle of fables, legends, and myths. He chided himself. *Stop worrying*, he muttered. *Remember Sarah: she is recovering. Everything is on track, and Josh is coming home. And you've got fifty thousand pounds in the bank.* Peter even promised that he would take care of the girl and the accusation! His family now had a bright future.

It was at that moment that he knew – this is what had been niggling in his gut; in the last two days, all of these unsolvable problems had been solved by Peter's interventions. *Why*? He spoke into the void. Was it just a coincidence, or had he been craftily manipulated all along? Had they orchestrated everything? Was this all to lure him into a trap? He stood up to shake off the nagging doubts. Trying to invoke reason he said out loud, "*This is good news! Embrace the future, man.*"

He reminded himself that he was about to be introduced to the most powerful people on the planet. He would become a part of their influential club. Peter called him a member of the elite. *How could that be bad?* And yet he shuddered! What kind of power is shaking up this planet? He stopped himself this time. It was time to get rid of the doubts and the gloom. He needed something to work this kind of magic. In the end, he decided there was nothing else he could do. He had to follow Peter.

Chapter 12

Introduction to the members

Punctual as usual, Peter entered the apartment, bringing a certain energy that brightens up a room.

John was struck again by his good looks. He was at least a foot taller than him, stunningly handsome in a craggy, robust kind of way. John felt totally mesmerised by this charismatic figure in his expensively cut dinner suit. *Some people just ooze a kind of quality that is difficult to define.*

As they travelled in the limo towards their dinner engagement, John strained to see where they were going. Peter laughed at his efforts. "There's no point in trying to guess where we are going, my friend. This is privacy glass. Our hosts would like to keep the location off the radar. There will be many rich and famous present tonight. Discretion is necessary on such occasions. We certainly don't want media predators getting wind of our meeting."

John was feeling nauseous again. He had never been good at parties.

Sensing John's unease, Peter reassured him: "Don't worry, people simply want to meet you. There is no need for any in-depth conversations. You will be at my side most of the evening; otherwise, Gloria will look after you. Ah. Look, we have arrived."

John noted that they had driven on for at least another five minutes before the car pulled up at the entrance of a grand stately home. They were led into a huge hall with a checkerboard tiled floor. Grand, intricately carved pillars stood proudly at either side of the symmetrical curving stairways. Beautiful paintings, exquisite tapestries, and objet d'art adorned every wall and flat surface. Whoever owned this house was super-rich and obviously liked to show it.

As guests poured in, John grew increasingly uneasy. *Oh God, I don't belong with these people.* He recognised a few politicians, a famous movie star. As he expected, there were a few members of the aristocracy – most of the guests he had never seen before. Everyone seemed keen to meet him and were all introduced by their first names. *Probably to protect their identities,* he figured.

When they moved into the dining room, he felt a sense of relief when Peter and Gloria flanked him on either side. Dinner was sublime – he had never tasted food quite like it.

Later, they moved into a large ballroom, set out with rows of beautifully handcrafted Georgian chairs.

It was fascinating to observe Peter as he moved effortlessly through the room. He stopped and chatted with each group with uncommon ease. Obviously he knew these people very well. He was charming, witty, and comfortable within his own skin.

Surprisingly, it was Peter and not the host who stood upfront to address the crowd. He welcomed the members and indicated that there were a few new recruits in their midst. Everyone turned towards John and clapped.

John smiled, somewhat proudly. He had been accepted into this elite club.

Cracking a few jokes with uncommon ease, Peter then

introduced the entertainment for the evening. A young solo singer and a violinist began a beautiful rendition of the haunting Goreki symphony number 3. This piece of music was one of John's favourites. He remembered that – unusually for Sarah – she had cried the first time that she heard the song.

On the way home, Peter asked John if he had enjoyed the concert. The song was about a group of sorrowful mothers grieving for their lost children. The Holocaust had robbed so many mothers! Poignant and intensely meaningful, the song seemed deeply relevant. The stirring in his heart felt strong enough to produce a stabbing pain. He remembered a quote by Emmanuel Kant – *Music is the language of emotions*.

Did he answer Peter? – he wasn't sure. Turning away and deep in thought, John realised that yesterday he had identified with the sorrowful mothers. Powerless, he was losing both his son and his wife. Today, thankfully, it was a different story.

Interrupting his thoughts, Peter asked him if he would like to walk back to the apartment.

They ambled slowly along the Southbank, taking in the crisp autumn air. As they came alongside the Tate Modern Gallery, they discussed the age old debate about traditional versus modern art. While John straddled both genres, Peter was very much a traditionalist. He loved the works of the Old Masters like Titian, Rembrandt, and Turner. Still his favourite painting was the *Stubbs Horse,* whom he called "A magnificent creature." Peter explained that the artist's love for horses had not prevented him from dissecting many animals in the quest for perfection.

John noted that disturbingly, Peter seemed to enjoy this ghoulish aspect of the artwork.

Although sharing Peter's love of traditional art, John

began to talk enthusiastically about an exhibition of Wassily Kandinsky he had visited at the Tate Modern. He spoke about the innovative way the curator had arranged the story of the artist's life in his paintings that revealed his deepest fears. From humble beginnings of Russian folk art, many of the works were painted on cardboard to his later works, grand in scale and more vividly optimistic and full of colour. At the beginning of the world war, he produced huge apocalyptic canvasses; works of chaos and destruction. Then, the grey gloomy post-war abstracts evoked feelings of a man without hope.

John spoke again: "You could see his depression in the paint. The futility of life sung out of the canvas like a lament."

They both agreed that art – like music – was an incredibly powerful medium to communicate concepts that could not easily be explained in words.

John knew that Kandinsky's later paintings were a mirror of his life only a few days before.

They stopped at a bar for a nightcap. As he sat across from his mentor, he watched Peter as he enjoyed the Southbank's atmosphere and the multitude of riverboats traversing haphazardly over the fast-flowing River Thames. This allowed John some time to study the unusual species of a man.

He couldn't help himself as he blurted out, "Are you for real Peter? I can't pretend to understand everything that is happening. This fantastic story you have been unfolding to me, well, you know it's . . . a lot to take in. I'm not sophisticated like you. I'm just a simple guy leading a very ordinary life. I can't understand how I can be the right person for you."

"John, my friend, let me worry about that," Peter said with a warm smile. "I've had my eye on you for a very long time. Believe me, you are not only the right man but you are uniquely suited to your new role. You can say goodbye to your old simple life. Tonight you are holding the destiny of all mankind in your hands.

Do you feel the weight of it? Not many people can say that. Let me assure you, John. This is real. Nothing will ever be the same again!"

John leaned back in his chair. He felt satiated in every way. Without a doubt, it was time to move up in the world. For the first time in his forty years, John felt at ease in another man's company. It seemed obvious now that his father had spoiled his ability to trust other men.

"Is Peter your real name, or should I call you Cain?" *The Immortal* chuckled. "Oh, you have found me out. My given name is Cain. Peter is just my little joke. You know that it means the *rock that everything is built upon*. Everyone calls me by my immortal name. Why don't you?

That night John drifted off to sleep immediately his head touched the pillow.

Chapter 13

Outside of time

John woke with a thud on the floor. Familiar feelings of night terrors hung over him. His inner core was shaking. He'd heard his mother's voice in a dream. Her voice replayed over and over, warning him to be careful or he would be deceived. *Mutterings of a delirious old woman – ridiculous!* he thought, and yet his clothes were soaking in sweat. He shuddered as he remembered the pain he felt as he watched his mother disintegrate before his eyes. It hadn't been a long illness but it wasn't easy. He resolved once again that he would not die like that, and neither would his family – Cain had given them the way out.

It was 3.16 a.m. on the third day; decision day. When he looked back at the clock, he felt troubled: acutely aware that he had changed his mind a thousand times in the last 48 hours. There were moments of complete certainty – like when he saw Sarah with renewed hope in her eyes or when he thought of the future that lay ahead for his son.

Of course, he admitted; it wouldn't hurt to be one of the most powerful men on the planet. A new bloodline – *The Immortals*!

He thought about the unlimited information to which he would have access. It would be like possessing an unrestricted database of knowledge.

Surely with that kind of knowledge, all of mankind would benefit. They would be able to solve every problem known to man! He reasoned.

New technologies would be opening up with quantum computers. Something he had been totally unaware of two days ago. He had listened to the inventor describe innovative methods of processing information at phenomenal speeds. He explained how these computers could access other dimensions and bring back information into this timeline. It sounded futuristic, but amazingly, he discovered that this technology was already being adopted by major corporations worldwide.

He continued to imagine this new world and how it was like a great treasure map unfolding before him. Surely this was the holy grail of knowledge seekers.

Cain and his people seemed to own the keys to this unseen realm of meta-knowledge. He pondered for some time about the power they would possess. Systems would be able to access all data in an instant.

Like any new era, with significant change, there would be a downside. People would have nowhere to hide. He was aware that in this new world, everyone's lives would be transparent.

Still, he concluded that it would be a small price that would have to be paid for immortality.

He reasoned that it would happen anyway, so it was best to be on the winning side.

It was at that moment he admitted – humanity would polarise! This technology would create a great divide, and he knew that it would be terrifying for those who wouldn't participate! They would be like an underclass in a new world where everyone else had been upgraded. Ironically, free will would give everyone a choice to live forever or die.

It was hard to admit that until now, he had no understanding of the powers controlling the world. Until three days ago, he had been like a castaway on a square metre of land. Stranded and helpless; he was waiting there, as the sea roared on all sides. He considered his plight once more. Had God and his army of angels rescued him? No! It was Cain who came with a lifeboat full of incredible gifts and promises of a better world for him and his family. He was becoming increasingly convinced that he was on the right side.

As John drifted back to sleep, he saw his mother standing over him. "The whole world is about to come under a hypnotic promise of peace and prosperity."

"Stop!" He shouted out in the dream. "You can keep your God. What did he ever do for you?" He spent the next few hours grappling with ghosts. The gentle beep of the alarm clock brought him little comfort. His head was pounding. The bedclothes were wrapped around his body like a shroud! Surreally, it felt like he had taken part in a great cosmic battle.

John was fully aware that this was the day of the deadline. *If only I had a clear sign*, he wrestled. Rubbing the sleep from his eyes, he looked towards the window blinds as a shaft of light filled the room. He stared for a while as if expecting the light to speak to him.

Pulling himself up from the pillow, he laughed at this absurd notion. It was certainly not a mystical experience, just the rising sun breaking the night from day. He lay back in bed for a while, thinking about Sunday afternoons when he was a child. After lunch, his mother would clear the table before laying out the *Good Book,* telling him stories, and encouraging him to learn their meanings. In his formative years, he had loved this ritual; somehow the words had brought him comfort.

Strangely, one particular verse was playing over and over in his mind. "Do all you can to get wisdom, even if it costs you all you have, search for her like hidden treasure." Why was wisdom described as a woman? The story went on to show how Lady Wisdom could keep foolish men from wayward women. He remembered sniggering as his mother warned him about certain ladies who could *lead a man down the steps to hell with sweet seductions and enticements but, in the end only want to ruin you.* As a young man, he had discovered this was indeed true, so afterward had avoided that particular road.

John spoke into the room, "Alright, mother, I'll be careful! But I'll decide what kind of world I want to live in!" Not realising the significance of that fateful day until now – he froze! It was the day his father had walked out and had never come back. He had repeatedly tried to talk to his mother about his father's disappearance, but she refused to discuss it. He could never quite work out why. He always wondered if some wayward woman had led his father down the steps of hell.

After that day, John never sat at the table to do his lessons. Indeed, it was the last day he truly listened to his mother. He had never stopped loving her, but he had chosen another path.

Strangely, his mother never threw out any of his father's belongings. Their bedroom remained untouched, almost like a shrine, until the day she died.

He had found a way to remember his dad by gathering a few little trinkets and mementoes. Every year on his birthday, he would open his keepsake box – an old biscuit tin. Carefully, like a sacred ceremony, he would take out his bounty. A Swiss Army knife, a hazy old photograph torn at one edge, and a broken pocket watch. He always meant to have it repaired, but it seemed symbolic of their broken relationship, and the day time stopped.

Performing his yearly ritual, he would hold the faded photograph next to his chest and vow never to give up hope of seeing his father again.

They had been so very close. Nothing made sense anymore. His memories were fading, just like the photograph. Maybe it was time to grow up and accept the truth – his father was never coming back!

John ate breakfast to fuel up on some calories. Neither hungry nor enjoying his food, he thought he would need the extra energy to get through the day. After refusing a second helping he gulped down two very strong coffees.

Gloria was busy working in the kitchen. He'd observed that she was a woman of few words. She was singing a non-descript tune under her breath. Curious to find out what she knew, he hesitantly tried to start up a conversation. "Ahem . . . do you live nearby Gloria?

"Oh!" She seemed surprised by the interruption. "No, I live quite a few stops away on the tube, but it's easy enough to get here."

John tried again to engage her in conversation. "Peter, oh, I mean Cain – is an incredible man, he looks really good for his age, don't you think?"

Gloria turned from the cooker and looked directly at John before she answered: "He rescued me too. I was probably in a worse state than you." With a piercing look, she added, "I know everything."

John thought he saw a fleeting darkness film over her eyes, but the moment was gone when Cain entered the room. As he looked towards John, he grinned, "You will be delighted to hear that Josh will arrive in London tomorrow morning. His flight arrives early at Heathrow so all going well, you should be reunited at breakfast."

"This is so wonderful; I can't thank you enough." John was longing to tell Josh all that had happened, but especially the good news that he had found a cure for him. He started to plan how he would tell him about their good fortune. *We will have to go to visit his mum straight away.*

Somewhere in the distance, he vaguely heard Gloria and Cain discuss something about a document that had arrived by courier. She had left it on the desk. He was slightly curious about the content, but he had other things to think about. *Yeah, I'll need to organise some celebrations.*

"Thanks Gloria, you finish up and take the rest of the day off." Cain courteously guided her towards the door with an unmistakable air of authority that did not expect to be challenged. She obeyed him without question, immediately putting on her coat, and was gone without a backward glance.

John admired the commanding quality this man possessed. He was so self-assured! People like that were a rarity. Confidence poured out of every fibre of his being. No-one could feign such faith in oneself without any hint of embarrassment or uncertainty.

Kings and politicians, celebrities or geniuses . . . scratch the surface and all that would remain was a colony of zombies – dead men walking! All of them had a certain appointment with death. Power, wealth, and status were all transient and meaningless. In the end, life was like going on a journey, boarding a train at one station, and yet knowing that the last station had no platform. Only a gaping void! This was the destination for every human – apart from Cain. He was unique!

John shuddered. He had never given his future much thought. Until this day, he'd been content to leave his mortality to chance.

Cain jolted him out of his daydream as he asked: "Can I pour you a coffee?"

John shook his head. "Better not, or you will have to

scrape me off the ceiling!" They both laughed.

"Yes. Well! That very timely comment introduces the subject of going into higher dimensions. Do you think you can handle it now?"

John nodded, but inside he was terrified. "I guess it will make all this real for me. I need to see some evidence. I find it hard to completely believe without seeing for myself. I guess it's like having faith in . . ." he stopped short.

Cain raised his eyebrows, then grinned. "It's okay, you were about to say – that's like having faith in something you can't see." They both laughed heartily at the absurdity of the statement.

For over thirty years, John had not believed in a God or in the existence of a spiritual dimension called eternity. Now Cain was about to prove it was all real. He would no longer be able to claim ignorance or remain as one of no faith. Today he would have to make a choice. Which path would he take?

Cain left the room for a few moments before returning with a long wooden rod – it was roughly hewn like a shepherd's staff. "I know this looks outlandishly biblical, but you need something to hold onto and well . . . I've used this rod for a very long time. We shall be gone for a few seconds, but when we return, time will have altered – just slightly, though. We don't want to cause any glitches in the cosmic clock – do we?"

John's eyes widened.

"Don't worry, you won't have grown a beard or have aged a hundred years. Although when we come back, it will feel like we have been away for days."

John's knees were buckling, and his whole body began to shake. However, his destiny was set out before him, so he braced himself for what lay ahead.

"Okay, my friend," Cain spoke gently but firmly.

"Hold onto this rod and see that you don't let go. Not even for a second! It's probably best that you close your eyes initially. You will feel disoriented, and I don't want you to be sick all over the universe. That would be awful!" John looked horrified, but the ancient man just laughed "I'm just teasing you!"

John obediently closed his eyes. He felt nothing at first. Then terror seized him as he became aware they were travelling at great speed as if they were rocket-propelled. It felt like his skin was being dragged backwards as his innards were catapulted forward simultaneously. His senses were playing tricks on him as he no could no longer tell if he was the right way up or not.

Unable to bear it any longer, he opened his eyes. At first, he peered out of one eye, trying not to look at everything at once. Then he gazed in wonderment, his eyes now a pair of lenses zooming in and out of the spectacular scenes all around him.

A sea of colours swirled around them as plasma clouds formed Auroras; they danced playfully in every direction. Planets came hurtling towards them, swirling and spiralling as they moved beyond the huge fireball of the sun. They seemed to be following the elliptical course around the sun. Somehow he knew that they would soon be flung out of the solar system.

In a dreamlike state, they passed over Saturn with its mysterious gaseous rings surrounding the planet reverently like a halo. There seemed to be a sound or frequency emitting from the rings. Awestruck, John pointed to the top end of the strange planet. A mysterious blue smoky cloud capped the North Pole. It looked like a storm, and yet its geometric structure was that of a perfectly formed hexagon. Six straight lines. How could this shape exist here? It seemed impossible and so out of place!

But there was no time to work it out! He gasped as a massive planet – hundreds of times bigger than the sun – came into his vision. They came so close that he could no longer see the outline of the planet. He could hear himself shout, "We are too close." His heart pounded as he felt the gravity of the planet almost swallow them whole. Cain indicated that everything was okay.

Exhilarated and relieved, John wanted time to stop to assimilate this experience. Remembering his school days, he recalled the name of the giant planet, Regulus. It was impossible to conceptualise from reading a book. The sheer size of the planet took his breath away. In comparison, his own sun was a tennis ball and the earth a speck of dust.

They moved through the visible colour spectrum and beyond towards an inky darkness, leaving behind gas clouds pouring forth fountains of colours he had never seen the likes of before. John felt like a child as bubbles of light washed over them like iridescent raindrops.

Then everything changed, and he felt bereft as they travelled beyond the light show and indigo blackness engulfed them. There were no stars to pierce the darkness. It felt to John as if he was hovering in a void of nothingness. Before he had a chance to scream, they changed direction. They stopped and turned 180 degrees as if to go back the way they had come. Standing – or more accurately, hovering – in the darkness, he could see far off into the realm they had just departed. All of his senses were being challenged. They had neither spaceship to contain them nor spacesuits to protect them.

No oxygen tanks either – and yet they were breathing something. All of his understanding of what it meant to be in space no longer existed. Defunct! Nothing made sense. His eyes had to be deceiving him. He watched in awe as the universe began to roll up like slowly like a paper scroll.

It appeared as if they had just escaped out of the edge of the scroll before the tubular shape folded up before his eyes. He found himself trying to narrate this vision in his head. He wanted to remember every second of this journey, but words were failing him. Indeed, it was impossible to describe. A total mystery!

Am I standing outside of the universe in a different dimension, far outside my perception of space and time? Is there a universe within a universe? Am I dreaming? Stomach churning and senses reeling, asking him a whirlwind of questions. *Oh no, I'm feeling sick – no joking this time! Stop yourself!*

Turning to Cain once more, he sought reassurance. The rod was firmly in his grip. Then he looked again at the awesome sight. Something caught his attention. Some kind of material or objects were flowing in one side of the tube and out the other end. Without anyone explaining, he just knew that the substance was *life*. Incredible fragments of *life* were flowing in and through and then out of this . . . what could he call this shape-shifting universe? A multi-dimensional organic living entity?

If only his tongue could become the pen of a writer. People had no idea that they were living in some kind of multiverse. He needed to tell everyone when he got back, although how would he convince them? They'd probably think he was high on some mind-altering drugs – maybe he was! Maybe Cain had slipped some hallucinogenic substance into his coffee? He couldn't remember how long they had been there nor feel the flow of time passing. Maybe it had been days or even minutes – but in some way, he was simply existing.

"Where are we?" John whispered reverently. Cain responded. "We are at the end! This is what the end looks like. Everything you know will get rolled up like a scroll. It's all going to be destroyed."

"You can't destroy it." John protested angrily. "It's so beautiful. It's perfect!"

Cain turned from John, looking again at the incredible scene. "Oh, it's not me, John. I'm not going to destroy it. Don't you remember, this is what I told you about? Blame *The Maker* because that is his plan!"

"Get ready! Hold on! We have to go back now."

John held on to the rod so tightly that his hand felt like glue. At first, they moved slowly towards the visible universe. As they came closer, it was as if they were accelerating through the cosmos at breakneck speed. It was thrilling and terrifying all at once. They passed by a multitude of galaxies, but it was impossible to identify home as they all bore a resemblance to the familiar spiral shape of the Milky Way.

They had made a time shift. A space shift. Impossible! And yet John knew it was real.

Chapter 14

The Rewards

Back in the room, John crash-landed on diamond-hard rock. *Well, that's what it felt like*, he reckoned. His body was shaking uncontrollably, and he was burning up.

Cain quickly helped him into the shower, running the cold water over his body, clothes and all. This relieved some of the pressure, but John felt that at any moment he might spontaneously combust into a million fragments of fire.

He heard someone scream then shout out something in a language he did not know. "What the hell!" he groaned, realising that it was coming from him.

Cain held him tightly as they both slid to the floor as a waterfall of freezing water poured over them. He was well aware of the shockwaves John was feeling in his body. "You'll be fine, but it will take a few hours before you recover. I'm sure you must be starving. Honestly, you have no idea how many calories that trip used up."

"What, you mean I could have lost a few excess pounds?" John spluttered excitedly.

It was an awkward situation, but they both laughed.

The experience had completely changed his thinking.

My perception of reality has altered beyond belief. He couldn't recall feeling so highly charged. It felt like some kind of electrical energy. *What now?*

"Get some dry clothes on. Quickly, we need to eat now!" Cain's commanding voice conveyed urgency. "Questions can wait."

They ate a hearty meal in complete silence, both unable to speak and ravenous from the calories expended during the journey. John had no idea where the meal came from but was grateful that it had been laid out for them.

All of his senses were heightened as if they were functioning at extreme levels simultaneously. He tried to work out how he was feeling, but nothing made sense. It was as if his whole being had been expanded during the experience. He had no grid for this. His current vocabulary was redundant as he was trying to analyse his new position.

Yes! That's it! I feel like a child in a new world, and this child needs to learn a new language!

John looked at his ancient relative with admiration and was now sure that he had found a true father. Someone who would teach him how to function in this new life! Neither of them moved from the table; transfixed. John decided it was best to stay put as he needed to keep his feet firmly on the floor. Feeling the need to say something, he simply offered: "I feel totally disoriented."

Cain responded. "Don't worry, I do too. No matter how many times I go there, it still takes a while to recover. Let's just sit here and talk. What do you want to ask me?"

John searched for his voice again. "I . . . Peter, oh, I mean Cain . . . I don't know what –".

The Elder responded, "It's okay, John. It's all a bit much to assimilate into your human psyche. You've gone beyond the edge of the universe into the second heavens and way beyond the threshold of your current five senses.

It will take time to get used to your newfound sensory experiences, the explosion of new colours, and the heightened awareness of everything around you. Everything you have known has shifted. Your simple little world has multiplied into at least ten dimensions. No wonder you are feeling confused. Nothing will ever be the same again. Would that about sum up how you are feeling just now?"

"Pretty much."

Cain began to fill in the gaps in his story. "It's like this, John. First of all, *The Maker* is real and this universe has a beginning and an end. Humans find it difficult to grasp how vast the universe is, but now you know that it is only a fraction of what exists. This universe exists inside another, and so the story expands."

"It's like those Russian dolls," John added naively. He then asked, "Is this what we call infinity?"

Cain agreed. "You've answered your own question, dear boy. If we had been able to stay longer, you could have looked into history – right back to the beginning – to my time. What I've been looking forward to revealing to you is that we now know how to change the end! It has taken us millennia to develop the technologies to achieve our dreams. We are going to stop *The Maker* from carrying out his destructive plans. He said there will be a new heaven and a new earth. Yes!" The ancient man thundered, "There will be, but this one will be ours. He can take his faithful few to his golden palaces, but we will have this universe.

For the first time since they met, John saw Cain's face darken. He practically spat venom out of his mouth as his rant about *The Maker* and his followers intensified."

Hearing these words, John instinctively recoiled. He felt as if he'd been bitten. After all, his own mother was one of these faithful followers that Cain had just spewed out of his mouth.

Seeing John's reaction, the elder realised that he had stepped over the proverbial line on the maternal front. Bad move! Knowing that John had been starved of paternal love and that his late mother had been his only source of nurture. "Oh, I'm so sorry, I've upset you. I appreciate the deep feeling you have for your mother. My outrage was expressed towards *The Maker*. Forgive me for being insensitive.

You see, I've been searching for a son for a very long time. I think today I have found one. I want to share everything I have with you, and I mean everything. All my possessions are yours. My vast wealth of knowledge will be available to you. I'm even going to share the building blocks of my immortal body with you! We may be separated by thousands of years of genetic transference, but here we are today – we share the same bloodline. The ancients called this life force *Nephesh* because it literally exists in the blood. I promise you, son, I will never leave you nor abandon you."

Cain's strategy was working. John felt something awaken inside. It felt like his *Nephesh* was beginning to vibrate with life. *I am standing here talking to a father! Albeit from ancient times.* John strengthened himself with this thought: *I am no longer an unwanted rejected soul. I have Cain now. We are blood relatives.* At that moment, he decided that it was his destiny to follow this man. "What happens now?" he asked his forefather.

"I transfer my unique, *immortal DNA* to you, Son!"

John eagerly replied, "When do we start?"

The *Immortal One* smiled but cautioned John that he would have to go through the formal signing of contracts. He continued to explain how the hospital needed his permission to carry out procedures. "They have to be sure you are not being coerced. It has to be your decision for obvious ethical reasons, and of course, they don't want to be sued! It's just formality. Everything above board, eh?"

"Of course," John agreed.

Cain continued to explain that the second part of the agreement stipulated that under no circumstances could he transfer his *recombinant DNA* to any other person without permission. "You remember from the research papers that we can combine two sets of *DNA* using *CRISPR editing*. When the geneticists insert my *immortal DNA* into your body, you will become a saviour to mankind."

John flinched at that remark but kept his thoughts locked up.

The Immortal continued. "Your *DNA* will be an extremely valuable commodity. The members have contributed vast fortunes to develop this technology, so they don't want it falling into the wrong hands. You must understand that they have asked for specific guidelines to be put in place to protect their investments.

They have stipulated that for a short time, you will not be left on your own. Of course, this is not my idea, but I am sure that you can appreciate their concerns. The restrictions will only be in place for a twelve-month period, and by that time, all the procedures will be complete. Would that be a problem for you, John?"

John shifted in his chair; he hadn't expected the one-year confinement clause. Cain saw his hesitation, so explained: "The plan is to take you and your family to a private island where we have all the facilities we need. There is an excellent hospital where we can continue to treat Sarah, and you will receive all your tests and procedures."

John felt uneasy about being taken to some god-forsaken island where it sounded like they would be held captive. He expressed these reservations. "I'm not too sure about being locked away in a prison for a year, and I don't think Sarah would be happy about that."

Always resilient, Cain immediately responded. "Come, let me show your prison," he chuckled. "I know you won't be disappointed."

The room lit up again with holographic images of an enchantingly beautiful coralline island surrounded by sapphire seas. A luxurious villa sat atop cliffs overhanging a pristine white sandy beach.

John was given a guided tour of the property with its sumptuous interior and the house surrounded on three sides by a walled garden leading to orchards and stables beyond. It looked idyllic. The view panned out over the island again, where a few kilometres away, he could see the state-of-the-art hospital Cain had described.

John was surprised when the staff all came out to greet him – in real-time! The head consultant greeted him like an old friend. He liked this feeling of being important.

The doctor explained some details of the forthcoming treatments John would receive and assured him that procedures would be simple and virtually painless. "There will be a lot of needles," he conceded but emphasised that he was sure John could handle it. He went on to explain that John would receive the best treatment to maximise his health while there.

Once again, John enjoyed being treated as special. *All the medical staff and the beautiful house. My God, a whole island specially prepared for me! I must be chosen*! He consciously straightened his frame. He had gotten into the bad habit of slouching again, so he made a mental note: *Must remember to stop that.*

"Why don't we get this boat on the water? We don't

have time to waste." Cain said, trying to mask the rising note of urgency in his voice: "Get all the formalities seen to. The core team are waiting for the green light. Then we can go out for dinner with a few select members tonight and for some celebrations later. They are waiting anxiously for your answer. Although I confess that I anticipated your response, so I've booked a top-class restaurant with fabulous entertainment. I also have a wonderful surprise for you."

"I'm in!" John simply stated.

The Immortal made a phone-call that brought a team of people to the apartment within a few minutes. Apparently, they were waiting on the fifth floor, "not too far to travel," Cain informed him. They were just a short ride away on the elevator.

Handshakes and excited congratulations energised the room as a group of people exited the lift. John felt quite giddy with this amount of attention. An older man sat down to explain more fully about the medical procedures and his need to stay on the island. This was agreed upon, and the contract was signed.

Shortly afterwards, another man, fresh-faced and full of youthful energy, approached him. He produced documents that effectively made John the proud owner of the penthouse and a country estate. Millions of pounds of real estate would belong to him with the stroke of a pen.

He signed the missives before anyone could change their minds. An attractive lady, who introduced herself as the managing director of a central bank, produced papers to open up a bank account with an unbelievable deposit of money. John tried not to gasp as he signed his name.

Another stranger handed over the keys to a top-of-the-range car. So the rewards piled up extravagantly, one on top of another. John looked around the room, observing a sea of faces, all talking with great enthusiasm. He couldn't remember anyone's name. It didn't matter. Surely, they needed him – or perhaps more accurately they would all be indebted to him for what he could give them – eternal life!

Within hours they were driving towards an exclusive hotel somewhere in the centre of London. By this time, John had lost his bearings. He felt giddy, confused and probably a little drunk. Countless bottles of champagne had been consumed to celebrate the occasion.

"Enjoy, son." Cain said. After tonight there will be no alcohol for the next year!" He guided him to a corner table to speak with some business acquaintances. A small orchestra played unnoticed as people came to introduce themselves. Everyone there was dripping with wealth. They were all friendly, but John wasn't naive; he knew that none of them would have glanced his way a few days before. He didn't care. These people were going to be his friends and part of his new life. Soon he was going to possess the confidence of an *Immortal* – just like Cain. He was going to be mentored by his ancient father figure or perhaps more accurately, ancient grandfather. He would watch, listen and learn from this great man.

A few minutes later, while in deep conversation with a geneticist, his attention was interrupted by a communal gasp echoing around the room.

She was in a self-propelled wheelchair heading straight for him. Sarah looked stunning. A real beauty. John could never understand why she married him. She was way out of his league! The entire room burst into applause. Even the orchestra changed to an upbeat tempo, mirroring the hope and enthusiasm she radiated into the room. It was thrilling to see his wife come back from the dead. As good as!

They embraced to the sound of shouts and cheers from their newfound friends. Sarah could only stay for a short while as she had to go back to the hospital for ongoing treatment. He wanted to go back with her, but his beautiful wife insisted that he stay and enjoy the rest of the evening celebrations, content that they would be reunited soon.

Later, while alone in the apartment, John held out his arms. He gathered in the day, holding it close to his chest; he didn't want this day to end. Everything had changed. He was reluctant to go to bed in case he would wake up and discover that it had all been dream. Instead, he picked up a pale blue cashmere throw from the chair and draped it around his shoulders like a mantle. Spreading out his arms again – he felt like he had wings. Dancing around the apartment with pure joy, he started singing, *"Come fly with me"* until he collapsed laughing. *"Hey, whoever is listening. One day I'm going to have wings and I will fly!"*

John fell into bed after savouring a few single malts. *The best whisky anyone could buy*, he thought – *No more scrimping and scraping for this family*. Twenty minutes later he collapsed into bed. Content. He slept like only the inebriated could, snoring loud and deep.

Chapter 15

Josh's story

Nothing could have prepared Josh for the news that his mother had been diagnosed with a potentially fatal degenerative disease. Somehow it was harder to swallow the bitter pill about his mother than the possibility of his own imminent demise. He couldn't bear to watch her suffer, but the possibility that his mother had passed the faulty gene to him was unthinkable.

Going for genetic screening seemed the only way to go. His Mum and Dad echoed the doctor's opinion that he should get tested, so he relented without really understanding the consequences of a positive result.

He did all that was required. While sitting numbly in the consulting room, he nodded his head in at appropriate times as the counsellor talked him through the possible outcomes. Obediently he rolled up his sleeve to bare his skin, ready to receive the invasive needle into his unwilling arm, while every cell in his body was screaming out – No! He complied silently. The doctor was speaking but Josh no longer registered his words.

Two hours later, he regretted his actions. He wasn't ready to know his future just yet. Although the doctor had given him a choice to hear the results in his office or take away a sealed envelope, he was afraid of the outcome.

The letter was to be opened now or later when the time was right. He chose the latter; painfully aware, he needed time to prepare himself for the result.

That night while lying in bed, he denied himself sleep to organise his escape plan. Fortunately, his gran had left him a small legacy meant to help fund his degree course. His life had been on track to study medicine at Glasgow University. The family were all delighted when his application had been accepted. Embarrassingly, his mother had thrown a party for him, but secretly he was pleased. He guessed they were genuinely proud of him. Matriculation was in four weeks.

Life would soon be over, he reckoned, so what was the point in wasting time. Seventeen years wasn't enough. *Is life pre-planned, and am I destined for this cup of suffering?* This was unfair, he reckoned. Legs crossed, he curled into a ball on his favourite rag-rug that his mother had spent months making. Hands holding up his head, he closed his eyes and dreamed of a better day. Pictures of a world waiting to be discovered filled his inner vision. *This will be my only opportunity to taste the sweetness of being free. I want to live without restriction – if only for a short time. No responsibility or ties. No intense period of studying.* The only *tomorrow* that seemed bearable.

Intuitively, Josh knew if he told his parents they would easily dissuade him from going. They would tell him about being sick and needing his family nearby. His mother might be able to cope, and he knew that she would understand, but his father would use emotional blackmail to make him stay by his mother's side. "*No!*" he exclaimed. It was best to leave without the drama – which he knew would follow if he disclosed his plan.

Before accepting his university place, a few mates had asked him to join them on a gap year to Australia. He decided: *To hell with everything – I'm going!*

A few hours later, he had booked a flight and arranged visas. Surprisingly, he discovered it was easy to book everything online. His passport had recently been renewed so, he had the green light to go. Josh packed his rucksack and quietly slipped out the backdoor before sunrise. Leaving home somehow seemed right and wrong at the same time.

He had to find a way to face his future but he knew he was abandoning his parents, which caused him great pain. In fact, the moment he left home, fear and guilt became his travelling companions.

After travelling extensively throughout the east coast of Australia from Sydney to the Great Barrier Reef, he turned inland.

The bus arrived in the late evening at Uluru, and so the landscape remained hidden behind a curtain of mystery. After a few hours of sleep, the tour guide awakened the weary travellers, encouraging them not to miss the sunrise. They all piled back into the bus and travelled a few miles from the campsite.

There must have been thirty to forty camper vans and cars full of expectant tourists waiting to see the sunrise over the ancient Ayers Rock. It was still pitch black when the bleary-eyed passengers spilled out of the bus. Headlights were turned off. Everyone sensed that the Spirit of the Land was about to reveal its treasure. Excitement and anticipation contained in every breath as people waited in quiet contemplation. A contract of silence existed in this temporary community.

Josh became aware of something bigger than himself. Truly, he felt that he was experiencing something sacred. Waves of emotions flooded his soul as the morning light revealed the first glimpse of the sun as she extravagantly set the red rock ablaze. It looked like a giant meteorite had fallen from the sky into the vast plains of the ochre red desert. It was the first time Josh cried since leaving home.

For the next few hours, he explored the base of the rock. Strangely, the dry red dust had managed to produce a blanket of delicate tiny yellow flowers. This was a mystery to him as it looked like it hadn't rained there for years.

Anger welled up as he watched his fellow travellers ignore the request of the indigenous people to not climb the rock. Their sacred lands were continuously trespassed by inquisitive uncaring tourists.

Josh walked half a kilometre from the blaze-red rock to look for … he knew not what. Somewhere to think, something he needed to capture.

Finding a spot behind a lonely rock provided deep shadow, a welcome shelter from the scorching sun. As he lay down on his back, a lone desert eagle flew overhead. He was fascinated watching the huge bird circle overhead in an ever-increasing unseen whirlwind, catching the thermals to rise up unto new heights. The small dark speck hovered for an age. Josh meditated. *What's he thinking? Is he simply enjoying the pleasure of flight? Can he tell me secrets from his lofty view?*

Something that Josh had never experienced before began to fill his thoughts. Peace. Lack of fear, or whatever it was, began to spread like liquid honey through his veins. He guessed that this was the holy grail that drug takers exchanged for the stark harshness of reality. At that moment, it felt like he had escaped from the gravitational pull of the earth and was flying with the eagle.

Stars twinkled in the night-time sky when he woke up many hours later.

The tourist had retreated to the comfort of their

temporary homes, desert hotels, and camper vans. Josh, feeling fully awake and hyper-alive, walked with newfound purpose along the deserted road to the campsite.

In the morning, he decided to travel to Alice Springs.

Even at a very young age, his father had awakened an interest in art. Josh decided to have a look at the galleries displaying the work of the local Aboriginal people. Most of the artists were happy to talk about their paintings, and one woman kindly offered to give him a demonstration.

He soon discovered that the simplistic dot paintings were more difficult to master than he initially believed. Their paintings incorporated fantastic stories of the sacred relationship between humans and the land. Not something understood in his poor western mind-set. The artist encouraged him to have a go, but his effort to capture the essence of their history was both lifeless and amateurish.

The next few hours changed Josh's life. He was genuinely heartbroken, listening to the stories of how the Aboriginal people had become a lost tribe, without place or purpose. The modern world was alien to them. A few made a living selling their artworks, but more than a few had turned to alcohol to ease the pain of a meaningless existence. He met some people who were working alongside the tribes to regain ancient land rights and so restore their purpose and dignity.

Witnessing these volunteers doing something worthwhile stirred up a lot of questions. Most of the young people he knew, including himself, were hung up on the material world. These people were different and made such an impression on him. And so it was in Alice Springs that Josh decided to give up his self-centred lifestyle.

If my life is going to be short, I'm going to make it

count for something.

His new friends put him in touch with voluntary services in Sydney.

Within two weeks, Josh had given up his nomadic backpacking lifestyle and was on his way to the Philippines to help build an orphanage. From there, he travelled to Tibet and then on to India. Struck by the extreme excesses of the rich compared to the abject poverty of the majority, he often felt helpless.

The first time he saw young children abandoned on the streets begging for food shocked him to the core. He couldn't believe that it was possible for any modern society to tolerate such neglect.

So much for progress! he thought.

It was amid such cruelty that he understood his calling to be a doctor had been the right way to go.

Currently, he was asymptomatic. Perhaps he didn't have ALS?

He'd have to open the envelope soon, but meantime, he had work to do to help finish another orphanage. Having no particular skills to offer when he started out on this journey, he quickly realised that the only way he could help was to do manual labour.

Over time he was able to master a variety of building skills. He wasn't an expert, but he'd become reasonably competent at laying bricks and could do some decent plastering.

Many times he felt homesick as he shared mealtimes with grateful families. He longed to see his own tribe. One day he saw a woman slowly pushing herself along the sidewalk in a makeshift wheelchair. There was something about her vulnerability coupled with sheer determination that reminded him of his mother. He knew that it was a sign: it was time to go home!

Josh knew that he had to stop running and return to face his destiny. He took out the plain brown manila envelope from a secret pocket inside his backpack.

Over the last eighteen months, he had learned to quieten his soul. Sitting in silence for an hour or so, he lit a candle as he prepared himself for the outcome of the test.

Before booking his flight home, he decided to visit Jodhpur in Rajasthan. The famous blue city was overlooked by an ancient fort – set high upon a rocky outcrop overlooking the walled city. It came to mind that he'd watched a documentary with his Dad about this tourist's jewel. Although a long time ago, he remembered how it had stirred his imagination. It wasn't too far by train, and it would be a shame to miss it, so he seized the opportunity.

The local hostel was basic but clean enough.

Handing him a ticket for room number three on the upper floor, the clerk smiled and pointed to a flight of stairs. The accommodation was the typical backpacker's metal bed with a wafer-thin mattress. Experience had taught him to choose a bed at the back of the room against a wall with clear views of other travellers bunking in the room. He had nothing of great value, but still, it was wise to be careful. The door was a threadbare curtain – and all that separated him from the highly populated insect world of India. He made a mental note to use his mosquito net! As was his custom, he threw his sleeping bag on the mattress to claim his territory.

A quick look at his watch confirmed that he had just about enough time to catch the travel agent before closing time then go for something to eat.

Josh spent the next day exploring the city. His first call was the Meherangarh Fort. He wandered through the palaces enjoying the artefacts, especially the brightly coloured Marwar paintings. In another room, he marvelled at the *Elephant Howdah* and wondered how any animal could bear such a burden. The Howdah resembled a huge golden birdcage: intriguing, as legend says the hill upon which the giant fort sat – was known as the Mountain of Birds.

The tour guide told a gruesome story of how the Chief of the Rathore Clan decided to build a fort but had to seek help from a female warrior – Shri Karin Mata – to evict a hermit. Locals called him *The Lord of the Birds*. He, in turn, cursed the city, declaring that it would always be short of water.

This was not the end of the story. Pointing down to the bottom of the wall, the guide related the ghoulish tale of how the ruler considered it necessary to break the power of the curse by burying a man alive in the foundations so that the hermit's curse would be broken.

Apparently, Raja Meghwal, agreed to be a human sacrifice in order that his family would be looked after forever.

Josh pondered, what kind of man would volunteer for such a horrific death in order to release his family from poverty? This man made the ultimate sacrifice to release them from the eternal misfortune of being of the Untouchables.

The enthralling story both fascinated and troubled Josh. He had come to hate the inequality and elitism that he had witnessed on his travels.

In fact, the story affected him so much that he had to sit down on a low bench underneath a fig tree to steady himself. His stomach churned with anger. What kind of man would condemn another human being to such a gruesome death in order to enjoy his own life of luxury? The story gave him the chills.

He was within earshot of the guide as he gleefully finished his gruesome tale. The chirpy guide was happy to point out that, alas, there was a good ending to this story. The poor man's descendants still lived in the nearby gardens bearing the martyr's name.

"Not such a good ending for Raja Meghwal," Josh muttered.

He walked along the ramparts then stopped to survey the scene before him. *India is such a paradox,* he concluded. There was such a divide between rich and poor, yet many of the poorest looked the happiest. *How can this be?* He shook his head. It was time to shake of his gloomy thoughts.

Marvelling at the mesmerising array of the colours of India, he gazed over the city walls to the town beneath, with its bright cobalt roofs reflecting the cloudless cerulean skies. Breathing in the scene before him, he thought, *It's good to be alive.* He vowed that day that he would make a difference in the crazy world he lived in. After closing his eyes, he raised his face to the sky and whispered, *Thank you.* He saw the liberating words again. *Test negative!*

Funds were running low after paying for his flight tickets, so Josh decided to use the community kitchen for dinner before setting out to do some more sightseeing. The dining room was fairly empty. A group of people filed out of the door, leaving a couple of travellers who sat at the back of the room. Deep in conversation, they hardly looked up when Josh entered. He took their cue and sat at the other end of the room.

As Josh was pouring his second cup of tea, he turned from the stove, surprised to see an older man hovering at his table. Dressed formally, he was sweating profusely, looking stiff and uncomfortable and totally out of place in the humble hostel.

Josh cautiously approached his table. "Can I get you something?"

The man shook his head. "No, thanks, but if you don't mind, I would like to speak to you."

Immediately Josh was on his guard. He'd heard many stories of fellow travellers being approached to carry packages back to the UK. "Look. I'm not interested in any courier work, so I suggest that you move on."

The man seemed genuinely offended. "No, no! I'm not a drug dealer or anything like that."

Josh looked over his shoulder at the young couple. They were still deep in conversation. Trying to work out his options, Josh was wary of being left alone with this stranger.

The man sat down, indicating for Josh to do likewise. He remained standing.

"Suit yourself. I have a message for you from a family member. It's good news, I assure you. I work for Mr. Peter Kayin, and he would very much like to meet with you. He has asked me to give you this parcel and a note to arrange a meeting with him tomorrow morning."

Josh was speechless. Could this be a relative of his father? He'd never met any of them. In fact, his father was always reluctant to talk about his side of the family. "How did you know that I was here in India?"

The man replied. "Oh, that's easy, my boss owns the travel agency, and he recognised your name on the flight list." Before he had the time to open the parcel, the man got up, shook his hand, and left Josh scratching his head.

What just happened there? Josh ran his fingers through his long wavy sun-bleached hair. He looked down at the envelope and then the parcel. Intuitively, he knew that he had made a mistake. Opening the envelope, he frowned as he read the note. It was an invitation to meet with the travel-agency owner. He wanted to discuss a business proposal with him.

The driver would pick him up at 8am in the morning. As Josh looked at the package, he broke out in a cold sweat.

Damn it! I've been duped, he muttered under his breath. Tentatively he picked open one side of the package. He could see that it contained a lot of money. Stuffing the note and the package in his haversack, he looked around to check if anyone had witnessed the transaction, then rushed upstairs. Fortunately, there was no one there. It would be useless to count the money, but it was obvious there were tens of thousands of pounds. *What to do next? No time to panic! I need a plan – no point in running. The travel agent will most likely have contacts at the airports.* He concluded that he wouldn't be able to leave the country.

Before long, he decided that he would have to meet with the enigmatic Peter Kayin in the morning and hope that he was a genuine relative. Meantime he would have to hide the money somewhere on his body. Fortunately, he had some strong tape in his backpack that he'd bought to repair a small tear in the bag.

The toilet block was empty, so he went into a stall and spent the next ten minutes taping the money around his waist and legs. Worried that he might be robbed, he resigned himself to the fact that it was going to be a long night. He settled down in his sleeping bag to read a book. A couple of guys came and went, nodding in his direction, but like himself, not keen to engage in conversation. It was around 10pm when Josh was startled by a commotion in the room. He hadn't realised that he had nodded off.

A large figure loomed over his bed. The intruder attempted to speak, "Got a light, mate?"

Josh shrunk back against the wall. As his eyes adjusted to the low light, he saw the face of a guy, with a cigarette hanging from his lower lip; obviously drunk.

"No! Get off." He yelled.

"Sorry, mate, didn't know you were sleeping."

"Try the night porter," Josh answered, to get rid of him. Fortunately, the guy was so drunk that he immediately fell onto his bed, sound asleep. It was hours before Josh finally settled.

In the morning, the night-time visitor woke Josh from sleep again. "Hey mate, you okay? You sleep like the dead!"

Within five minutes, Josh was packed and heading downstairs with a voice trailing behind him, "Hey mate, was it something I said?"

The stranger was waiting for him at reception. "Ah, Mr. Kayin, I was just about to send the porter to find you. Did you sleep well?"

Josh nodded. He lied but had no inclination to show any fear. He just wanted to go home. Reluctantly, he followed the stranger to the waiting car.

Chapter 16

A different genesis

They drove through the morning traffic, trying to avoid various obstacles such as street markets, wandering sacred cows, and beggars. It took all Josh's willpower not to extricate himself from the car. He had bad vibes about this meeting but knew that he would have to give the money back personally to the elusive Mr. Kayin.

After they broke free from the chaos of the city, Josh breathed more easily as they'd only travelled about a mile before pulling off-road. The sweeping driveway led up to an ochre painted villa perched high on a hill overlooking the blue haze of the city. During the entire journey, he remained alert; at every stage was planning his escape.

The driver led him into the main lounge. Every window was covered in open bamboo blinds to stop the searing heat of the sun and allow a gentle breeze to flow throughout the house. Josh looked around, calculating the wealth of the owner.

He looked towards the bar, thirsty and ready to get himself a drink.

Just then, a voice attracted his attention. "Can I get you a cold beer?"

Josh shook his head. "Don't drink alcohol! Any coke?"

Peter sighed silently, noting that he would have to be careful as he introduced Josh to his *Proposal*. He could tell that by the young man's response that he carried within him the skeptical, cocksure attitude of youth.

"Why don't we take a seat, and I'll explain why I invited you here?"

Josh shook his head, replying, "I'd prefer to go outside!"

Peter reluctantly led the young man out to the veranda. It was still early but already hot, and he was not keen to sit in the bright sunshine. A touch sharply, he ordered George to pull out the awning to provide a bit of shade. Feeling slightly disarmed by this young man's attitude, nevertheless, Peter outlined his *Proposal*.

He tilted his pitch towards the humanitarian benefits, aware that Josh was not the type to be persuaded by either financial or personal gain.

Peter plunged into his story, relating his plan to overthrow a cruel and uncaring tyrant-creator who left the world to fend for itself. What they lived in now was an unsustainable planet ridden with wars, famine, poverty, and sickness. Peter argued that the world needed drastic intervention to end the perpetual cycle of madness.

It took most of the day to tell the young man about both his history and his plans for the future. And to explain details of progressive science that would facilitate the new world order.

If Josh was fazed by Peter's story about being an *Immortal*, he showed no sign of it. His body language and facial expressions gave nothing away. Stories of miraculous scientific breakthroughs that would cure all sickness, including death, held his interest. *Yeah! But at what cost?* He refrained from expressing his views too soon.

They talked about whether human upgrading would be

voluntary or mandatory. Political and legal structures were discussed, and they argued back and forth about morality and ethics. Peter had answers prepared for every question Josh fired his way. After a day of rather heated debating, Josh remained circumspect. He concluded that even if Peter was an *Immortal* and if it were at all possible that he could overthrow the Creator, his grand plan was intrinsically flawed. In his mind, the lure of immortality was a trap. *This is all wrapped up in eugenics.*

He reckoned that human upgrades would be on a tiered system. It was obvious to him that not everyone would be included, and those in power – as they always have done – would use advanced technologies to their own advantage. At that point they hadn't even discussed the non-compliers.

By the end of the first day, Peter knew that he had a lot more work to do to win Josh over, although he still had a few tricks up his sleeve. He reckoned that it was time to impress this young man.

"I think that all of this talking is not convincing you, Josh. Perhaps it would be best to show you! This will provide all the evidence you need. Are you ready for that?" It was the first time that Peter noted any reaction, as Josh flinched. His eyes widened then he stood up and started pacing the wooden deck

"Where do you want to take me?" he asked warily. Aware that no-one knew where he was, he hesitated because he was a lone traveller and knew that people go missing all the time.

At this point, Peter felt that he was back in control, so he confidently related his intention to take Josh into the fourth dimension. "What we are about to do will totally change your perspective of your tiny little planet and how everything works. Very few have ever seen what I'm about to show you. Most people would give up everything they had to share this experience, so relax, son, I want you to enjoy every minute!"

What young man could resist this opportunity. Travelling through the cosmos was not something he was going to miss. Setting aside his previous reservations, Josh agreed.

The older man gave strict instructions to his student to be hyper-cautious and hold onto his staff throughout the journey. There would be grave consequences if he disobeyed. He made it clear that he may not be able to retrieve Josh if he let go.

Josh thought it was worth the risk to experience something that no-one else had done. In his heart, he was an adventurer.

Freaking out as they stood beyond the edge of the universe and watching everything recede was surreal and utterly terrifying! He looked around the enormous sweep of darkness. All of Josh's senses were now on high alert. The blackness was closing in on him, suffocating him. He didn't know if this was *dark matter,* but it seemed to have substance. He was lost in a horrible void. All light extinguished; darkness was complete. There was no wind, no sound; he could not even hear the familiar systole and diastole of his own heart. This felt like nothingness.

Panic set in he and let go of the staff. He couldn't count time or feel where he was in space. His body seemed to be floating down but somehow not falling. He'd lost his bearings. Although he could see Peter, there was no means to reach him. His only hope was to be rescued by him, but there was nothing to hold onto or any means to propel him back. He shouted and screamed at

Peter, but it was as if he was unaware that Josh was unhitched.

"Oh, God! What if I'm stuck here in limbo for all eternity," he moaned audibly? *What if I never find my way back, and I'm trapped here in another dimension.* Peter had tricked him, and he had foolishly let his curiosity lead him instead of common sense.

He closed his eyes to the scene around him. Overwhelmed, he hoped he was dreaming. He knew this must be the end as his whole life flashed before him. He saw his beloved gran and remembered her ways. Silently, he pleaded: *Please help me, Gran.* When he opened his eyes, the outline of a *Light-being* beckoned him to come towards him. He could see that it was the figure of a man, emitting ultra-violet light. Pulsing, rivulets of light flowed in his body as if through some kind of circulatory system.

Although Josh felt unsure, something about the man's presence made him feel safe. The man then communicated to Josh. "I am the messenger, Ruel." Then pointed to the distant universe signalling that Josh should follow him. To stay unhitched – was not an option! He looked back at Peter. It was as if he was frozen in time, totally unaware that he had let go of the staff or that they had a visitor.

Although he wasn't touching the light-being, Josh felt himself being pulled behind him by some kind of magnetic wave.

As they approached the edge of the universe, everything unfolded. Together, Josh and the strange being stopped moving and looked on in wonder. It was as if all of time could be observed. Somehow the past, the present, and the future existed in a continuum, and Josh could see it all at once.

Ruel looked at Josh with a kindly face; they both

smiled. No need for words. Josh knew that he had been given access to incredible knowledge.

The *Light-being* handed him a strange-looking garment and indicated for him to put it on under his shirt.

When Josh looked up, he was holding onto the staff again, and Peter was talking. "*The Maker* is going to destroy all of this, and we have a plan to stop him." Time had shifted.

Oh! He doesn't know! Josh surmised.

"We have to go back now. Hold tight!" Peter shouted.

"Quick, you have to cool down. You need to go into the shower. Peter went to follow him, but the warning look from the young man stopped him.

"Of course! Come into the kitchen as soon as you can. We need to eat."

Josh quickly undressed and laid the garment reverently underneath a pile of towels. The pain was excruciating, and he was burning up, so he turned the shower on and stayed under the freezing water as long as he could bear it. He dressed quickly, wearing the mystical garment next to his skin. Instinctively he was aware that the raiment was precious and could be misused if it fell into the wrong hands. He knew that he would have to guard it with his life. A few minutes later, he and Peter sat at the kitchen table eating more calories in ten minutes than he would normally eat in a day.

Josh had so much to say but was reluctant to speak. "I . . . wow! What a trip! That was mind-bending!" Josh decided that he had to play a part so that Peter would believe he was going along with him. They talked for another half-hour before Josh admitted: "Hey I'm whacked. I need to crash out, so can we continue this in the morning?"

Peter nodded. "Of course. It's not every day you get to

witness the mysteries of the universe.

I've got some people coming to meet with us tomorrow. I'll be going to the airport to pick them up. Make yourself at home. Maria will make breakfast for you so just tell her what you want. Check out some of the science we've been talking about. You can use the computer in the study. I'll be back before lunch."

Josh went to the bedroom, relieved that he could get away from Peter. He needed time to make a plan to get back home. Sleep was the last thing on his mind, but exhaustion forced him to lie down. Still feeling weak from expending so much energy, he crashed out as soon as his head touched the pillow.

The rising sun woke him from a very deep sleep. An overwhelming sense of well-being filled his mind and body. There was no explanation for his time-travel experience, but there was no doubt that it was real. The precious garment was still nestling under his nightshirt. It made him feel strong! Protected!

He looked at his watch, and it was still early, so he had plenty of time to do some research, but first, he must eat. Ravenous again, he wandered into the kitchen to find some food.

"Good morning sir, what can I get you for breakfast?" The woman smiled pleasantly and ushered him into the dining room. "Oh, I'd rather sit outside. What's on the menu? I don't suppose you could rustle up a full English?" Again, the woman smiled deferentially as she worked about the kitchen. Fifteen minutes later, Josh was sitting eating a hearty breakfast on the veranda. The saffron yellow sun spread her sultry glow over the mountainside. India once again threw him off balance. The scene before him was spectacular in its jewel-like splendour, but just a short ride away, children would still be living in filth and squalor. And yet he was still able to believe: *It's good to be alive.*

Once he had satisfied his hunger, he entered the study and logged into the computer. He knew exactly what he was looking for; there was something familiar about the garment he was wearing under his shirt.

Hardly aware of time passing, Josh heard excited voices in the courtyard outside. The morning had slipped away. Flipping the blind open, he saw Peter with three young people. Two girls and a guy. They looked around his age, give or take a few years.

This is going to be interesting!

Peter introduced Eli, Havah, and Angelina and explained that they had flown in from Geneva to meet with him. They chatted over lunch and politely expressed an interest in Josh's travels and humanitarian work. Relieved that the spotlight shifted from him, he spent the remainder of the afternoon listening to their stories. Although Peter stayed with them, he let the young people do most of the talking.

The threesome openly spoke of their origins. Josh momentarily stopped breathing when he learned that none of them were the offspring of human parents.

They frankly discussed their unusual entry into this world – how they were created by genetic engineering. They had no biological mother or father. Josh had no idea how that was possible.

They were the first children exclusively designed by scientists. All of them seemed proud of their origins and boasted of their high IQ and athletic prowess.

Josh leaned back in his chair. There was no need to say it, but Josh admitted that they were good looking people. They seemed pretty well adjusted, friendly and happy, and not robotic as he would have imagined. Still, it unnerved him to think about it. Josh had so many questions but wasn't sure how to ask them.

The moment arrived. All four faces were looking at him for a response.

"Oh, do you want me to comment? Unnervingly, they nodded in unison.

"Don't you miss having a family, parents? Who is your mother?"

Eli seemed to be the spokesperson for the trio. Sidestepping the question initially, he was keen to talk about his life and how he worked at CERN in Geneva as a particle physicist. He noticed Josh frown. "Perhaps you think I'm exaggerating. You think I'm too young, but we have all been intensively trained since babies."

Josh was impressed; he looked closely at Eli and reckoned he was of a similar age; around eighteen to twenty years old.

They seem to have artificially enhanced super intelligence. Josh surmised.

Eli continued to relate his life story. He owned a house in Geneva, a New York apartment and a villa in southern France. The list of cars was just as impressive. Then he dropped the bombshell: "Family is over-rated Josh. This social model is just a source of pain and suffering."

Josh concluded that if that was meant to impress him – it failed miserably. He surmised that Eli was a cold-blooded materialist. Josh loved his parents, and being part of a family – even the painful part – was what made him human. It was definitely time to go home! Josh continued to listen to Eli, but at the same time, was planning his exit.

Angelina spoke up for the first time. "You know Josh, it's not that we don't have a family; it's just that our family is different. We don't have biological parents, but we were born the conventional way. Peter has always been there for us and has been like a father to us – and we three are equivalent to what you would call siblings."

Josh was reluctant to ask any more, aware that his views would be confrontational.

Peter sensed the tension in the atmosphere, so he cut in to suggest that they all go out for dinner. "We must go to a local restaurant, the cuisine is renowned as being superb, authentic Indian food. It's only a short drive from here and a bit of a hidden gem! Why don't you all go and get changed, and I'll book a table?"

Josh was relieved. He needed a plan to get as far away from Peter without coming to any harm. He was rebuking himself for ever having left home in the first place. His stomach was tied in knots again. He wanted home, his parents, and familiar things.

An hour later, they entered a building that looked pretty basic on the outside. However, the waiter led them to a horseshoe style booth with surround seating filled with sumptuous multi-coloured Indian cushions and a magical view across the valley. They all watched in silence as the gigantic ball of orange sun slid lazily down behind the distant hills.

Much to Josh's relief, the conversation was pretty neutral. He began to relax as they enjoyed the ten-course banquet. Josh observed the strange *family* as they chatted easily amongst themselves and wondered if he had been overly harsh about judging their non-human status. Perhaps they had more in common than he first believed.

They returned to the house just after ten o'clock. Angelina approached Josh, asking if he would like to check out the gardens. "They are really beautiful; I had a walk around earlier today. Honestly, it's worth a look."

Feeling that would be impolite to refuse, he followed the blond-haired girl down the well-lit path until they reached a wooden gate. He was pleasantly surprised as they entered an enchanting walled garden. Each bed was laid out with different species of roses. The perfume was intoxicating. The path naturally led them to a seat under an archway laden with sweet honeysuckle.

Angelina sat down and beckoned Josh to do likewise. "I can sense your reluctance to be alone with me. Honestly, I'm just the same flesh and blood as you! Pinch me if you like," she teased. "It would be good just to get to know one another – without the audience. Please, come, sit here next to me. You can ask me anything you like."

Josh initially hesitated, but she seemed friendly enough, and so he sat down but measured carefully the space between them.

They spent hour or so circumventing the hot topic and so ended up talking about India. Angelina had never been there before, so Josh was quite happy to describe the time that he stayed with local people in each region he visited. They had a long conversation about the caste system and how Josh couldn't understand why a country would still operate this way in the twenty-first century.

She expressed her surprise that so many people were living in poverty and yet still chose to have children. "Why bring more children into this kind of misery?"

Josh turned and looked at the girl, curious, asking: "Wouldn't you like to have children?" She laughed openly. "Oh no, not me . . . I'm not a breeder! I'm made for intellectual pursuits."

Josh inhaled sharply.

"Hey, don't worry, I am free to be with whoever I want. We don't have restrictions in our circle . . . we are very liberal."

Josh felt his body tense again. "You mean you go both ways?"

"Oh Josh, don't be so old-fashioned. We are all family, and it's a free world we live in. There are no rules!" Josh was still trying to work out what that meant. Did she include Peter in that scenario too? He decided not to ask.

She sensed his disapproval. "I think I'll go see what the others are doing. Perhaps I've shocked you, Josh, but think it through. You know where to find me if you want some company."

Josh watched as the beautiful, sterile, clone-girl walked back along the path. He didn't know what to make of her story. She certainly wasn't an *Immortal,* but her genetic origin was a mystery. He looked at the pure white rose in front of him. *Even a flower can produce offspring after its kind. Does she even have a soul?* He stroked his chin. This whole ideology was disturbing.

He had to find a way to leave but was genuinely worried that Peter wouldn't let him. He went over the terms of *The Proposal* in his head. Peter told him that all he had to do was listen for three days, then he was free to walk away. He didn't care about the money, but he was fully aware that he knew too much!

I'm gonna have to play along for now until I can find an escape route.

On the way back up to the house, he met Havah on the path.

"Oh, hi Josh, I was just coming to find you. We are all having a nightcap. Why don't you come and join us?"

Josh wasn't sure how to react, and his protestations about not really being a drinker seemed to fall on deaf ears. Thankfully, Peter had gone to bed. It was getting harder to keep up the pretence. *God! I need to relax. Maybe one drink?*

It was decision time. The morning of the third day and Josh had an angry hangover but paid it no attention. He went looking for Peter and found him in his study; he'd decided not to wait until the deadline.

Peter looked up, immediately noticing the hesitant look. "Ah Josh, I was just about to come find you. Is there something wrong? I can see the look of a troubled man? Here, sit down and tell me your concerns."

Josh cautiously sat across the desk from Peter, strangely feeling like he was sitting opposite the headmaster of his old high school. On more than one occasion, he was sent to his office for some minor misdemeanour. Although he was always commended for his academic work, he had a bit of a reputation of being stubborn and rebellious. He preferred to believe that he was principled.

"I need to go home Peter, I just think that this *Proposal*, the whole thing, you know. . . it's too much to carry on my young shoulders. I need to get some guidance from my parents. If it were just about me, it would be different. What you are planning will change the whole structure and fabric of the world. I understand the whole relationship thing and that I'm a suitable candidate. I get what you are planning to do and everything. It's just too much responsibility for me. What if I get it wrong?"

Peter resisted the urge to roll his eyes. Instead, he stood up and walked around the desk. He put an arm around the young man's shoulders, announcing: "I suspected you might come to that conclusion. This strange story I have presented to you is a great deal for anyone to process. I understand your reservations. You are a conscientious young man, and I guess I hadn't made allowances for your age, son."

Relieved, Josh breathed more easily until Peter continued: "However, this is easily rectified. We can go to London today and talk with your parents. I'm sure they will be able to help you come to a decision. Don't worry about it, son, we can be ready to fly out this afternoon. I'll book the flights right now. Why don't you go and get some breakfast and then go pack your things?"

Josh wasted no time. Immediately, he went back to his room and packed up in record time. He had barely finished when Peter announced they would be leaving in thirty minutes. Relieved, Josh went into his room to pick up his bags. Not sure exactly what to do with the money, he decided it was best to hand it back to Peter in person. He didn't want any accusations hanging over him.

Peter accepted the package without ceremony but handed him a bundle of notes. "You are going to need some of this for expenses." Before Josh had the chance to refuse, everyone was piling into the mini-bus, ready for the short journey to the airport.

The conversation on the way to the airport was lively and light-hearted. No-one would have known that Peter was annoyed, but Josh was aware that the old man was pretty adept at covering up his rage.

Going through customs should have been a formality – given Peter's profile – but the security guard at desk number six pulled Josh out of the line.

Josh went to protest, but Peter intervened.

He spent some time talking with the customs officer turning a couple of times to look at Josh. He shrugged his shoulders. "It's something to do with an irregularity with your passport. You cannot travel today, and you must go to the consulate to update some information."

I'm being deliberately delayed. If Peter wanted him on that flight, he was pretty sure that he could have made it happen. This was good news as far as he was concerned as he dreaded spending the next twelve hours on a plane with this tribe.

Peter and the three Swiss teenagers left on the scheduled flight with the plan that Josh would join them in London in a couple of days.

Standing outside of the security control, he sighed deeply with relief. He was sure his parents wouldn't fall for Peter's enticing proposal.

His first port of call was at the British Consulate's office. Irritatingly, the office was closed due to some local holiday and would not open again for three days. It almost felt like Peter had thrown a plethora of obstacles in his way, but surely he didn't control the British Consulate? *Now, that would be ridiculous,* he muttered to himself.

He picked up his backpack again, resigned to accept there was no option but to travel to another city a half day's journey away. Thankfully, upon arrival, he was rewarded with good news: the surprisingly helpful clerk assured him that his passport would be ready to be picked up within 24 hours. The empathetic clerk also gave him access to a phone. Josh made several attempts to contact his parents. No-one picked up. There was nothing he could do but wait.

Knowing that he didn't have the luxury of exploring the city was frustrating, but he wasn't in the mood for taking any chances. This wasn't due to un-explained paranoia. It was a time to remain circumspect. He was pretty sure that Peter was having him watched and that he wouldn't be able to walk away.

The thought of being on his guard in another hostel was not an option, so he booked into a reasonably-priced hotel. It was worth it to have some privacy. Maybe he was hyper-cautious, but he decided to stay nearby the hotel for the remainder of his time there. The ticket he had previously purchased was for a flight two days away, so he decided to use this ticket rather than be beholden to Peter in any way.

Knowing what Peter was planning gave Josh an

incentive to find an Internet cafe near his hotel, where he spent most of the next two days checking out the sinister world of *Genetics* and *trans-humanism*. Alarmingly, what he discovered as he dug a little deeper confirmed everything that Peter had told him and had far-reaching consequences for the whole of humanity.

It was frustrating that he had to wait another day but at least he could spend the time doing some research. How he was going to use this information to alert people was still beyond his understanding. Somehow, he was going to raise a clarion call to the world. It was a mystery, but he had seen it during his *cosmic experience* although it was difficult to explain – even to himself!

The next twenty-four hours passed by uneventfully, and thankfully his concerns about Peter sending some of his people to kidnap him didn't materialise. However, the journey back to Jodhpur and then onto the airport was nerve-wracking. The security check was his last hurdle, but he passed through without a hitch. It was a relief to be sitting in economy class, albeit with restricted legroom. He had cancelled the first class ticket Peter had paid for. Being in debt to him was not an option!

On arrival at London Heathrow airport, he winced as he entered the baggage hall. He had worked out a number of scenarios in his head about where he would go first, but he hadn't expected to encounter George in the arrival hall.

"Hello, Mr. Kayin. I've been sent to pick you up and take you into the city. Your father is meeting with Peter. I have been instructed to tell you that they are getting along well and have struck up a deal!"

Chapter 17

Josh returns/The Kosmocratoras

John woke up, startled by the sound of loud jingling in his ears. The tight band around his head reminded him of his overindulgence the night before. "Oh God! Josh is arriving any minute," he groaned inwardly.

He'd just finished dressing when the door opened and Josh walked in as if it had been only a few days since he had last seen him.

George followed a few paces behind, apologising to John for Mr. Kayin's absence, explaining that he was attending to some urgent business. He planned to join them in a couple of hours. John dismissed George gracefully but firmly. He had learned this authoritative approach from his mentor.

As soon as George left, father and son ran towards one another. Neither able to speak as tears of reconciliation flowed.

John spoke first: "I have so much to tell you, Son. You won't believe what's happening here. It's . . . it's like something out of a fantasy movie, but we need to talk –"

Josh interrupted. "Wait, Dad . . . let me get changed. I've been cooped up in an aeroplane for the last 24 hours, so I really need to stretch my legs. Why don't we go for a walk?"

As they left the apartment, John shouted to Gloria: "We are going out for a while." He didn't wait for a reply.

Fifteen minutes later, they were walking through Hyde Park, along the winding path by the Serpentine River. They stopped at the Riverside Cafe for a drink, and John related a brief outline of his encounter with Peter.

He looked at Josh, hoping for some feedback, but his son's response was not at all what he had expected. John could sense a gaping void between them. He observed that the muscles in Josh's face attempted to smile, but his son could not hide the deep sadness in his eyes.

John could feel all the excitement and celebrations of yesterday dissipate. His back began to hunch forward, finding solace in his familiar posture. Burdened and perplexed by this response, he wasn't sure what to do next.

He had just outlined a way for Josh to be free from a dreadful genetic disorder that threatened to destroy both him and his mother. *Why is he not jumping for joy? Why is he not relieved . . . a bit more positive?* John pondered this for a while.

"What's wrong, Josh? I thought you would be ecstatic – or at least curious. This is good news. I've found a cure for you, Son!"

John carried on speaking, although he could feel Josh resisting him. "I've been so worried about you, Son. Your mum and I had no idea how to find you. I understand that you had to work your way through the awful news about your illness, but we are a family, and we need to stick together. Don't you see, Josh; this is our only way out of this nightmare."

He went to put his hand on his son's shoulder, but Josh recoiled, then replied without hesitation: "No, Dad, this is not the answer. And you didn't find a cure for me because . . . listen, Dad, I need to tell you . . . I didn't open the envelope until a few days ago. The tests were all negative. I don't have ALS, and I don't need a cure!"

"You're not sick?" John pushed back his chair and stood over his son. "What do you mean? You had the genetic test and then disappeared, so we assumed –"

"I know, Dad. I ran away. I was so confused. I couldn't stand by and watch mum deteriorate, knowing that it would be a vivid picture of my future. I was terrified – that I might be dying! It was all too much! Everything I knew and believed was being challenged. I needed to find some answers.

John closed his eyes and shook his head. "But, we would have helped you, Son."

"No, Dad, you couldn't. I had to find my own way.

Tears welled up in John's eyes. Feeling lightheaded, he felt like his legs were about to give way.

Josh continued, "Dad. I know Peter. He came to me seven days ago and told me everything."

He what! John yelled. He stood up suddenly, upsetting the table and chairs – everything scattered.

He wasn't sure if his anger was directed at Josh or Peter. "What! How can that be true . . . surely he would have told me that he met with you. No! No! No! This can't be happening."

"Look, Dad, I get it. Really, I understand why you were so excited to tell me. I went along with his ideas for a while – but to tell you the truth, I had so many niggling doubts from the beginning. On some level, it just sounded so fantastic, tantalising, enticing! Who wouldn't want a world free from death, disease, and poverty? Who wouldn't want a world without wars?

Everything I believed was being challenged, and I almost fell for it. I needed to buy some time. In the end, I told Peter that it was all too much for me to make any decisions, and I just wanted to speak to my Dad."

John turned ashen, his pupils dilating. He felt like he was going into shock.

"Dad! You haven't . . . you know . . . signed the documents have you?"

Looking aghast, John wasn't sure how to tell him? He stood up again and paced around the table for a while before shouting out: "Of course I signed Josh because I did it for you and your mother. Hell! I did it for mankind."

Josh looked at his father in disbelief. "Can I ask you this Dad, did you know I was on my way home before you signed?"

John practically spat the words at his son: "Of course I knew you were coming!"

The son remained silent for a few moments while looking straight at his father. He asked another question, "If you knew I was coming, then why didn't you wait for me? This affects me too!"

Flummoxed, John fabricated an answer.

"Your mother was at death's door, so I had to make a decision to save her life, and time was running out . . . but Josh, you should see her now. She can sit up, feed herself, and even brushes her own hair. It's a miracle, just wait till you see –"

Josh cut him off midstream.

"Did she agree? did she sign?"

John nodded his head. "She knew it was for the best for all of us, and she was thinking of you!"

"Oh, God! Josh cried out. What have you done?"

John tried to comfort his son by putting his arms around him and pulling him close. "It's all for the best. They are going to take good care of us. We will be healthy in every way – mind and body, and even financially. We're going to be billionaires. We will be full of energy and never-ending life.

Damn it! They've even set up a private island with advanced technology to help your mother make a full recovery. We have everything we need to start our new lives, Josh! We'll never need for anything ever again. We will know everything . . ." his words trailed off as he saw the look in his son's eyes.

"Yeah, Dad, but at what cost?"

"It's all free son, they are paying for all the treatments."

"I don't believe you're that naive, Dad. Don't you remember anything Gran taught you?

Until the day I got the test, I sort of believed in a general way that God existed, but I couldn't face the test results until I found out the truth. I needed to know what this life is all about. Who am I? Could I still believe in a *Creator* if I found out that I had a degenerative disease?

Do you know Dad, that everywhere I went, I found the same old story? Every religious organisation and every culture had the same systems. All had created a hierarchical structure where a few top dogs rule the sheep below. I found lots of good people, but no-one who could answer my question. No-one could tell me why I exist!"

John was about to speak, but his son cautioned him with a look. John bit his lip.

Josh continued: "Night after night, I lay awake. The envelope would call out to me to open it. I resisted. Then I had a dream. I saw Gran sitting at the kitchen table. You know the one. That old wooden one that came out of the ark. We would sit there most Sunday afternoons, and she would teach me about life. She was amazing."

John was scrambling for words, his brain awash with clashing thoughts. He didn't want to hear this. It was too close to the dreams he had been experiencing. He dismissed it as a coincidence.

Josh said, "Yeah, Gran and I had amazing conversations. I loved those times. She never wavered. She was just . . . so sure! We talked about everything. Love, life and death, suffering – you know, Jesus and all that. She knew all the people in the sacred book as if they were close relatives. Abraham, Moses, and David were her favourites. She knew their characters well. They all were heroes at one time but also indelibly flawed.

The early autumn sun was beating down on them. John pulled at his collar as sweat began to trickle down the back of his neck.

Aware that his father was uncomfortable did not deter Josh as he dug his heels in, determined to finish his story. Throwing a twenty on the counter, he walked back along the path, indicating to his father to follow. Josh found a quiet bench set back from the river. They needed to continue this conversation in private. Both had strong views, and emotions were running high.

Josh spoke softly: "It was in the dream I saw Gran had it right all along. She knew." He paused and looked up towards the sky. "I miss her so much." Tears began to run unashamedly down his cheeks. Turning to look into his father's eyes, he continued: "I decided to come home that day. Ironically I had travelled the globe to find the truth and discovered it had been in front of my eyes every Sunday around that old wooden table.

The next day I went to the travel agent to book my flights, and within 24 hours, Peter, or should I say *Cain* turned up with his incredible deal. For the next two days he offered me a world full of unimaginable wealth and immortality. Then he took me to a place outside of space and time."

John winced.

"Yeah, I can tell by your reaction you have been there

too, Dad. There were . . . I don't know . . . a few seconds when I was able to zoom in, right into Gran's kitchen where she was telling me about the Ancient One, the Special Messenger. You know that part, Dad . . . the bit where someone took him to a high place and offered him all the kingdoms of the world. I knew instantly I was standing in the same place. *Temptation*!"

John froze!

"Cain was oblivious when I accidentally let go of his staff. Somehow it broke the spell, and I knew exactly what was happening. I saw everything."

John bent over, his eyes closed as if in prayer. "I can't listen to this; it will ruin everything."

As Josh looked at his father, he felt sorry for him but carried on regardless. "I was told by Ruel – one of the Messengers – that a group called *The Fallen Watchers* had been looking for a suitable candidate, so when I went for the genetic screening test, it flagged up my name. Apparently, my genes are 40% pure so they would make great material for splicing and dicing my *DNA*. What power my genes possess! I would be able to give the gift of immortality to the human race and enable the top dogs to have control. I could have singlehandedly created a superhuman race. How neat is that, eh?" Josh said sarcastically.

John interrupted. "It's not like that. Cain wants to help humanity. He wants to cure mankind of every disease."

"Come on, Dad! You got sucked in. You need to ask yourself. If the super-rich are funding this and they have exclusive rights to your *recombinant DNA*, then what about the others?"

"What others, what do you mean, Son?" John answered defensively.

"Really! You haven't given any thought to the majority of people who don't have the millions of dollars required to join this exclusive club. You're not that stupid. You have already considered it, haven't you?"

John bowed his head again, but not in shame, he was scrambling for an answer. "Everyone is going to have the opportunity to receive immortality. Cain told me that we are going to cure the world." John tried to defend his stance, but his son was a persistent opponent.

"You really don't get it, Dad! Everyone will be offered immortality, but the elite will have exclusive access to the upgrades. Is that morally acceptable to you?"

John stood up and turned his back on his son.

"You can't do this, Dad," Josh pleaded.

"Oh yes, I can," his father responded sharply. I'm not prepared to die, and I want your mother to be free from this awful disease. What has your God ever done for us? He got us into this mess, so don't expect me to trust him. All we've had is thousands of years of chaos. He could have intervened at any time and made himself known to us, then we could all become his faithful little sheep."

Josh softened his voice. "That's just it, Dad, he already has."

John stood up, enraged, "Don't give me that Jesus story. It's pathetic. Why would an all-powerful being let himself be killed like that? No, don't answer. I know what you are going to say – it's because he loves us. Well, I don't feel the love. I'm not buying it. Look! It was all just a big show. The truth is, he is as helpless as the rest of us. He has lost the battle. He's just a – Josh interrupted desperately.

"No, Dad! Please don't. That makes you sound like the Antichrist."

John glared at his son "I'm not anti-anything. I'm definitely pro-life!"

Josh buried his head in his hands. Exasperated, he

sighed deeply before continuing: "Dad, do you know how ridiculous that sounds? Pro-life is an organisation that campaigns against the killing of millions of unborn children.

What about your friend Cain and his geneticist friends? Why don't you go ask them how many humans embryos they have used in experiments in pursuit of their pure bloodline?

Oh, of course, they call these humans non-viable, and that's supposed to make it okay. Does it, Dad? Don't fool yourself; this whole thing is a *eugenic programme*."

John felt nauseous. Here he was, a grown man being chastised by his only son, but there was no way back.

Determined that his dad would hear the truth, Josh forged on. "Did you know that Francis Galton was Darwin's cousin? And that he is known in scientific circles as the *Father of Eugenics*.

You see, Dad, most people don't realise that Darwin's famous book about evolution has a dirty little dark secret. The title as we know it today *The Origin of Species* was altered."

John frowned. "What do you mean? What dark secret?"

Josh responded, "They deleted a subtitle from the original book:

On the origin of species, the preservation of 'Favoured Races' in the struggle for life.

They most likely realised that it was not politically correct, as we call it. Where do you think Hitler got his ideas about ethnic cleansing to let the *Favoured Races* rise up? – Yes! Dear old Galton and Darwin. There's not much *natural selection* in the practice of *eugenics*. It's more like an *artificial selection* by the elite. And now your friend Cain is peddling the same propaganda of

Transhumanism. It's just a continuation of the *Nazi Eugenic Programme*. If you go ahead with his proposal, be assured that Hitler would be proud of you!

John swayed backwards.

"How does it feel to fulfil his dream?" Josh accused.

For the first time in his life, John raised his hand and struck his son.

Josh wiped the blood trickling down his face, knowing that he was losing his father, but he had to keep trying.

John was foaming at the mouth, exasperated by his son's accusations – although deep down, he knew that he was speaking the truth.

"You need to ask yourself one question, Dad."

"What bloody question?" John yelled.

Josh calmly reminded his dad about the dream. "Please, just listen for a few minutes," he pleaded. "This might be our last chance. When I saw Gran in the dream, she told me about the question God asks all of us. The most important one we will ever have to answer."

John paced in front of the bench.

"Please, Dad, sit down. If you don't want to talk, please give me this chance to explain." John sat at the end of the bench with teeth clenched then nodded to his son to continue.

"What would a man give up for his Neshama?"

John frowned "I have no idea what that means."

Josh explained, neither did I but I looked it up. "In the Hebrew tradition, man was made in the image of the Creator, and then he breathed his life into him. After much reflection, I realised that it means that somewhere within us exists a different type of consciousness. I guess you could call it the spirit of man. It's said to be the link between heaven and earth. It's a delicate connection, like a silver thread that needs to be nurtured. That's why we are different from animals."

"Stop preaching at me!"

Josh shook his head. "I'm just telling you the truth. I've made my choice." He turned to face his dad. "What about you. Whose side are you on?"

Josh could see that he had made a dent in the wall. His father's defence system was beginning to crack, affording him the license to carry on.

"Don't you understand that Cain and his people have a sinister agenda? God has a name for them: *The Kosmocratoras*. They are a group of beings currently ruling over our world: princes, powers, and dark rulers. There is a war in heaven that has been raging since the beginning of time. In the beginning, everything was good but the *Kosmocratoras* have been on the attack ever since. Their intention is destroying, not only God but his image in man. These dark rulers have been pursuing mankind with a vengeance because they hate us! They are the ones who incite hatred and discord."

The father said nothing.

The son understood his decision.

"I guess we are on opposite sides now, Dad.

Do me a favour though, at least stop deceiving yourself. Stop pretending that you are doing this for your family." Josh looked at the stranger with deep sorrow. Today they had become enemies. Groups would be polarising soon. Sadly, he remembered his gran saying "One day, a father will be against his son, brother against sister," but he never thought this would happen in his lifetime.

"Just let me see Mum before I go," Josh pleaded.

"No!" His father was adamant. "That's not possible now!"

Just as he was about to protest, a young child fell off his bicycle, and his mother was far off. Weeping and wailing, the child shouted at his distraught mother.

"You let me fall. You let me go!"

Josh rushed over to the crying child to pull the heavy bike off his legs. He helped his mother lift the young boy onto a bench to mop up his bleeding knees and assess the damage. "Nothing too serious," he said and reassured the boy that he would be fine.

The mother thanked him and asked him to help her carry the boy to her car.

Josh agreed, "I'll just have to ask my Dad . . ." He looked around, but John was gone. A distant figure walked over the Serpentine bridge without even a backward glance. Josh felt that he had been orphaned. He whispered the traitor's name, *Judas!*

Chapter 18

Father and Son

Josh didn't see the tears running down his father's face. Rivers running into torrents. It was too late now – there was no way back. Couldn't bring himself to tell his beloved son that he had begun the first treatment.

Cain had insisted that they start right away and had casually joked with him: "Why don't we sign the deal in blood?"

They had both laughed, but that statement had made John shudder. His benefactor had already donated his red treasure, which the doctor carefully infused into John's body.

Everything that Josh said had greatly disturbed him. It was all true. Walking along the riverbank, he stopped and caught sight of himself in the still water. What he saw sent chills up his spine. *Oh dear God*, he moaned, *I'm one of them.* The reflection he saw was that of a *Kosmocrator.*

John began to panic as the enormity of what he had done flashed in front of him like a bad dream, or more like – a waking nightmare. Voices in his head were harassing him again. *You've traded your soul for all of eternity? You've abandoned your only son.* What was he going to tell Sarah? She was expecting to see Josh today.

What was immortality anyway, and did he really want it? Would he be locked into a prison system forever?

Just as a pressure cooker has to let the steam out, John needed to do something before his head exploded. In a fit of madness, he jumped into the river. He had to stop the tormenting voices, but the water was only a few metres deep, so not really deep enough to drown in.

An unexpected calmness overcame him as he allowed the current to carry him downstream. Turning on his back, he looked up at the empty sky. People were shouting from the riverbank. That familiar feeling of numbness returned. He longed to die but was now indestructible.

A group of swans gracefully swam by, ignoring the intruder's body. As John floated under the Serpentine Bridge, he saw a multitude of eyes staring accusingly at him. A flock of birds had taken up shelter under the bridge's arches, sheltering from the upcoming storm. Unlike humans, he recalled that birds possessed an inbuilt warning system to alert them of danger ahead.

Someone had jumped in to save him. He didn't struggle but let his rescuer wrap his arm around him and pull him ashore. The lifesaver offered him a hand, but John managed to stand up unaided.

The lifesaver tried to put his arms around him, and John tried to push him away, but a voice responded, "Dad, it's me . . . it's Josh! I've got you, and I'm not letting you go."

In a daze, John collapsed into his son's arms. They both could feel the loud painful sobbing pass through John's weary body as they locked arms around each other.

The son took on the weight of the father; it was a poignant moment of role reversal. The past three days had been a rollercoaster. Random thoughts were swirling around John's head. Nothing made sense anymore. He'd got it all so very wrong.

"Oh, God! What am I going to do, Josh? It's too late." Josh looked with compassion on the broken man: "What's too late, Dad?" Josh was anxious to hear what had transpired between Cain and his father.

John took in a sharp breath before admitting his transgression: "You know that question you asked about what would a man trade in exchange for his soul? Well, I've done it because I traded everything I have for immortality, even worse – for money and power. He could not find the words to voice his sense of shame." He wept inconsolably.

Josh pleaded with his father to listen. "No, Dad! I was too harsh. I see that you were trying to help Mum and me. You just wanted to save us by finding a cure."

John looked totally defeated as he tried to explain to his son. "At first, that genuinely was my motive because I really thought that I'd found the solution for all of our problems. But I got greedy for power and wealth. Truthfully, it was just too hard to resist. They offered me everything I could possibly want. How could I resist, Josh? I tricked myself into believing it was all for the good of the human race and ignored all of the warning signs. It sounds totally foolish now, but I signed and traded my body. You see, I sold it! I belong to them now because I took a blood transfusion from that man, Cain. That makes me an Immortal."

Josh hesitated, "I don't know how to tell you this, Dad. It took me a while to work out why they couldn't do a straight transfer from Cain to the members. Why do they need a middleman? Didn't that strike you as odd?"

They sat down on a bench nearby.

"Of course, but I guess I avoided asking the right questions. There was so much information to take in.

What do you know, Son?"

"I know how persuasive Cain can be, but the truth is that he didn't have your best interests at heart; in fact, it's just the opposite."

"What do you mean? You have to tell me!" John implored.

Josh looked down and shuffled his feet. "Cain only told you a fraction of the story for sure; he conned you, Dad.

He took you into his world and revealed amazing knowledge to you, but most of it was half-truths. Just enough to hook you in. He knew your Achilles Heel, Dad. Sick wife and a missing son. All he had to do was solve your problems by offering you the right sweeteners. It's classic psychological manipulation. Does that sound about right?"

John nodded but decided not to add insult to injury by mentioning the accusation of molesting a student or the unpaid medical bills.

Although acutely aware of his father's discomfort, the young man knew that he had to push on. "I know this is extremely difficult for you, but the *Kosmocratoras* have been operating in the shadows for a very long time, so I guess they know our weaknesses and fears. Humans are no match for them. That is unless you know how they operate! Otherwise, we are helpless against them. We can't outsmart them without superior knowledge."

John interjected: "But who are these *Kosmocratoras?* How do you know about them?"

"That's easy, Dad; the answer is in the sacred text. They are a ruthless cabal who want to dominate mankind. The thing is, Dad – they hate God, and they know that their rule over this world is coming to an end."

Josh waited for that to sink in as he knew Cain had painted a twisted picture of a malevolent God who would destroy humankind.

"So, what do they really want with us?" John asked with trepidation.

"What do you think, Dad?"

John's frame shrunk again as the truth was laid out before him like an illuminated path.

"They want to destroy us or enslave us because we are made in God's image!"

Josh wanted to cry, but he couldn't afford to stop the flow.

"That's only part of the plan."

The father looked deeply into his son's eyes. "Just tell me."

Josh moved closer to his dad. "It's quite shocking, so prepare yourself.

Cain intended to sell your *immortal DNA*.

Your body would be the most valuable commodity in the world. Everyone would want a piece of you. Literally! You would merely have been a host body because your *DNA* was compatible, a good genetic match. Like a lab rat."

A deep groan reverberated around John's innards. This was the truth! He knew it.

"And that's not the whole story." Josh continued, "They not only planned to change what it means to be human. The members would be given all the privileges of immortality and the power to rule. Everyone else would be enslaved not just in this life, but for eternity."

Shaking his head, John couldn't believe his naivety. He winced. "So their strategy is to entice us into this *New Age* of immortality and world peace. Then lead us step by step to relinquish our humanity?

It was hard to watch his father's embarrassment as he realised the truth. Josh tenderly touched his father's arm as he continued to explain: "You see, Dad, *Trans-*

humanism is humanity's worst nightmare!"

Josh paused, to let that sink in.

"It's the first step towards us becoming *Cyborgs*. I mean, organic beings linked to computers. We are partway there with our obsession with smartphones and digital technology. They want to hook up everyone to the *World-Wide-Web*. It's the ultimate mind control. And they will get many to sign up using the immortality ticket. Can you imagine what it would be like being controlled by machines with no means of escape – ever!"

John remembered something that Cain said about *The Web* being important in the future. The truth shocked him to the core!

"Oh, Son, what have we got ourselves into? I can't believe we are sitting here talking about all sorts of strange beings – *Nephilim, Watchers, Kosmocratoras, and Immortals* "What the hell are we going to do? We have to stop them. Jumping to his feet, John almost knocked his son off the bench. Oh no! Son! Your mother, we've got to go and get her out of that hospital. What if they've moved her somewhere? What if –"

"Dad! Hold on, you need to calm down. We need to act wisely. We've got to think this through. Cain doesn't know we've sussed him out. Let's use this to our advantage."

It was Josh's turn to pace around the bench, but he was aware that his dad was utterly freaked out.

Tentatively, Josh unfolded his plan, but it would be the last thing his father would want to do.

"We have to create a diversion, Dad. We need to rescue Mum but make it look like everything is going to plan. We can't let them get suspicious."

John knew what Josh was thinking. "You want me to go back, don't you? I . . . I don't think I can. I'm terrified of what they'll do to me."

"Look, Dad, technically they haven't started the gene manipulation. They will wait until they take you to the island. It's a tricky science. The blood thing . . . I think that was just for effect, to get you to sign. There's no *DNA* in red blood cells! You need to go back, tell them I just want to spend some time with Mum and you will come later for a family reunion. We need to buy some time. I'll go to the hospital; the prodigal returns and all that. They won't suspect a thing if it looks like you are going ahead as planned. Meanwhile, I'll find a way of getting Mum out of there."

John knew that it made sense if they wanted to see Sarah again. "I have to do it," he said. "I was the one who got us into this mess! I just hope I can play the part without them suspecting what we are up to. But where will we go – we can't go home. Do you know of anyone who will hide us?"

Josh was quick to answer. "Yes, I do. I've got friends in south London. I'll give them a call and tell them that you are coming. Dad, – I know a lot more, but we don't have time. I'll fill you in when we meet later. Come on, let's get going, but . . . you can't go like that; they will want to know why you're soaking wet. Let's swap clothes. I'll go home and get changed into dry clothes, then make my way to the hospital. I'll meet you at this address at 2pm. Explain to Cain that we need a bit of time together. He won't want to upset you just now, so I'm sure he will agree."

John looked at the address in Dulwich. They planned his route by tube and train to get there, deciding that it would be unwise to use a taxi.

"One more thing, Son. I can't understand why Cain let us meet. He knew we would talk. Why not keep us apart? He's bound to ask what we discussed."

Josh sighed: "I don't know the answer to that one but

he must feel pretty secure that he has sealed the deal."

John cringed, then turned to look at his son with admiration. He wished he could be as resourceful or even capable of handling this bizarre situation. There was no point in denying that he was floundering.

Father and son parted company at the park gate, both acutely aware that they were on a dangerous mission. Without ceremony, they nodded and went off in different directions.

Chapter 19

Sarah's meets Ruel

The last few weeks were a blur; she seemed to be living in a dream-like state, but still, she knew she was dying. It was in one of her waking moments that Sarah had resigned herself to quietly sleep away her last days. It was easier, and the medication made her drowsy.

John was standing at the door, hesitating.

"What's wrong? Come here, John, sit beside me."

Tentatively he explained what had transpired after his meeting with a distant relative called Peter. It took a while for the story to sink in.

John was urging her to say yes to the treatment. If it was true, then how could she make this decision? *Is this some kind of sick joke? Is it ethical?* She shook her head. It was the kind of philosophical question that would have academics arguing about for years. She wasn't sure if she had the qualifications or even the right to enter this moral maze. *I must be the least qualified person in the world to make this life-changing decision.*

How could a person be objective when offered such a controversial cure while lying on a hospital bed attached to tubes coming out of every orifice?

She wasn't fully aware of the universal consequences of this path. She had no idea at that time that John had already made the choice on her behalf. All she knew was that she was feeling much better. Her body felt as if it was gaining some strength, and compared to a few hours ago, her mind was razor-sharp. Still, something was niggling in the back of her mind, but she tried to push it away.

Burying her head in her hands, she tried to clear her mind. Peering through her fingers as John gazed intently at her, she cried out. "Oh, God! What about all the conscientious objectors? What will happen to them?"

She tried to think objectively. *Yeah, but what about my family!* This was indeed a moral dilemma. *Maybe we have to think about ourselves!* Her thoughts rolled back to the day Josh was going to the hospital for his genetic testing. He looked so vulnerable, but he had tried to put on a brave face. Rolling further back – before *D day,* when life was good, and they were functioning as a family – that was her light bulb moment. In her mind, she picked up a pen and signed the contract!

Half an hour later, the tubes came out, and the physiotherapist spent time tutoring her how to use a self-propelled wheelchair. Relief overrode thoughts about coincidence or, indeed, spending any time considering what the future new world would look like. It didn't take her long to realize that John had already given his permission for the treatment, but she didn't care. It was good to be alive and feeling so much better.

The room was buzzing. Nurses and doctors were coming and going. Everyone seemed upbeat. Nurse Graham came in next; she was in an extremely cheerful mood. It didn't take her long to coax Sarah to improve her disheveled appearance. Apparently, she had a mystery appointment that night. She only had a couple of hours to shower, apply some miracle make-over and have her hair done.

When the doors opened, and her arrival was announced at the venue, a sea of faces welcomed Sarah. For the first time in many months, she actually felt like a human being. Every head turned in her direction, but when her eyes met with John across the room, it was magical. His face beamed like a lighthouse. It was like being on a first date, only this time there was an audience cheering them on.

Although she could only stay for a short while, it was exhilarating. They actually had a bright future! The rehabilitation team had devised a plan to work hard with Sarah to rebuild her atrophied muscles. Although the treatment was already working, months of inactivity had weakened her body. It would mean sessions of painful rehabilitation, but Sarah was genuinely grateful for the medical team's unending enthusiasm.

The day Josh turned up at the hospital became her *V day*. She told him with great enthusiasm that it was a day of celebration and victory. Ignoring his obvious embarrassment, she hugged and smothered him with kisses. "I can't believe it; everything is reversing. This is the best day I've had in the last two years. I'm just so –"

Her voice trailed off as she saw Josh's mood change as his face took on the familiar look when things weren't quite right. A mother knows! Her brows knit together as she questioned him: "What is it, what's wrong, Josh?"

"It's not quite *Victory Day*, Mum. I've got a lot to tell you, but there's no time. All of this . . . it's not quite what it seems. You need to trust me and do everything I say."

Sarah saw the urgency in his eyes. "Of course, what should I do?"

He held her again, whispering instructions about how he was going to get her out of the hospital and would return shortly.

Sarah found it difficult to gather her thoughts. The dilemma she faced was ridiculously unfair. She had approximately thirty minutes to decide whether to leave the hospital and risk relapse or trust in her son.

Within half an hour, Josh was wheeling her towards the garden at the rear of the building. Strangely, they were heading towards a massive hedge, but Josh had already opened an old concealed gateway that led onto a path by the River Thames. As he helped her into the waiting car, she handed him a small bag full of vials of medicine she had hidden under the blanket.

"Mum, this is Ruel; he is going to help us escape!"

Feeling panicky, she hesitated before getting into the car but sensed the situation was too dangerous to express her concerns.

They whisked their way through the traffic with uncommon ease. The traffic lights seemed to change every time they came to a junction. She wondered if Ruel possessed an electronic device, like a special kind of remote control that changed the lights as they approached. When they cleared the Vauxhall Bridge, Sarah began to relax a bit.

Looking sideways at the young man in the driver's seat, she gasped; he looked familiar. If someone had asked to describe what a Greek god looked like, Ruel would fit the bill. He was strikingly handsome with the profile of a Michelangelo sculpture. His long dark hair seemed to glow with health or strength or something undefinable.

When he became aware of her staring, he turned and gave her such a warm smile that she immediately breathed easily and relaxed into the seat.

As they passed through the noisy crowds in Brixton Market, Sarah started to shake her head. "What is that noise? Have you turned the radio on? Who is that speaking? Someone called Peter! It sounds like he's inside my head!"

Ruel scowled as he turned to look at Josh. "I think they've put a tracking device in your mother!"

Sarah screamed: "Get this thing out of my head! Oh, God. He's telling me that I can't get away. I have to come back to the hospital – now!"

The Messenger put his hand on Sarah's arm. "I know this is difficult, but we are almost at the safe house. I need you to be completely silent until we get there. They can only track us when they pick up the frequency of your voice. No matter what he says. You will be safe. Do you understand? Just nod."

Sarah complied, but the voice inside her head – although muffled since Ruel touched her – was difficult to ignore. It threatened that she would die unless they all returned.

They drove down Coldharbour Lane and then over Herne Hill towards Dulwich in complete silence. Sarah was exhausted by the time they pulled into the driveway of Ruthven House.

Two men named Micael and Samu were waiting expectantly at the doorway to help. They also seemed to be *helpers* and had a similar appearance to Ruel. The *helpers* guided Josh into the sitting room. Ruel carried Sarah into the house, deliberately taking her into a separate room, before laying her down on the couch. Holding his finger to his lips, he reminded her not to make a sound. He then placed his hands on her ears.

Sarah relaxed a little. All she could hear now was a beautiful sound that drowned out the threatening voice.

In the other room, Micael quietly asked Josh: "Do you have the garment?"

Josh opened his shirt to reveal the mysterious raiment.

Micael indicated to Josh to take it off.

"Do you know what this is?" Samu whispered as he helped him take off the garment covered with jewels and twelve strange symbols.

"Yes, I did some research. Is it really the *Breastplate of Judgement*?"

Samu nodded: "Yes, this is just what we need to help Sarah. Come, we cannot waste any time."

Josh stood back as the three men gathered around Sarah. Ruel. He then placed the breastplate on Sarah's body.

Heads bowed and eyes closed, the three strangers waited together expectantly. Josh held his breath in wonder as he looked on at the sacred scene.

The precious stones began to glow as if powered by a hidden source of energy. Sarah's body began to shake uncontrollably.

Alarmed, Josh went to help her because she looked like she was having a fit.

The three men didn't appear fazed at all. Then Sarah sat up and spewed something out of her mouth.

Ruel picked out a small metallic-looking object and examined it carefully. "We must leave now!

Samu – take the device. You know what to do. Go now! We'll see you later at the meeting place. Come, everyone. Follow me!"

Sarah didn't even think about it. She simply got up and walked unaided. It wasn't yet the time to celebrate, but they all cheered together anyway.

As Samu drove out of the front gate, the others scrambled into a camper van, escaping through the electric gates at the back of the property. Micael locked the gates and as a double measure, he padlocked the central pillars with a massive chain. It wouldn't stop Peter and his team, but it would buy them some time.

Samu headed east along College Road to the private tollgate and alongside the college grounds – it was a local shortcut. He paid the fee, then moved forward and waited until the barrier went down. He then stopped to speak to the gatekeeper. They were deep in conversation for a few minutes before he returned to the van.

"That's fixed," he laughed heartily. He looked behind him as a queue of cars were stuck in a jam, unable to pass the broken barrier. The toll-keeper stood with his toolbox pretending to repair the payment machine. All the while, he was in ecstasy because his arthritis has been cured when the mysterious stranger touched his head. He was completely pain-free for the first time in twenty years. Following instructions, he had to give the stranger a ten-minute head-start before he fixed the *broken* machine. Meanwhile, the camper van headed west to avoid Peter and his people.

Sarah felt exhausted and energised at the same time. The sheer excitement of moving about freely was exhilarating, but this fast pace of life was overwhelming her body. She would have to take time to rebuild her strength after the long period of inactivity.

The trip was reasonably comfortable, so she slept most of the time in the fold-down bed.

Ruel briefed them on their current status each time she woke up. Apparently, Peter had reached the Channel Tunnel on the south coast before realising that he had been tricked. Samu had done an excellent job of leading them on a wild goose chase. They all experienced great joy as they heard about his exploits at the college tollbooth.

"Samu sounds like a bit of a prankster," Sarah laughed. "I really like him."

Ruel responded kindly, "You should Sarah, he has fought many wars on your behalf!"

Sarah swallowed hard, totally overwhelmed that anyone would do such a thing for her. She wanted to cry but sensed it just wasn't the right time. They were all still in danger until they got to the safe area. Ruel had cautioned them not to ask too many questions until they reached their destination. All they had been told was that a group of people were waiting for them and they would explain everything when they met.

Sarah woke up startled. A loud whirring noise seemed to be circling round about the camper van. She looked to see what the two men were doing. Both of them were deep in discussion, but Micael continued to drive even with the powerful headlights shining in his eyes.

"Oh, God, it's a helicopter; they've found us!" she exclaimed. Micael kept driving as Ruel made his way to the back of the van.

"Listen, Sarah and Josh. As you see, we are surrounded by Cain's people.

Sarah looked startled at the mention of that name. "Yes, that's his real name, Sarah. They won't be able to tell for sure if you are with us, so they will try to stop us." Sarah recoiled. She really didn't want to meet the man behind the voice in her head.

"What can we do?" She tried not to scream at him, but Ruel heard the terror in her voice.

He sat down beside her to explain the new plan. "We are going to use a technology that we are only allowed to use in extreme cases, and frankly, this is one of those rare moments. We could easily upset the balance of time, so you must stay as still as possible. It will be a little uncomfortable but only for a few minutes."

Sarah responded, "Okay, but it would be helpful if you tell me what is going to happen."

Ruel looked at Sarah with a broad grin. "We are going

to travel faster than the speed of light. It will look like we have vanished. They won't be too happy."

"You mean we are going to time-travel?" She said.

"It's the only choice we have!" was his reply.

Ruel sat between Sarah and Josh, a hand on each of their shoulders. Trying to lighten the mood, he said with a mischievous smile: "Well folks, you won't get to do this too often. We are going on an adventure. It's just like the Tardis in Dr. Who." he chuckled. "Just hold on to me, and you'll be fine."

"You mean you watch *The Doctor*?" Josh scoffed.

"Don't you?" The mood lightened as they all laughed.

Micael shouted, "Ready!" The whole van started shaking.

Sarah felt like she was blinking in and out of existence. It wasn't physically uncomfortable, but her grasp on reality was slipping further and further away. Terrifyingly, she felt totally lost, immaterial! She couldn't work out if this is what it felt like to be dead. Still conscious but without substance! When the shaking stopped, she breathed again.

"Did we make it" she shouted.

"The eagle has landed," Micael replied.

"Please don't tell me we are on the moon!" Sarah exclaimed.

Both Ruel and Micael burst out laughing.

"Oh! You are wicked!" Sarah joined in the laughter: "Okay, so the joke is on me!"

Josh shouted. "Mum! We are in your homeland!" He recognised the distinct peaks of the Isle of Arran across the water.

Turning to Ruel, she asked, "Why are we here: why Scotland?"

Ruel smiled: "Because Cain cannot follow us here. He is banned from entering this land."

Mother and son looked at each other, perplexed, they were both about to ask more, but Ruel pre-empted their questions. "All will be revealed shortly. Let's go and meet up with our hosts."

A short while later, they reached their destination. The house was tucked away from the main road. After approaching the property through a narrow lane, they entered a small courtyard. She half expected to be taken to a dingy old cottage but was surprised to see a charming red sandstone house with a beautiful walled garden hidden behind a narrow archway.

The entire west wall was covered by a cleverly-pruned network of purple wisteria, inviting the viewer to enter a labyrinth of flowers and exotic plants.

Sarah, though exhausted, insisted on spending a little while to bask in the fragrance of the place. She hadn't realised how much she had missed the simple things in life. *Most people don't*, she reckoned, *until it's taken from you!*

After entering the house, Uzel tentatively opened the door to let them see that John was already there, but he was obviously tormented with the same intimidating voice that Sarah experienced. He sat with his hands covering his ears.

Quietly closing the door, Uzel led them to the adjoining room, promising that they would be reunited as soon as possible. Thankfully it was only a few minutes before Ruel retrieved the tracking device, and they were able to be together as a family for the first time in almost two years.

Chapter 20

The safe land

After leaving his son at the park gate, John clenched his jaws as he made the short journey to the Alpha Towers. The glass lift was the least of his problems.

Cain was waiting for him. He practically, pounced on him as he walked through the door.

"Ah, John. I was just about to send George to find you. Oh! No, Josh? Where is he? What have you done with him?" Cain laughed, but his face told another story.

"We went for a walk in the park. He's gone to see his mum at the hospital. They haven't seen each other for eighteen months. They need some time together, so I'll go later, and we can have a proper family reunion."

John was aware this man would have no understanding of the bonds of family love.

"Yes, yes, of course. And how is Josh? I'm sure that he will have told you that we met in India."

John scrambled for words. "Yes. He told me that you offered him the same deal, but he wasn't sure what to do, and that's why he came home. But . . . I don't understand why you didn't tell me you'd met my son?" John wasn't sure if he should have asked that question.

Cain responded. "It's all a bit complicated." Then explained that he had a small window to find the right person. Basically, he only had three candidates, and Josh was the best suited due to his age. John was a good candidate, and there was also a third, but this man was less suitable in terms of compatibility.

John's made a mental note. *A third person?*

Cain reminded him that he had limitations placed on him. "There has to be no coercion either from me or the other candidates. We have to maintain the laws of free will."

John's eyes narrowed.

"I had to withdraw my offer to Josh before the boy returned from India."

He admitted that he had manipulated the situation with Josh. His flight had been deliberately delayed so that they wouldn't have the opportunity to discuss the matter. Although he had temporarily kept back this information from John, he pointed out that it was well within his mandate. If John had refused, he would only have had six more days before the window closed. The timing was crucial for the success of the project.

Pulling on all his resources, John responded: "Oh right, I get it. It makes sense now. I hadn't realised that you had these restrictions on you."

It was satisfying to watch Cain wince. It must be galling that his power was indeed limited. John was tempted to push a bit further and make him squirm. He had no idea how he would defeat this man, but he would find a way. Mercifully, he had just discovered his weak spot!

They spent some time discussing plans to move to the island and the logistics of travelling with Sarah. Cain assured him that she would have a full medical team in attendance at all times.

John had to summon his acting skills to feign interest

as *the imposter* enthusiastically talked him through the journey. Casually glancing at his watch, he tried to estimate where Josh would be, roughly calculating that the alarm would be raised in the next thirty minutes or so. John was never very good at drama class, but he was secretly pleased with his performance.

Just then, the telephone rang. John braced himself when he saw the rage in the old man's eyes as he walked towards the door.

Oh lord! I'd better find a way out of here! Foolishly, he realised that he hadn't made an exit plan.

Okay, so the lift is out: fire escape! As soon as he stepped onto the balcony, he was startled as he bumped into a complete stranger – and yet there was something familiar about him. He looked remarkably similar to one of the men from the Mountain Rescue Team who'd rescued Sarah.

The tall man beckoned him to follow. John wasted no time debating; he knew instinctively to obey.

Clambering down the fire escape to the tenth floor they found an open window into the hallway. From there, the man opened a laundry hatch, indicating that John should follow him. He had to trust this man.

They landed with a thud on a pile of dirty linen. No bones were broken!

As they made their way up the exit ramp, a white transit van drew alongside, barely stopping as they climbed on-board. They sped across town before Cain's people discovered that he was gone. John was fully aware that he was hot property: Cain would never let him go.

The two men sat in silence. It was comfortable enough in the back of the van sitting on a pile of freshly laundered towels, but John's mind was racing. *Who are they?* He could only surmise that they were helping him escape, so must be *the good guys*!

Looking through a small crack in the blacked-out window, he could see they were travelling west. As they left the busy streets of London behind, John's breathing slowed.

They stopped on a side street, and one of the men came in to join him in the back of the van. He indicated that John should not speak. John's brows knit as he mouthed, "Okay."

The young man wrote something in a notebook, then handed it to him. "Please remain silent; we suspect they have placed a transmitter in your body so that they can track your whereabouts. It is activated when you speak, so we will only use written communication until we reach our destination. Our plan is to meet up with the others. They have the technology to remove this chip. Don't worry, John, your wife, and son are safe." John breathed deep as he reached out for the pen: "Who are you?"

"My name is Uzel, and the driver is Mazu, and we are here to guard you. You know that you are in great danger. We must take you to the safe land.

"What safe land, where is it?"

Uzel replied, "I know this is difficult, but it's best for you not to know too much just yet. I'm asking you to trust us for the next twenty-four hours, then you will understand."

What option do I have? They seemed to genuinely be looking out for him.

They drove for many hours – continuing west, or more likely north-west, John guessed. Travelling mostly by minor roads to avoid detection. This made the journey long and tedious.

Finally, they arrived at *The Twelve Keys Ferry Terminal* in Birkenhead near Liverpool, just managing to catch the last ferry of the day to Belfast.

Uzel explained apologetically that John would have to

remain hidden in the back of the van during the eight-hour journey. Cain would most likely have access to on-board CCTV cameras.

This was a daunting prospect for John but he knew that he'd have to endure it.

Uzel and Mazu did the best they could to make him comfortable, but he'd never been a good traveller.

As soon as he started retching, a menacing voice broadcast in his ear.

"Ah dear John, what a pity you are not enjoying your trip across the Irish Sea! You should try some ginger; it works a treat. I'll bring some with me when I meet you in Belfast."

Once again, Cain's manic laugh gave John the chills. He frantically searched for the *Messengers*. "Help me, Uzel! They know where we are. They heard me throwing up. Cain says they'll be waiting for me in Belfast! What are we going to do? I can't go back!"

The two guardians glanced at each other, they did not speak, but John knew they were communicating. Uzel wrote: "You might as well come onto the deck – but don't speak. Time for some drastic action! We knew that all the border roads were being watched, so we took the long route via Ireland.

Uzel smiled warmly at John. "Don't worry, my friend, we have a *plan B*. We are only permitted to intervene in the affairs of man on rare occasions – and this is one of them. Don't be alarmed, but we are going to have to turn the ship."

Without any further explanation, they climbed upstairs to the control room. John took the opportunity to get some fresh air, but Cain's constant talking was extremely disturbing. "We have a contract John, so don't think anyone can get you out of this. Make no mistake, we will find you, and it would be better for your family if you come without a fuss."

It was hard to ignore the threats. His hands were shaking as he held on to the rails; he could feel the pull of the dark waters of the Irish Sea.

Someone touched his shoulder, breaking the spell.

Uzel scribbled another note. "The safe land. Cain cannot follow: he is forbidden to enter." Although John had no idea what he was talking about, he felt a great surge of relief.

John saw that the boat was turning towards the Scottish coastline.

How had they managed to persuade the captain to change course? Perhaps they would tell him later.

They arrived at *Cairnryan Ferry Terminal* within an hour. Although the voice was still bombarding him with threats, Uzel had done something that had muffled the accuser's voice. The sound of the music calmed him – well, perhaps he wouldn't describe it as music, more like a muted frequency of soothing sounds. It stopped him from listening to Cain's threats.

Mazu informed him that they had another drive ahead of them. Meanwhile, Uzel encouraged John to settle down to catch up with some sleep. He wrote: "We have to meet up with the others. They are in a safe house a few hours drive from here."

When John woke up, it was a beautiful clear morning, and the early morning sun was rising along the Ayrshire coast. As he stepped outside the van, he stood on the sandy beach at the water's edge and breathed in the fresh clean air whipped up by the rolling waves of the Firth of Clyde.

Looking across the firth, a familiar outcrop of jagged purple mountains pierced the clouds above. Goatfell was hidden from view by the mysterious mist that often clung to the mountain range. He looked at Uzel, who somehow knew what he was thinking.

Uzel replied in his notebook to his silent question, "Yes! You've been here before many times, and it's where we first met.

"It was you! You rescued Sarah!"

"I've been with you for a very long time, John."

Puzzled. John was about to ask, but Mazu interrupted as he wrote in the notebook.

"Teams have been working tirelessly in this place, so this is a very special location.

This land has been cleared of predators. There is no frequency to which they can attach. The gates are closed to them. Come, dear friend, it's time for a family reunion."

John smiled as he heard Cain's shouts of protestations now buried under the sound of victory.

A group of friendly locals greeted them as they entered the old stone-built house. John was led into a large sitting room with panoramic views over the sea.

Uzel returned a few minutes later. Shaking his head as he warned John to remain silent. He indicated to John to sit on a nearby sofa. He wrote some instructions. "Sarah and Josh are about to join us, but we have to extract the tracker before you greet one another. We must keep the mystery of how we do this hidden." John heaved a great sigh of relief as he saw his family.

Uzel then placed the mystery breastplate upon John's chest. The gemstones began to vibrate with light. John shook violently before sneezing, as the metal chip landed on the well-worn carpet. The Messenger chuckled as he picked up the object before heading towards the door. He turned and, with a nod and broad smile, indicated that it was alright to break the silence. The grateful family fell into each other's arms and wept.

John spoke first. "I'm so sorry for getting us into this mess. How could I have been such a fool?"

Sarah gently kissed his forehead, whispering, "It's alright, John. We're safe now!"

John looked at his son with repentant eyes. He wondered if he would find mercy or judgement. "I'm so sorry, Josh. I've been a very foolish man!" John spoke in quiet tones as his son put his arms around him.

"Dad! We came up against the most powerful man on the planet. Very few would be able to stand against him!"

John looked with admiration at this young man who was still effectively a teenager and stated: "Yes, but you did, Son!" John shook his son's hand. "You are more of a man than I will ever be. I'm so proud of you!"

Sarah put her hand over John's. "We are all together now. We're safe. Let's not give that man any more victories. All of these people are here to help us."

The family spent some time together, gently repairing the places where trust had been damaged.

An hour later, Mazu entered the room, announcing that lunch was ready. "A group of people are excited to meet with you," he said. The dining room was crammed full. John reckoned there were around thirty people present. Everyone clapped as they entered the room.

A local man named Duncan and his wife Rhona came forward to greet them. "Come, there's lots of time to talk. Let's eat. You all must be famished!"

John had no idea what he ate, but he knew that he enjoyed it.

After the meal, Duncan led father and son into the sitting room. Sarah had to excuse herself as fatigue overcame her once more. She desired to keep up to speed with current events but reluctantly had to go to bed.

John related his story about *The Proposal*. Eyes

widened as he told them about Peter's true identity. They all wanted to know every detail of Cain's plans, often stopping John to ask questions.

Josh remained quiet while his father related his experience. Surprisingly, no-one seemed shocked by his revelations.

"The prophecy told us that someone would come from the south and would bring about great unity between our two countries." Duncan looked around the room at every expectant face then back to John. "We've been waiting for you."

John almost choked. "No! no! not me. I'm a weak man. Cain had me in the palm of his hand. It was my son that rescued me. I think he is the one you have been waiting for."

Duncan wrinkled his face and laughed. "He's just a lad How could he come against the most powerful man on the planet?"

John looked proudly towards his son: "He's got something I would love to have – integrity!"

Duncan looked at the young man again. "Well, son, that's what we all need!"

Stepping forward, Josh spoke up: "Can I ask a question?"

Duncan nodded in response. "Sure, son, ask away!"

"What did Ruel mean when he called Scotland *The safe land*? How come Cain is forbidden to enter this territory? What is so special about this place?"

Duncan, a fit man, strong muscled, built over a life time of walking the rugged hills and mountains of Scotland. Aged around sixty years and a well-respected elder of the community. He was known locally as *The wise man*. He stood up, slowly walking around the room before answering. Finding a spot next to the great mantlepiece where a glowing fire filled the room, he began to relate his story.

Expectant faces waited for his answer. The Kayin family wondered about some great event that had driven out Cain's hellish influence and power from this land.

He began: "You had all better get comfortable because this is a story about great spiritual battles that have raged for centuries." He went on to describe the wars against great evil powers who sought to crush and destroy mankind.

"Many campaigns had been sent against the Scots, and for a long time, the people had been fooled and subdued. However, for the past three months, something has changed.

"It's been remarkable to witness." Duncan proudly stated. "There has been a silent revolution in this land to bring about an unprecedented rising against the evil powers who reign over this world."

Rhona joined her husband, anxious to share about the restoration of her people. She described how the Scottish people now understood the real battle raging was not against humankind. "Our people have been granted knowledge about the true enemy. The revelation of *The Kosmocratoras* has been given to many people through dreams and visions. Now that they have been exposed and we have realised how we have all been manipulated and controlled, we now understand that we have a common enemy. This knowledge has brought about a great sense of peace, unity, and purpose amongst the people."

"The revelations have given us incredible powers to clear the land of these evil predators. You must understand. There has been a great uprising here. The *Kosmocratoras* have been evicted, and most of the contaminated land has been repossessed. Although there are still pockets of unbelief – but that will not be for long."

Duncan and Rhona felt extremely proud of their people. They were happy to tell the Kayin family about their great victory. "Cain and his co-rulers cannot re-enter this land without permission. That can only happen if the people choose to open that door. Now everyone understands that they have free will to choose who will be their landlords. Thankfully the land is transforming into a safe place for people to live without fear. We've had a great awakening in this land. It's like we are coming into a period of paradise regained."

Chapter 21

To Iona

The group set out on a road trip to the islands, arriving too late to catch the last ferry from Oban. To pass some time, Duncan drove the camper van up the steep Battery Hill to a popular tourist spot. He and Rhona had accompanied the Kayin family on the journey north. The Messengers had led this family to them, and now they were aware that their paths had crossed for a greater purpose beyond their current understanding.

It was a balmy, early autumn evening as the group crossed the gardens to the McCaigs Tower. It was unusually warm, but from time to time, the Gulf Stream carried warm weather to the Scottish shores unexpectedly. Strangely out of place, the skeleton of a building that dominated the Oban skyline was reminiscent of a Roman Colosseum.

Duncan explained, the owner had originally intended it to be used as an art gallery, but he died before it was completed.

They all went separate ways to explore the site. John and Josh went out onto the viewing platform. Far below them, the vibrant town was busy with seasonal tourists keen to explore the enchanting west coast islands. Car ferries shuttled the explorers at regular intervals to nearby islands and further afield to the Outer Hebrides.

Silently, they stood together, looking over the horseshoe bay beyond the Isle of Kerrera towards the distant mountains of Mull. In this serendipitous moment, father and son knew instinctively that destiny was calling them across the shimmering greyish-green sea and beyond the hazy blue mountains towards the Isle of Iona.

John tenderly put his arm around his son's shoulder. Both sensed the importance of their journey, although puzzled when Uzel told them that they would meet a man on the island who would explain everything.

As Sarah was about to pass through the gateway, she stopped and looked in awe at the scene before her. Her heart leapt with joy – but at the same time, she wanted to cry as she thought about what had happened just a few days before. It could have resulted in a completely different scenario.

Something deep was being repaired between father and son, so she quietly withdrew and returned to the van.

As Sarah was deep in contemplation of all that had transpired in the last few months, Ruel appeared next to her. He placed his hands on Sarah's shoulders to reassure her. Looking into The Messenger's warm and friendly eyes made her feel safe. Even when he reminded her that he could only manifest physically for short periods, she was not unduly distressed. He would have to leave soon, but he would return at the appointed time. Taking a deep breath, she relaxed and smiled, knowing that she would never feel alone again.

Closing her eyes and feeling as if she were cushioned on a cloud of peace, she leaned on Ruel's shoulder.

As she rested, she remembered how she'd left her homeland not long after graduating. The pull of the vibrant art scene in London had drawn her south – but her heart had always belonged in Scotland.

Marriage, family, and employment had kept her busy and fulfilled, but it was her time to come home, and she never wanted to leave her beloved land again.

They left for Mull on the first morning crossing and landed at Craignure before driving across the island to Fionnphort. From there, it was only a short ferry crossing to the Isle of Iona. Like a dependent child – the tiny island drew all resources from the parent Isle of Mull. Everyone was surprised by the crystal clear, turquoise waves that carried them across the small channel between the two islands. It looked more like a Mediterranean setting than a typical west-coast Scottish scene.

Nestling snugly into the shoreline, an ancient stone Abbey dominated the skyline to the north of the harbour.

The Messengers had explained they would meet a prophet in the sanctuary who would help them. Anticipation mounted as they all walked a well-worn path – *The Street of the Dead*.

Before the rise of tourism, it had been known as the place where Scottish kings had come, but most – like Macbeth – for their funeral procession. Rhona pointed to the burial mounds, along the side of the road, then to a small chapel to the side of the Abbey where legend says it contained the part-remains of St Columba's bones.

As the small party entered the building, they stopped abruptly; collectively entranced by the beautiful sound of the Taizé singing. Mystical chanting – like the sound from a distant age – filled the building with a tangible sense of peace. They all took a seat at the front in the only vacant row.

As the music quietly concluded, a man at the far end of the row stood up and made his way towards the pulpit.

A loud gasp filled the sanctuary, prompting the congregation to turn towards the source of the commotion.

All eyes fixed on John. He was oblivious to the mumbling coming from the pews.

A desperate shout swirled around the building: "What the hell are you doing here?"

The speaker looked up, peering over the rim of his spectacles. He calmly took in the scene, then with uncommon ease, he announced: "Waiting for you!"

The congregation turned to measure John's reaction. He stood transfixed, a stifled scream caught in the back of his throat.

The audience turned to the speaker for direction. He didn't disappoint. Slowly, he walked into the body of the people, looked around, and then announced, "This is my Son, the one we have been waiting for."

Everyone fell to their knees. Some prostrated themselves on the stone floor. Many were weeping. Then John folded to his knees and wept along with them.

The speaker came towards him, helped him up, then held him tightly.

John sobbed. "Why did you leave us? You've never been in touch. It's been 33 years!"

The humble man answered: "I know Son, I'm sorry. I've missed you so much; at times, it's been too difficult to bear, but I had no other choice." Time ceased to exist in that place, and it was as if all the empty years had been swallowed up in a moment.

Matthew spoke softly to the congregation as he continued to hold on to his son. "The waiting is over. Today we witnessed the fulfilment of the promise. The overcomers are here! This is the day of new beginnings and the start of the restoration of everything."

Sarah, Josh, and John had no idea what was happening

but realised they were part of a great unfolding plan. No one knew how long they remained in a state of awe. It could have been an hour or even a day. In the stillness, a lone woman sang out a haunting song. John felt that 33 years of pain had turned liquid and evaporated into the universe as his father held him tight.

It felt like a thin place between worlds!

His father held on to him as he raised his hand to usher the people out of the building.

John tried to tell Sarah about the anger and hatred he felt towards his father, but the more he tried to explain the less important the idea became.

The singing faded, and one by one, the people slipped out of the building. Matthew invited his guests: "Come, let's eat. I'm sure there is enough food for five more guests."

John corrected him: "Oh, father, there are nine of us." He turned to introduce Uzel and the others, but they were gone. It wasn't the right time to explain, so the Kayin clan, along with Duncan and Rhona, made their way to the dining hall.

Sarah stumbled as they entered the refectory. John rushed forward to help her but Sarah held up her hand. "Hey! I'm fine. I just need to have a lie-down. Remember, Ruel said I'd need to rest to let my body recover. We've been travelling for days so I'm going to catch up on some sleep. Go spend some time with your father. I'm just feeling a bit worn out."

John had so many questions, but he knew they could wait. He was enjoying the reunion with his father, yet there was one which he couldn't resist asking: "Why did you come to this place? This remote island?"

"All in good time, Son, I'll explain everything. Dinner awaits!"

And so began a new family relationship as they sat

chatting about island life. Wrapped in his father's presence – he felt his muscles relax for the first time in years. All the feelings of abandonment and rejection were gone. He knew that in time his father would explain his disappearance.

As they sat around the table enjoying a simple but wholesome meal, John looked around in awe. "This must be what if feels like to have a heart transplant," he whispered to Josh."

He watched Josh interact with his grandfather with ease and laughed freely as Matthew retold stories of island life.

To his surprise, he heard Matthew talking about himself to Rhona – that he'd been born at home on the island and that they had moved south before registering his birth. There was a bit of a mix-up and John's place of birth was registered as London. So technically, he had a Scottish birth-right. John had never heard this before, but then again, there was so much he had to learn about his family.

After dinner, father and son gravitated towards a small private sitting room., "It can get a bit chilly in the early autumn evenings." Matthew put some logs on the fire.

John chuckled. He loosened his shirt collar.

"Would you like some tea, or is it too late for something stronger?" his father asked.

John glanced mischievously at his father. "I think I need something stronger. I want to hear everything – so it's going to be a long night."

"I'd better join you then."

Just then, Josh appeared at the door, but John signalled with a shake of his head, so he left without disturbing them. They sat in silence as Matthew thoughtfully and ritualistically, poured out a glass of malt whisky. John noted that his father's slow, easy manner had a calming effect on him. Although he seemed unhurried in whatever he was doing, nevertheless, his intense attention to detail was a joy to watch.

Matthew handed his son his drink then settled back in his chair. "So, where would you like to start?"

John wasn't sure how they could cover the missing years in one night, but he had one pressing question. "Why did you leave us?"

Matthew hung his head and closed his eyes for a few moments before he replied. "That's quite simple. To stay would have put your lives in danger. You see, a man called Peter Kayin contacted me with the offer of an amazing job, and that's how we ended up in London."

John sat forward in his chair.

"It took me a few years to realise who he was and what side he was on. I thought I was working for a humanitarian organisation. I believed Peter was a philanthropist, setting up projects to help people, mostly medical research, to look for cures for people with degenerative diseases."

Matthew then told John about the day Peter came to him and said to him that he would have to leave his family, saying that one day in the future, this man would offer John a position in his empire.

He explained: "Peter said you had to go through a time of struggle before he approached you." Matthew's frame seemed to fold as he told John: "He threatened to kill us if I didn't comply. There was nothing I could do. He has people everywhere. It has been a battle every day to stay away, particularly when your mother passed."

Matthew paused. His voice wavering.

"I've had to learn to persevere and trust that you would be strong enough to stand up to him when the time came. Look, Son, I'm not going to go on about how difficult it has been for me. It's just that I had no choice. He would have wiped us out. Make no mistake, he is a cold-blooded killer."

John felt his gut heave. He thought he'd need to throw up but swallowed hard. He had to hear his dad out.

Matthew explained that he had a receiver inserted in his hand to track his movements, and that's why he couldn't ever come home. John was both horrified and relieved at the same time.

It was comforting to know that his father hadn't abandoned him. Still, he was furious that Peter had robbed him of his childhood while virtually imprisoning his father.

Matthew's eyes watered as he looked at his son. "Your mother wrote a letter to me every month. Friends had to use couriers to deliver them. Even the regular post was monitored."

John responded. Tears welling up: "You mean Mum knew?"

Matthew nodded. "That was the hardest part because we couldn't tell you. Then the letters stopped. It was the worst time. I couldn't come to you in your time of distress."

Both men cried. Their family had been torn apart. The cruelty of the situation impacted them.

"His real name is Cain; not Peter; that name is just a smokescreen." John vented.

His father frowned.

"I'll explain later."

They talked for hours. John told his father about *The Proposal* and how he had succumbed to Cain's persuasive powers and that it was Josh who saved him from his own greed and stupidity.

Matthew tried to comfort his son. "Look, we are

talking about the most powerful and influential being on the planet. He knows exactly how to tempt us. He watches over our lives and then attacks when we are at our weakest. Just be glad that you were able to get out before it was too late."

John felt somewhat relieved that his father understood. "How did you know . . . that I would make it?"

Matthew stared into the fire, transfixed by the yellow glow of the flames. He turned again to look at his son, grieved by the vulnerable look in his eyes. He thought about the loss of not being with his son as he grew up and missing his important milestones. John had no idea how much he was truly loved. He saw the pain in John's body language. His stance was of someone searching for approval. This was a tragic loss for him. Both of them had lived for so long in a state of mourning.

"The answer to your question will sound strange, but over the years, I've had many dreams about this day. I saw you returning to the place of your birth. I saw that you had overcome the *Dark Ruler* and then came back to help us."

John started to protest, but Matthew told him that in the dream, he'd seen many helpers. "I don't know how to say this, but – I don't think they were human! They seemed to have supernatural powers."

John responded enthusiastically. "Yes! they are *Messengers* and have come to help us win this war."

Matthew was glad to hear his son confirm this and told him that there were many people across Scotland who'd had similar dreams. "That certainly helped me keep believing that you would come one day."

John couldn't think of anything to say. He knew that he didn't deserve any recognition for the overthrow of Cain's wicked plan to take over the earth. It was really down to Josh and the intervention of Uzel and the others. He looked troubled as he stood up and turned his back towards the glowing fire. "I don't think we are out of the woods yet. Cain told me that there were three suitable candidates. We need to find the third . . . oh no! Dad!"

Matthew stood up too, aware of the grave situation they were still in. "Yes, I think you will find that it's me, Son!"

"Oh God! How do you know, has he contacted you?"

Matthew answered softly. "I think he will activate this thing in my hand somehow!"

John reacted quickly. "Look, we haven't got much time; I'll go fetch Josh. I'll explain later!"

Josh was outside, obviously enjoying chatting with a local girl. "Hurry, Son, you've got to get the breastplate. Your grandfather has one of those tracking devices in his hand."

Josh returned within a few minutes and placed the ephod on Matthew's chest, copying what Ruel had done. Nothing happened! Josh and John exchanged glances. Both men were at a loss about what they should do next.

Matthew examined the breastplate looking closely at the arrangement of the gemstones, then exclaimed. "Three stones are missing! There should be twelve."

He hesitated for a moment. "I think I can help you find one of them. Come with me."

They all followed him to the abbey. As they entered the sanctuary, Matthew headed towards a Celtic cross. Everyone gathered around the cross as Matthew pointed to a gemstone in the middle of the Celtic knot. "This stone has been hidden here in plain sight for centuries. We all knew that it was important, but no one knew exactly why – until today!"

John carefully removed the stone and inserted it into

the golden clasp. A perfect fit! He then placed it on Matthew's chest again. This time the stones were activated.

Matthew was alarmed as his body began to shake uncontrollably but quickly recovered as the implant surfaced under his skin on the back of his hand – then exited his body without a single tear in his skin. Relieved, Matthew started dancing up and down the aisle and shouted, "I've had that thing in my body, keeping me prisoner for 33 years. I'm free! Come on, boys, celebrate with me!"

The three men were ecstatic, laughing, and dancing together until they saw Duncan standing at the entrance. It looked like the whole village had followed him. "You'd better take a look at this."

Chapter 22

Echad

The Kayin men followed Duncan outside, where they were confronted by a drone hovering just above the small chapel. Two hearts froze as they heard Cain's voice address them from the attached device. "Oh, I see you are enjoying a family reunion. How wonderful that must be. I hate to cut the celebrations short, but I don't have much time.

Matthew, I would like you to take the motorboat I have sent and visit me here in Ireland. It should only take you a couple of hours to get here."

John stepped forward and replied, "None of us will be coming to join you in your crazy plan to overthrow the Maker. We have our own plans."

"Oh, my boy, aren't you full of bravado. Don't waste my time!" dismissing John with a wave of his hand, he continued. "Matthew! I need you to go down to the harbour and get on that boat. You see, I have your precious little island in my sight as we speak, and it won't take much to blow it out of the water. I have a fully armed warship ready to fire some pretty nasty missiles. You have thirty minutes before I give the order to annihilate your little haven, your family, and every living thing within a fifty-mile radius."

Matthew did not respond. There was no point in debating with this man; they all knew his threat was deadly serious.

John, however, continued to protest.

Cain ignored him. He was losing his patience. "I want you all to leave Matthew," he commanded, "I need to speak to him alone. I think we might settle this without an audience."

John stepped forward to interrupt, but Matthew held up his hand to stop him. "Go back up to the house. I'll meet you there shortly. I need to do this alone!" As John looked into his father's steely blue eyes, he knew there was no point in protesting.

Moments later, when the two adversaries were alone: an eerie light filled the building. Matthew had to look away before adjusting his eyes. When he looked back, he shuddered. A holographic image of Cain filled the sanctuary. The haunting green image looked like a ghost. Matthew tried not to flinch, but this man had such a grip on his life, and it had been impossible to stop him.

"So Matthew, you are not willing to sacrifice yourself to save your family and the islanders. I really didn't have you measured as a coward! Don't you know that they are looking to you to save them?"

Matthew spoke, ignoring the question he responded: "Your name is Cain. John told me who you are."

"Yes, but it changes nothing. Can't you see that there is no other way? Or maybe . . . hmm! Perhaps there is."

"What do you mean, . . . another way?" Matthew responded hesitantly.

"Well, if you are not man enough to come, send me your son. I only need one of you. John has already been prepared. He is the obvious candidate. He has already signed the agreement. The judges have already declared that I can have whichever one of your family that comes willingly." Cain sneered, his eyes dark and brooding.

Matthew started to protest, but the *Immortal* interrupted: "There is an edict out against him, so wherever he goes will become a war zone. You know me – I will never give up my mission. This world is finished. It's time for all the restrictions to be lifted. Now it is my time to decide what the future looks like. You humans, you really think you have the power to become like *The Maker* and take back this world from me? You've had thousands of years, and no-one has defeated me. Not even *The Chosen One* could stop me!"

Incensed, Matthew responded with newfound confidence. "I know that many will believe your sales pitch. They will be enticed by your offer of a perfect world where everyone is immortal, but we both know that you hate mankind and intend to enslave us forever. You are like a spider spinning his deadly web to lure us, but you will not have this family."

Cain responded with a chilling hysterical laugh. "Oh, Matthew, I see that you believe in the prophecies written in the old book. Ha! No-one believes that stuff anymore!

Believe me, there will be little resistance! Don't you realise that every government, every politician, even major corporations are under my control? When I snap my finger, the banks will stop issuing money. Soon the markets will not have any food to sell without my consent. It's just a matter of time. You will all come my way in the end.

Sacrifices must be made. Just make the decision which one of you will come then I will leave this island in peace. If you can't choose, then why don't you throw lots," Cain scoffed.

"Perhaps the dice will make the best choice."

Matthew spat out his response. "I'd rather starve than live in your world".

The *Kosmocrator* mocked, "Really! So you are willing to die and let your people perish? What kind of leader are you?"

Matthew knew once more this man had him cornered. Unsure how to fight this monster on his own, he was relieved when Josh appeared at the door.

"Don't listen to him, Grandfather. No-one is going to die today! He's bending the truth. He's a ruthless psychopath. His days are numbered. Goodbye, Cain!"

The ancient man protested. "You are nothing more than a rebellious child . . . how dare you! –"

Josh grabbed the drone and took the device, smashing it underfoot.

"Well, Son, that's one way to deal with him!"

Josh smiled and put his arm around Matthew. "Come on, Grandad, let's go see the others. I've lots to tell you. Don't listen to him. All he has is weapons of words.

"How do you know this?" Matthew was intrigued by this young man. "What makes you so sure?"

Josh winked. "Because I've seen the future!"

As if on cue, everyone returned to the abbey. John approached his father as he ushered the people in. He put a comforting hand on his father's arm.

"Listen, everyone! I don't believe that Cain has the power to destroy this island or anywhere in Scotland for that matter! *The Messengers* told us that this country is called *The Safe Land,* and they have put some kind of covering over this place. I believe that Cain is bluffing – but I can't prove it. We can stand together as one and trust that the *Warring Messengers* will stop the missiles, or we can hand my father over to this man of lawlessness who aims to overthrow the Creator and enslave us. We have to make this decision together, but I can't guarantee that we'll not all die within the next twenty minutes."

A strange *hush* hovered over the sanctuary. One by one, the islanders began to gather around the family and sing a Taizé song. Matthew, John, and Josh closed their eyes and held one another. Their fate was now in the hands of the unseen warriors.

No one knew how long they remained there. They all felt that they had entered another dimension as heaven was touching earth.

A voice rang out. "Come look! They are here!"

Tentatively, everyone poured out of the building to witness an incredible scene. The sky was filled with strange wing-like clouds. Iridescent lights pulsed over the island.

John shouted, "I've seen the aurora borealis before – but this light-show is in a different league." They all danced and sang with total abandonment.

When John checked in on his wife, she was still sound asleep, oblivious to the spectacular events in the skies. Reluctantly he decided to leave her sleeping. He kissed her forehead whispering, "Sleep well, Sarah, I've got lots to tell you, but it'll keep till morning."

They heard nothing from Cain for another two hours, but everyone knew that he wouldn't give up easily. This time a drone dropped leaflets over the island. The message warned that Peter had international armies, unlimited ammunition, and hundreds of warships at his disposal. It was only a matter of time before they penetrated their defence system.

Cain had no inclination that they had no protection other than the unity of the people. They had to be in total agreement that they would stand together against their enemy!

Matthew spoke to the islanders. "I think we will ask this young man to help us out. Apparently, he has information that we need to hear. Is that right, Josh?"

The young man grinned. "I can tell you that Cain will not conquer this island. He will influence many people and take over many countries. Still, a handful of countries will be exempt, and Scotland is one of them! This will be a place of refuge."

"Why Scotland?" an islander asked inquisitively. "Oh. That's a good question. When I saw the future, I could see that many people here had joined forces against the *Kosmocratoras*. For years they had gathered together in small groups all over the country. This is what created an incredibly powerful force-field against Cain and the others. They could still harass but not harm the people within that area. It's simple, really. When people act together like one – oh, you know what I mean – it's as if all the people have one mind. Nothing can penetrate the unified field. Does that make sense?"

An old man stepped forward. "There is a sacred word to describe that. We call it *Echad*. It literally means acting as one! We have been pursuing this for many years, son. The prophecy says when we make *Echad,* we will change the world."

Josh replied with great respect. "Well, it is obviously working. You are truly holding back *The Dark Empire*."

The group breathed out a collective sigh of relief, in awe that their actions carried such weight. It was as if the young man had virtually torn a curtain revealing the workings of the unseen realms. Overcome with emotions – too raw to contain – many of the people sat and wept!

"Hey! This is good news." Josh was stunned by their reaction. "There's no need to be sad!"

Matthew answered kindly, "Oh, they're not sad, Josh. It's just that they have been waiting for such a long time for this moment. Some think faith is a simple thing, but it takes great patience and determination to believe in something not yet seen by anyone in this world!

Most people give up at the first hurdle! The world today believes in instant gratification."

Josh, slightly embarrassed, answered: "Yeah, I'm sorry, my generation has got a lot to learn. I've never had to persevere like you. To be honest, I don't understand why I was given this knowledge. I didn't seek it, and I certainly didn't deserve it. It's as if I was randomly chosen to see the future."

Matthew looked at his grandson with pride: "I think perhaps you are too modest young man; it took great courage to challenge someone like Cain. I believe what you were shown is your just reward."

The others cheered, and Josh responded cheekily with a bow.

"I know you have lots more to tell us, but it's been a very long day. I think tomorrow we shall make plans for our future. It seems like we have all been given different pieces of a jigsaw, and we have to find a way to put it together. Let's all meet in the dining room at 7am. Our minds will be clearer after a good night's sleep." Matthew turned to leave.

Both John and Josh had to suppress a laugh. The fate of the world was at hand, but it was only 9pm, and the islander way of life took precedence over the mighty battle happening all around them. "Now, that definitely takes faith!" John responded.

Josh nodded. "Hey! why don't we go for a walk around the island. We don't want to miss these fantastic skies."

The skies continued to display the beautiful light-show all night. People slept soundly in their beds, unaware that each flash of light was the force-field holding back the impact of multiple attempts to break through their defences. Cain was looking for a weak link. It only needed one defector to break the protection.

He knew people very well. It was obvious that Matthew, John, and Josh were strong together.

He just had to create a little breach in their wall, and he had a plan to do just that.

Sarah was alone in her room. The drone was a little primitive, but it was his only means of communication for now.

Chapter 23

Sarah's temptation

It was around 10pm when Sarah heard a voice calling her name. All day, she had been drifting in and out of consciousness. The travelling had drained her.

Like an echo from a bad dream, the strangely familiar voice roused her from a deep sleep.

She opened her eyes and squinted as she looked around the room for the source. It wasn't inside her head this time, but she had heard *that voice* calling her name before.

Please, dear, God! Not him! Although she had already recognised the deep penetrating tones of his commanding aristocratic accent.

Panic set in when she realised *the voice* was speaking to her from a device hovering just outside the partly-open window. *The voice* from the tracking device caused her stomach to knot in fear, surely seeking her destruction. She grabbed the sheet, pulling it over her body.

She was alone, confused, and paralyzed. She tried to cry out, but her vocal cords were frozen.

It's him!

"It's okay, I won't harm you." *The voice* promised.

It took her a while to rouse herself out of bed.

In a blind panic, she tried to make her legs walk

towards the door, but *the voice* spoke softly, imploring her.

"Please wait, Sarah; at last I have the chance to speak with you. You don't really know me, and I guess you've heard many distorted stories. Sarah, I don't blame you for wanting to avoid me, but I would like you to hear me out. Would you do that?"

Deep down, she knew this was a mistake. It was madness. He'd threatened her.

Run, now! she whispered, but truthfully, she was intrigued. Her gut feeling was to get help, but half-way towards the door, she looked back.

She conducted an internal debate. Her mind, literally in conflict as she listened to the voice of her family urging her to flee, but still, she felt justified in giving him the chance to explain. They had met briefly, but truthfully she hadn't spent time with him. However, it was an indisputable fact that her remarkable recovery was down to him. If it wasn't for his intervention, she would be dead by now!

In hindsight, it seemed odd that John, Josh, and Matthew were all totally against Cain. Everything had happened so fast. She hadn't really had time to think it through. They talked about him as their enemy, but apart from Josh and John's testimony Sarah had no real evidence of the malevolent monster.

Had she reluctantly been swept up into their war?

Family loyalty had made her trust their judgement, but niggling doubt had plagued her since the day she allowed Josh to carry her out of the hospital.

She backtracked to the day her son had spirited her away from her hospital bed. Until that day, she had been completely grateful to this man who had made her well again. She mulled over the possibility that her family had got it wrong, but memories of the angry voice in her head as they fled the hospital still disturbed her.

Sweat was dripping down the back of her neck. Was Cain's aggression justified? *After all, he brought me back from the brink of death*! As she considered how her family had repaid him by sneaking away without a word – she closed her eyes, ashamed. He had good reason to be angry. Knowing that her medical procedure was ground-breaking technology – and had cost millions – gave her all the more reason to be grateful. Her family could not afford to pay for the treatment.

The internal argument continued – she didn't really know him well enough to trust him, but in his defence – he had saved her! No one else really understood how near she had been to death. Or even what it felt like as she and life – whatever that was – were parting company. Sarah shivered! No-one would volunteer to feel that kind of pain, hopelessness, or loneliness.

She didn't want to be separated from her family. Not then, and not ever.

I'm going to have to make a choice.

In the end, she convinced herself that it was only reasonable to listen to Cain's side of the story. *Perhaps if I gave him a chance to explain, I'd be able to make them understand.*

Unusually, she was in a highly emotional state. Alarm bells were going off in every quadrant of her mind, but the desire to live was a potent force.

I can't go back. I don't want to die. I have the chance to live, maybe forever!

Cain witnessed her struggle; he knew not to rush her, but time was not on his side. He spoke softly again, like a deadly snake hypnotizing his prey.

"Sarah, have I ever done anything to harm you?" Interrupting her thoughts with his persuasive argument.

"First of all, I owe you an apology, Sarah. I admit that I was a bit heavy-handed with you all but let me explain! I was trying to protect you. There are many unscrupulous people who are trying to steal this new technology. Remember this dear girl, I have only tried to help you. Isn't that true?

Sarah could only answer, "Yes!"

"Honestly, it is so good to see you getting better, but truthfully, I'm deeply concerned."

Sarah felt the panic start in her stomach then travel through her nervous system like a bullet train, knocking her off balance. She sat down, holding onto the edge of the bed.

He noticed her agitation. "I've been speaking to the medical team, and they tell me that you only have another day or maybe two before the symptoms return. Believe me, it's imperative that you complete the treatment! I know that you took a good supply of the medication, Sarah."

She felt her face redden. He was being kind. Truthfully, she had stolen the phials.

She stood up. *I need to find John.*

"But you need to understand, Sarah, that your treatment will take another few months before you are completely out of the woods. Genetic medicine is a complicated business, so this is not a do-it-yourself project. Injecting yourself a couple of times a day will not work. This technology requires a lot of fine-tuning. Every person has unique *DNA*, requiring individual treatment plans. It's naive to think that you can self-medicate, Sarah!"

Aghast at this news, Sarah edged backwards towards the bed. The fatigue was overwhelming her. She closed her eyes. *I can't fall ill again.* The idea was unpalatable.

Cain could see her weaken. "It's so unfair, Sarah; all I

want to do is stop people from being sick and stop people dying. Is that so bad?"

"I … don't know! Truthfully! I'm not sure. You were really aggressive when I had that tracking device in my head. I was terrified!"

Cain responded apologetically. "Yes! I understand. I was panicking and lost it a bit! I can only say that I am sorry for upsetting you like that. You see, what we are doing is going to bring such massive benefits to mankind, and I thought we had lost everything, and the enemy had snatched you right out of my hands."

A master manipulator, the *Ancient Snake* continued to entice his prey. "This is such a big deal, Sarah. Please let me explain. You must understand: the tracking device was for your safety. Unfortunately, the truth is, they'll stop at nothing to destroy my plans."

Sarah responded. "I'm so sorry that your work has been undermined, but I'm baffled. One minute my body is being restored, and yet my family is against you. Now you tell me that I will get ill again, and that means . . . how can I choose?"

Again, the *Snake* reasoned with her. "This isn't just about me, Sarah. Dr. Savage and his team have worked tirelessly for years to develop this technology. So, the pathway of your recovery matters to them. If your treatment is a success, think about the millions of people that they will be able to help. However, they need to be sure that it works before releasing it worldwide. Do you understand why your recovery is so important to us?

Permission to carry out this treatment takes years. The medical world, with its interminable ethical committees, blocked our way. We took a chance on you because you were dying. Sometimes we have to take the risk for the sake of the evolution of a species. Don't you agree, Sarah?"

Sarah remained silent, acutely aware that she was deep in a moral maze. She wanted to throw up.

"If this is so wrong, Sarah, why did John gave us permission to give you this treatment? He was aware that we had to use you experimentally as a test subject to trial the drugs."

She replied: "I guess he knew that this was a massive risk and my only chance of survival. We had nothing to lose."

"Yes, indeed! Although the team was confident that it would work. Until now, no-one that close to death has ever recovered. You are a medical miracle, Sarah! If we continue with the right treatment, you will be fully recovered in one year, then you can indulge in incredible upgrades to your body. And that, my dear, will take you into the realm of *The Immortals.*"

"I don't know. I think it would be best if I go fetch John. I'm sure if I explained everything, he'd listen."

Cain remained calm, knowing that with one hint of aggression, he could lose her. "John has been mesmerised by these people, Sarah. I want you to understand that he is not aware of their agenda."

Sarah frowned. "What agenda?"

"They want to stop progress. Maintain the status quo. They don't want people to have any power. They want to keep you all as slaves until you die."

Sarah sighed. "Yeah! I've been a bit perplexed about why they can't see the benefits for everyone. Well . . . everyone who will comply." Then added, "I'm sure you now have sufficient evidence that the treatment is effective. Look at me; I'm living proof that it works. I'm going to have to find a way have to make them understand."

The *Immortal* smiled inwardly. The hook had found

the flesh. This was so easy for him. It was as if his tongue was a storeroom ready to deliver a constant stream of half-truth's in order to fulfil his plan. He cared for no-one – and would bend every rule to have his way. He had caught his little fish, and she was the bait to haul in his prime target.

Realising that they had come to an impasse. He knew that he had to offer her something to reel her in. He had to entice her to come to him quickly before anyone got wind of him talking to her. Sarah was sitting down again, trying to decide what to do next, when Cain interrupted her thoughts.

"Look, Sarah, I'm going to have to be honest with you, we don't have much time. Don't be alarmed, but Dr. Savage has made it clear. If you don't receive your treatment soon, he's not sure if he will be able to reverse the damage a second time. There is no medical research to support that theory.

We simply don't want to lose you, and as I explained, you are the first person we have been able to bring back literally from the edge of death. The world needs to know that we can offer hope to the terminally ill and that we can cure life-threatening diseases. No more sickness – no more dying. How can that be bad?"

It seemed like Sarah's heart and her head was in disagreement. She almost felt disloyal to Cain for thinking that he was some kind of monster as her family had led her to believe. The fact was unavoidable. He was her only hope! Cain put up a good argument, but she was pretty sure that the rest of her family wouldn't listen to him.

"So, why don't you take a goodwill gift from me. I have a doctor waiting on Mull. She will administer the new medicine and give you a supply for the next few days. This should buy you some time to convince your family that this is the right way to go. It's the only way you will have a future, Sarah! You need to come now."

Sarah bit her lip.

"Dr. McFarland is there now waiting for you. Then you can return to John within the hour. You will see that I mean you no harm. I am thinking of your welfare Sarah. We don't want you to become sick again."

Sarah was still hesitant. "Can't you get the doctor to come here?" she replied.

This negotiation was delicate. He had to tread carefully as everything depended on Sarah's choice.

"Dr. McFarland is taking a big chance even meeting you because she could be struck-off and lose her job. Although she is willing to risk coming to you, you must meet her half-way. Don't you think that is a reasonable request, Sarah?"

"I guess."

"Sarah, are your hands beginning to weaken?" Peter pressed.

She looked down at her trembling hands. "Yes!"

Cain could hear the frustration creep into his own voice. He breathed more deeply.

He had to hold it together.

"Right, we have to move quickly; there's not much time before it's irreversible. I want you to come down to the harbour as quick as you can. There is a boat waiting to take you across the channel. You'll be back before you know it. Don't say anything to anyone. Just hurry!"

Reluctantly but without remorse, she succumbed to Cain's persuasive powers. She slipped on her shoes and a light jacket then made her way along *The Street of the Dead* towards the harbour.

John and Josh were lying on their backs, looking up at the incredible light show. They had walked up to the north shore, where the beach seemed to glow iridescent under the floodlit sky. The white sand glistened like a sea of diamonds reflecting the extraordinary lights from above.

John broke the silence. "It's been an incredible day: I can't believe I've met up with my father after all these years. I thought I'd never see him again. For a long time, I waited, believing that he would come back. Years passed, but he never came." He paused. "Recently, I'd grown to hate him."

Josh smiled. "I guess I always thought he was dead, but today I'm overwhelmed because I've gained a grandfather. Now that's a good reason to celebrate!"

Just then, John looked over his son's shoulder; something strange was happening towards the south of the island. "Oh no, something is wrong. We'll have to put the celebrations on hold. Come on, we have to go!"

They ran like the wind. They could see what looked like a dark patch above the water just beyond the abbey. For some reason, the lights were not reaching the harbour. A dense fog hung over the water like an impenetrable wall.

John gave his son instructions, "Go back and check if the others are okay. I'll go down to the harbour and see what's going on."

As John reached the jetty, he saw a small boat crossing the channel. He was sure that he caught sight of Sarah, but it didn't make sense. Searching for a means to follow her, he spotted a small boat anchored a few feet beyond the jetty. The island folk were trusting people: the owner had left the key in the ignition. As he jumped in and started the engine, he heard Josh calling.

"It's Mum; she's gone! We have to go after her."

By the time Josh reached the jetty, John had untied the boat and was heading towards Mull. "I'll come with you,

Dad. Come back!" He realised his protests were in vain when his father called out.

"No! I got us into this mess. I'll bring her back."

Josh felt like he was standing on a cliff edge even although the ground was perfectly flat. One step into the darkness, and he knew that he would fall. The fog began to wrap around him, calling him in. He shuddered. It was a warning. He could go no further. He would have to trust that his father would not fail. Destiny was calling him in another direction. Josh ran back to the abbey. By this time, everyone had gathered, still in their nightclothes.

Chapter 24

The Song

Matthew closed his eyes and bowed his head when he heard Josh's report. The others followed his lead. No words were spoken, but everyone knew they had to focus on victory.

They remained in the quiet vigil until Josh broke the silence. "I know that the situation looks hopeless. Mum and Dad are missing, and we have to presume that Cain has a hand in this. However, as I explained before, two weeks ago, I was given insight into future events. I saw visions of this time, and I think I need to share something with you."

One of the villagers called out. "What exactly should we do? Do we wait here or follow them and bring them back?"

Josh paused: it was difficult to explain what he had seen. He looked to Matthew for support.

"It's okay Josh, we need you to tell us what you saw."

Josh explained that his insight into the future did not run in a linear pattern.

Stepping *out of time* with Cain had distorted his understanding of reality. The visions of the future that Ruel had shown him were still difficult to interpret. It certainly wasn't the same as predicting the future. He was aware of an inner sense of peace about the future, but somehow time wouldn't allow him to understand the visions all at once. He knew that he had seen everything right up to the end and yet the meaning of the visions was only released as events unfolded.

Realising the enormity of the burden his grandson was carrying, Matthew put an arm around his right shoulder. Everyone was looking expectantly to him for answers. Still, his earlier confidence seemed to have evaporated into the dark sea along with his parents.

Matthew gently encouraged him. "Just tell us what you see and what you remember, then perhaps we'll get the sense of what we should do next."

Josh nodded, then soberly tried to explain his understanding of his mystical experience. "Okay. So you might all think that I'm crazy, but I don't believe we have to go after my parents. I believe that they have been taken for a purpose. It's our job to find the missing gemstones from the breastplate. I'm not exactly sure why, but for some reason, they are going to help us win this battle."

A young girl around Josh's age came forward. Josh recognised her as the one who sang the beautiful Taize song earlier. She introduced herself. "Hi, my name is Emma. My mother used to sing an ancient song that speaks of the mystical stones."

Matthew called her forward. "Come up here and sing for us."

Emma began to sing out the Celtic ballad, narrating the tale of stones from Jerusalem in times past. She half-spoke, half-sang the words of the song, obviously struggling. She hadn't heard the song since childhood. Memories of her mother's voice triggered the melody, but it was as if the words were hidden behind a veil, lost in the midst of time.

Matthew came alongside her, resting both hands on

her shoulders. "It's okay, child, just take your time. Centre yourself. Put away anxious thoughts. Find that place of rest that you know exists inside your soul. The words will come to you."

Josh looked upon the scene in awe. He watched intently as his grandfather interacted with the girl. Matthew seemed to possess something deep within himself. Some kind of energy or spirit or something mystical that was difficult to define

His mind turned to Cain – his kinsman. Both men had some kind of intrinsic authority or power and yet were poles apart in character. Somehow, just being in Mathew's presence made him feel safe. His grandfather possessed a hidden store of strength that he could transfer to others by a simple touch or even by simply being in his presence. He had no language to describe it, but whatever it was – he wanted it. Josh surmised that Matthew had developed this inner state of peace through a lifetime of waiting. Just holding on, expecting the right side to win.

What about my Dad? Until recently, Josh would have described him as a real family man who cared deeply about his wife and son. But now, all he could see was a deeply anxious man who, without doubt, put himself and his family first but cared little for the rest of humanity. He hadn't noticed this before.

Emma tentatively started to sing. Her voice trembling.

"Sing to the land that one day will be free
Follow the path of the saltire
There you will find the precious stone
Leading you higher and higher
Seek out the place where the rulers anointed
High on a fortress hill
One foot below the mark of the King
Search for the stone for this is his will."

Emma stopped abruptly, weeping openly. "I'm sorry, I think there's more, but that's all I can remember. It's just so difficult . . . I have to translate the song from the old Scots tongue for you to understand."

Once again, Matthew comforted her quietly. "You did great, Emma, and this song has given us some good leads. Don't be upset; just let us know if you remember any more."

The girl sat down, relieved that she had been able to help. She desperately wanted to remember the rest of the song, but it seemed locked up in a vault of memories from long ago.

Matthew turned to the villagers asking, "If anyone thinks they have an interpretation of the song, speak up now." Without hesitation, a young man stepped forward.

"Ah, Angus McLeod, our history graduate. Of course! Can you enlighten us?"

Angus coughed before speaking. He was a quiet lad, not confident at public speaking. "I think the saltire could lead you to two places. The first being St Andrews. The national flag is based on a dream by my namesake King Angus." He laughed nervously, embarrassed; perhaps he'd been rather bold to compare himself to a king. His Scottish psyche had trained him to be careful about giving his opinion but rather to let others lead. His people had been crushed so often, and for so long, it was difficult to step out of the victim role. Nevertheless, he went on to explain that King Angus had invoked the name of St Andrew before going into battle.

King Angus had seen a sign in the sky. A white diagonal cross appeared over the deep blue sky. He vowed that if he won the battle, he would make St Andrew the patron saint of Scotland. And so the saltire flag was born that day as he prevailed against his enemies.

Josh was intrigued because it seemed that St Columba of Iona was the obvious choice to be the patron saint of the land.

Pondering for a few moments, Angus offered his view. "Perhaps St Columba's dark history would exclude him from that honour." He explained that St Columba had secretly copied some precious documents which led him to start an uprising against one of the Kings of Ireland. A battle ensued, costing two thousand lives. St Columba, disgraced, was banished from Ireland and as penance was given the task of saving two thousand souls. That's when he made his home on the isle of Iona.

In contrast, the legend of St. Andrew's bones being brought to the kingdom of Fife by a monk from a Greek island was compelling. Known as the first disciple, he was killed on the island of Patras and hung diagonally on a cross by an arm and leg in respect of his master who went before him.

Josh spoke. "Ah, so that's why the Scottish flag has a diagonal cross on a blue sky background! I get it now."

"Where is the second place? Matthew asked'

Now that he had found his voice, Angus replied enthusiastically. "After the great conflict and the cathedral was destroyed, the bones were removed from the town of St Andrews. Some believe they are now kept in a reliquary box in Edinburgh Metropolitan Cathedral.'

Matthew pressed for more information. "Do you have any ideas about the other verse?" "Yes, well, there are four possibilities. Iona, Dunadd hillfort, Scone Palace, or possibly Inverness. Obviously, it's not Iona. We've already found one of the stones here, so we can assume it is one of the others. I have some ideas about Scone Palace where Scottish kings were inaugurated, but the description sounds remarkably like Dunadd, and it's nearby, so I think that could be our first port of call."

Matthew looked towards his grandson. "Josh, do you have anything to add from your encounter? It's like we have the makings of a jigsaw puzzle, but there are so many missing pieces. We could do with all the help we can get."

Josh shook his head. "I'm sorry, I can't work out the meaning right now. If only we had *The Messengers* to help us. I'm sure Ruel and Uzel would know where to look."

Matthew shook his head. "Don't be anxious, son. We'll find them. A long time ago, mankind gave up its dominion of this world. Perhaps it is our destiny to change that. Perhaps *The Messengers* are here to guide us, but they cannot take back what we gave away.

It's the *Kosmocratoras* – Cain and his kind – who have ruled and reigned over us in the shadows. We all know it but have been powerless against them. Perhaps this is the final battle. Not a war with tanks and guns but with faith that these sacred stones have been hidden for us to use in some way to overcome our oppressors."

Josh, Duncan, and Rhona retired with Matthew's to his private room to make plans to leave in the morning to search out the other two jewels. They all agreed that it would be best to split up to save time. Matthew and a couple of others would go east to St Andrews.

Meanwhile, Josh would lead his team a few miles south from Oban to an ancient fortress at Dunadd then on to Scone Palace in Perthshire to follow the trail of the kings. They made plans to meet up in Perth in a couple of days, deciding not to use technology to prevent Cain from intercepting their calls.

The four treasure hunters were reluctant to retire to bed. All were aware of the mighty battle ahead of them. Finding the gemstones was just the beginning. Even if they found them; what should they do with the

Breastplate? The fate of mankind was resting on their shoulders. They had entered an almighty war with the powerful *Kosmocratoras*. Who were these beings from the unseen world? None of them felt equipped.

For our struggle is not against flesh and blood, but against, Archas; Exousia; Kosmocratoras and Pneumatica in the heavenly realms.   Ephesians 6:12

Chapter 25

Search for the Firestones

The islanders gathered around the six travellers to encourage them and send them safely on their journey to find the gems.

It was decided the previous evening it would be more effective to split into two groups of three. Matthew would travel with Angus and Emma. Everyone agreed that the two young islanders were the perfect candidates to help solve the riddle of the missing stones. They planned to head east to St. Andrews – an ancient town on the east coastline of the Kingdom of Fife.

As Josh, Duncan, and Rhona were about to set off for Dunadd, Matthew put his hands on their respective shoulders and said gravely: "Be careful. Legend says that one called *The Dark Ruler* has been searching for the three gems for a very long time because they are missing from his breastplate. It is said that he has only nine and needs the other three to gain full power over the earth."

"It is not a legend, Grandad." Josh looked directly into the older man's eyes as he stated: "The true name for them is *Firestones*. He needs the missing stones to alter time and space, but we are one step ahead. Destiny led us to the Ligure – we need to find the Agate and the Amethyst before he does. I don't know exactly why, but I believe it will be catastrophic if he finds them.

"Well then. We'd better make sure that we find them before he does!" Matthew slapped his grandson heartily on the back.

Although the island had been Matthew's sanctuary for many years, and he had long since come to terms with his confinement, it felt strangely unnerving for him as they boarded the ferry from Iona to Mull. It was only a short distance from his home, but it might as well have been a thousand miles.

Driving a car was going to be a bit of a challenge. He'd forgotten how but had kept his licence up-to-date. Sitting in the driver's seat at Fionnphort ferry terminal, he stared ahead for some moments before resting his head on the steering wheel. His day of freedom had come, but his mind was blank. He felt cheated. Wanted to roar.

Emma volunteered. "Why don't I drive for a while till you get your bearings. You can take over any time."

Although Matthew knew how important his mission was to find *The Firestones*, it took every ounce of energy in his body to overcome the shock of leaving the island. His normal calm state-of-being was being severely tested. As the car-ferry reached the town of Oban, he felt increasingly uncomfortable. Even with a constant stream of pilgrims, the island had never felt busy or chaotic. It was a long time since he had seen so many people in one place. Journeying east was an eye-opener as they passed through the big cities. He was appalled by the amount of traffic on the roads, and the speed of the cars made him feel ill, so they had to stop a couple of times when he was carsick. It seemed like the world had changed so much he hardly recognised it.

Time constraints compelled them to keep driving until they reached their destination, stopping briefly to eat.

They arrived at St Andrews by late afternoon. As they passed through the Pend Gate, the historical site came into view. Matthew now understood why the huge area was described as *The ancient ecclesiastical capital of Scotland.* But the largest cathedral in Scotland was now a ruin. Even so, the site was impressive, commanding attention from tourists and locals alike. The walled area housed the cathedral, a tower and various foundations of older churches, and an extensive graveyard.

Standing at the entrance of the vast site, they all felt perplexed about where they should begin the search for the precious *Firestones.* A guidebook in the Tourist Centre described how a monk named St Rule brought ancient relics of St Andrew's bones from Greece to keep them safe from the *Roman Emperor, Constantine.* It boasted that the venerated bones of the disciple were once kept in a nearby church. Angus was excited to explain, "There is a custom of keeping ancient artefacts in a reliquary box. These boxes are often covered in precious jewels." This clue led them to search the extensive grounds with great enthusiasm but to no avail.

"Didn't you say that the reliquary box had been removed to Edinburgh?" Emma asked.

"Yes, but no one knows for sure if it's genuine; perhaps it remains here in St Andrews." They persevered in the search.

Close by, the impressive remains of a castle perched over the cliffs, clinging on for dear life as the fierce waves of the North Sea battered the supporting rocks. This castle was once the epicentre of battles about religious superiority, spanning many centuries. Hundreds of people were tortured. Many died.

A small inscription on the road marked the site of an execution. A man burned alive at the stake. As they looked on respectfully at this gravesite, a car casually passed by, irreverently driving over the memorial stone with a loud clank.

On a nearby plaque, the story continued as yet another man – on the opposing side – was killed, then pickled in brine and hung from the castle wall. This gruesome deed was seen as an act of defiance against their opponents who'd held them under siege.

As the small group looked around the site, they marvelled that so many had fought and died for their beliefs, and yet all that remained – was a ruinous heap.

The late evening sun slowly moved over the site, casting long shadows behind the ghostly outline of the ancient stone buildings. The poignant scene troubled Matthew. A reminder of the passing of time and the futility of lives lost in battles long forgotten. He bowed his head in sorrow. Murder and carnage hung heavy over them. They all felt the shroud of death over the place.

Matthew shook his head as if to waken himself from dreaming. "Come now, let's not be distracted by this melancholy mood. We have an important mission."

He managed to raise a smile. "It's only the future of the planet that depends upon us unravelling this mystery.

Emma! Keep singing the song until you remember all of it. Angus, can you think of any more historical links to the *Firestones*?"

Angus scratched his head.

"What stones do you associate with Scotland?" Matthew prompted the young man to dig deep.

"I don't know, perhaps the Scottish Crown Jewels. They're covered in gems?"

Emma interrupted, "But what has that got to do with the Scottish Saltire in the song?"

Matthew agreed. "She's right. We have to somehow link it to the flag!"

Angus suggested they visit Edinburgh Castle and the

Museum of Scotland. "There are any number of gems and brooches to be found there. For instance – you have the *Monymusk Reliquary*. Legend says that it once contained part of the sacred bones of St. Columba of Iona."

Matthew was curious. "Are there any gemstones on this box directly associated with Columba?"

"I'm not sure. The only stone I know to be linked to Columba is the *Stone of Destiny,* but that's something completely different. It's a block of stone, not a gem."

Matthew's eyes widened. He felt his heart race a little. "Let's not dismiss the *Stone of Destiny*. What do you know about it?"

Angus rubbed his hands together. He loved the idea that history held so many secrets waiting for the appointed time to be revealed.

"It's the object of many legends, so it's hard to know what's true. Some say that St. Columba kept the *Destiny Stone* at Iona, and it was used for the coronation of royalty. He believed it was so sacred that he used to sleep on it.

There is a good connection to royalty here because we have evidence that many Scottish Kings are buried on Iona. And of course, Columba – in his role as the Abbot of Iona – was involved in the inauguration of the Kings.

"And if I remember correctly that centuries later, the *Destiny Stone* was kept at Scone Palace?" Matthew looked at the history scholar for confirmation

"Yes. It was kept at various locations for coronations before it was stolen by King Edward 1st of England. His goal was to –"

Matthew interrupted. "Yes, of course, he wanted to stop Robert the Bruce being crowned as King of Scotland."

Angus nodded.

He continued the story. "*The Destiny Stone* was

transported around Scotland for centuries. Obviously, an object of power, whoever had possession of the stone, owned the royal position over Scotland. There are many places mentioned in the checkered history of the *Destiny Stone*. It was said to have been continually moved to protect it. It rested for a time at Dunadd, Dunstaffage castle, Dunkeld, and finally at Scone Palace."

Matthew sat down on a nearby bench. He needed to think this through. "Where is it now?"

Angus, glad to show off his knowledge, answered cheerfully. "That's easy, it's kept in Edinburgh castle, waiting for the next coronation, and that will most likely be at Westminster Abbey. The last one was over sixty years ago. Do you know that the *Destiny Stone* was submissively placed under the coronation throne in London?"

"Really!" Emma exclaimed. "What! I didn't know that! Maybe it's true that there is some connection with the *Destiny Stone* and Dunadd, and whoever possesses the stones has the power?"

Angus added. "And one more thing, just to complicate matters. Many believe that the real stone was replaced before Edward's army seized it, and it is hidden somewhere until the end of days."

Frustrated, Matthew threw up his hands. "How are we to make sense of these legends? Are they just myths, or is there any truth in these stories?"

Tired and hungry, he suggested that they find accommodation for the night and go for something to eat. "We have a puzzle to solve, and we can't do that on an empty stomach."

Emma and Angus were relieved. Their search was leading nowhere.

Chapter 26

Place of The Kings

Josh's group were equally frustrated. After travelling to the Fort of Dunadd, they climbed the rocky hillock to the *Place of the Kings*. As they reached a small plateau, they looked around for signs of the coronation stone. Apparently, archaeological finds had confirmed evidence of jewellery making and metal-works. Brooches and various metal objects were discovered at the site. The fort had been renowned as a place of communication through artwork and rock carvings.

Rhona, a keen climber, scrambled ahead up a narrow stony pathway to an upper terrace. "I've found it! Come up here!"

She stood, looking slightly in awe as she pointed to a grey slab of stone that resembled an ancient gravestone. A carved out footprint and a small bowl structure were all that remained of the coronation site.

They thoroughly searched the area for clues of where to find the gemstone – without success.

Angus had written down some instructions on what they should look out for. He guided them to the *Ogam writings* and the head of an animal faintly etched on the coronation stone. However, weather and time had almost obliterated the markings.

Josh bent down to study the engravings. "They look like scribbles. Some kind of hieroglyphics. Does anyone understand this?"

After a fruitless search, they decided to move on to the Information Centre at Kilmartin to look for clues. While browsing through leaflets about the area, Duncan chatted with a tourist who'd visited the area many times. He cracked open a secret that was not generally known by the public.

Duncan started jumping from one foot to the other as he recited the words of the song. "*One foot below the mark of The King search for the stone for this is his will.*" Excitedly, he shouted to Josh and Rhona: "Come here, you've got to come and talk to this guy. He has some information that we need to hear." The man looked pleased that he could be of help. Duncan, eager to share, said: "Tell them what you told me just now about the coronation stone, please."

The tourist spoke enthusiastically: "I just told your friend that the true coronation stone has been covered up by a replica made of composite material to protect it."

"Protect it from what?" Rhona enquired.

"The Historic Society feared that it would be destroyed by the fifty thousand tourists who visit annually to place their foot in the king's footprint.

He continued: "This allows them to have their bit of fun, but the one who places his foot in the true stone will make an oath to take up the responsibility to protect the land and the people. He is saying he will be married to them and will protect them with his life. I think it's safe to say that tourists do not understand it or intend to keep this solemn vow. I guess that only a true leader will be able to place his foot in the royal footprint. And his mark will be as one who looks after his people."

They all thanked the helpful tourist then made their way back to the car.

Pleased that he had solved a mystery, Duncan took charge of their next move. "We need to find a hardware store!"

The others looked puzzled.

"Remember the words of the song. It says we should search for the stone, one foot below the mark of the king."

They drove back from Oban in complete silence. All of them aware of the seriousness of what they were about to do. It was the hour of the gloaming – that special time somewhere between day and night. The sun was just beginning to set over the hillfort as they approached the driveway, and all were relieved to find no other vehicles in the car park. Scrambling up the hillside, it was hoped that at this late hour, no stray tourists would be found at the isolated location.

Rhona looked anxiously at the two men. "Are you sure about this? What if you destroy the real stone?"

Duncan held the pick above his head. "No! I'm not sure but it's the only clue we have." He swung his arms behind his head, ready to strike the stone, but the pick stopped in mid-air as he a felt strong resistance.

"Ah widnae be doing that, lad!"

The three gem hunters jumped back. After the initial shock, Josh stepped forward, trying to look as though they'd every right to be there. "Who are you?" he asked.

The large man in highland dress answered confidently: "I'd be The Keeper! And it's my job to protect this place."

They all looked at each other. No-one had seen him approach.

"Are you even human?" Rhona asked.

"Well, lass, isn't there a bit of the divine in all of us,"

the man stated mischievously, with a glint in his eye.

The sun was now low on the horizon. They all followed the man's gaze as he looked out over the plains of the Moss Moine. The River Add shimmered golden as it serpentined its way around the hill towards the distant sea.

The stranger spoke softly: "There have been generations before me; everyone patiently waiting for this time!

Would this be what you're looking for?" He held out a wooden staff.

They all gazed in awe as they carefully examined the details of the ancient relic. The crooked top was covered in silver with a large jewel embedded in the beautifully crafted Celtic knot-work. As the last glimmer of light passed through the jewel, it radiated a bright shaft of light upon the coronation stone, and the shadows of the Celtic knots danced about upon the grassy knoll around them.

No-one dared speak: reluctant to spoil the sacred moment. The Keeper cried out: "Yes! This is the day we have been waiting for."

"And here is a gem that you will give to the ancient one." He handed it to Josh. "This is a replica, of course, but the *Kosmocrator* won't know the difference until it is too late."

Josh examined the replica carefully; although similar to the one contained in the staff, it lacked the brilliant glowing lustre of the original.

"When you bring back the man who fought the ancient one for 33 years, I will give him this staff and the true Firestone." He looked again at the glowing stone then left them standing in the darkness.

No-one moved, each lost in their own thoughts, trying to work out what had just happened. The last glimpse of sunlight slipped under the hills melting into the distant sea.

"Matthew! It must be him." Josh spoke into the air.

"What do we do now?" Rhona broke the silence. After a while, she suggested: "I guess we should head back to town and find a place to stay. There's nothing more we can do until morning."

The team in St Andrews had not been so fortunate. Matthew, Emma, and Angus had finished dinner then made their way into the hotel lounge. Surprisingly it was empty, allowing them to discuss their next move.

"Okay, Angus. Did the *Destiny Stone* ever come to St Andrew's?" Angus shook his head. Matthew continued, "Let's start at the beginning and trace the journey of the *Destiny Stone* and see if we have missed anything. Maybe we can find a link."

Angus recapped the history of the coronation stone to the best of his knowledge. He told them of a legend that says that Scota – a royal princess – travelled with the ancient stone from Egypt through Scythia then stayed in Spain before eventually coming to Ireland.

He pondered for a while, rubbing the stubbly hair on his chin.

"Of course! There certainly is evidence that the Hebrew people fled from their land after the Babylonian and the Egyptian exiles, and many of them settled in Spain. We know this from the history about the Spanish Inquisitions when the Hebrew people were tortured then expelled. That is when Christopher Columbus led them to The Americas."

Everyone was deep in thought.

"Another legend says that when Fergus – a high king of Ireland – raided Scotland, he brought the Destiny Stone to Scotland and was inaugurated on the coronation stone at Dunadd. It was there that he granted his nephew, Columba, the land known as Iona.

The *Destiny Stone* was kept in Iona. After Columba's death, it was relocated several times, and eventually, it was taken to Scone Palace."

Matthew jumped up, excited, as he pronounced, "I think I know where we should go."

Angus and Emma shouted in tandem, "Where?"

Matthew anxiously tried to piece together the story "I think we have to go to Arbroath Abbey! Come on, guys. Think about it. *The Destiny Stone* was returned there after a group of students liberated it from Westminster Abbey. What was draped around it?"

Angus looked stunned, "*The Saltire Flag*!" Matthew could hardly contain himself "And what else happened there?"

Emma laughed excitedly, "Of course. The Declaration of Arbroath."

Matthew was on a roll: the mystery was unfolding. "Everyone knows that this Document was a letter to the Pope in the 14th century, declaring that Scotland should be independent. Many can quote the line *We fight for our freedom* . . . but I remember something about a group of people from far away places mentioned in the declaration. "Does anyone know where the document is kept?" They both shrugged shoulders.

"No? Right. We haven't got time, someone, check it out on your cell-phone."

Emma found what they were looking for. "It's kept in the National Record Office in Edinburgh, but look, I've found a copy. Oh no! The declaration is in Latin."

She quickly scrolled through the small screen. "No, wait . . . I think I've found the translation. Wow! You all need to read this."

Most Holy Father and Lord, we know, and from the chronicles and books of the ancients, we find that among other nations, our own, the Scots, has been graced with widespread renown. They journeyed from Greater Scythia by way of the Tyrrhenian Sea and the Pillars of Hercules. They dwelt for a long course in Spain among the most savage tribes, but nowhere could they . . . be subdued by any race, however barbarous. Thence they came, twelve hundred years after the people of Israel crossed the Red Sea to their home in the west where they still live today . . . (and so it goes on to say) The most-gentle, St. Andrew has since kept them under his protection.   The Declaration of Arbroath. AD 1320

The three treasure hunters sat down – stunned by the evidence they had just uncovered. Angus broke the silence. "So much for having a history degree! I thought this was all a mythical story about the *Stone of Destiny* being a sacred stone.

And yet, here we have historical evidence – to the Pope no less – stating that the Scots came here from the *Holy Land*, and the document has over thirty official seals to authenticate it."

They all stared at the phone-screen displaying a peculiar ancient, crumbling parchment scroll with curled-up paper fringes, edged with a multitude of waxed seals on the lower borders.

"How can this be? It must have been common knowledge at that time." Emma stated.

"Does that mean we have replaced the Hebrews? The people of the book?"

Matthew scolded her. "In no way are we a replacement! No branch can grow without a root!

And, young lady, our blood is not totally pure Scots."

Angus, unable to offer any suggestions, asked

Matthew if he knew what they should do next.

Matthew replied, "All I know is we have to find the *Destiny Stone*; perhaps it will lead us to one of the gemstones!" We have to decide, Edinburgh or Arbroath. Why don't we have a good night's sleep . . ."

Just as he was suggesting they retire for the night, a tall stranger appeared in the room.

"Are you waiting for me?"

They were all mesmerised. Josh and John had told them about the *Messengers,* but still, they were unprepared.

"Come, we must go now. John must have told you about me. My name is Uzel. Follow me." They looked at each other in trepidation but nevertheless followed obediently.

Uzel held up one hand. "No! only Matthew. This is for his eyes only!"

Emma and Angus stopped in their tracks. They were slightly terrified and still recovering from the shock of Uzel's sudden appearance.

"Don't worry, go and have a good night's sleep," Uzel instructed. "We'll be back before breakfast!" He winked mischievously as he put his arm around Matthew then disappeared from sight.

The young ones sat down in silence until both let out a huge sigh of relief. Ella spoke first, "How? What . . . just happened?"

Angus shook his head.

Meanwhile, Matthew clung to Uzel's chest as they travelled through the darkness.

At first, he could make out the shadowy shapes of buildings. Later he knew they were travelling over hills and mountains but had no grid or map to identify where they were going. For quite some time, they travelled along the banks of a large body of water, possibly a loch. *Too wide for a river* he reckoned.

Then unexpectedly, they veered off to the left and uphill. The sound of roaring water below their feet caused him to tense every muscle in his body. Uzel reassured him: "It's alright, Matthew, we've arrived."

Matthew realised that Uzel had not spoken, but he had heard him nonetheless. As they set down on the land, they could see the source of the thunderous noise. No voice could ever be heard in this deafening place. Uzel signalled for him to follow as he walked down a narrow pathway that led them into a large cave hidden behind the waterfall.

Chapter 27

The Cave

Inside the cave, three *Messengers* warmly greeted Uzel then bowed their heads towards Matthew.

Uzel introduced them. "Matthew, these are my fellow companions, Mazu, Micael, and Samu." They had the appearance of light-beings. "These *Messengers* have come to bear witness on this special occasion."

Matthew fell to his knees. "I shouldn't be here."

Gently but firmly, Uzel helped him to his feet. He reassured him once more. "We are co-workers. Do not be afraid. Come, my friend, have a look around. After all, this is what you have been searching for."

As he surveyed the huge cave, he noticed many artefacts and stacks of boxes lining the walls on every side. Then his eyes rested on a familiar blue and white material that draped loosely around an unknown object.

Mazu followed his gaze. "Go on, hasn't this has been your quest – to find the *Destiny* S*tone*?"

Matthew remained circumspect. He found himself alone in a cave with three *beings,* one of whom had spoken telepathically and transported him by unaided flight. "I'm just feeling a bit . . . Who are you? Where do you come from? I just need to make sure that I'm not dealing with the powers of darkness."

Mazu responded, "And what does the sacred text tell you to do? Isn't there a test?"

Matthew inhaled sharply. "Oh, I guess I use the *sacred name,* and if you are from the dark side, you have to obey and will leave here!"

A round of laugher filled the cave as Matthew spoke the *sacred name,* then opened his eyes and whispered, "Thank God!"

"I'm sorry, but this is all new to me; I'm feeling out of my depth here, I don't know what to do. After all the years of waiting and hoping – I should be excited!"

Mazu put a comforting arm around him. "We understand. You're doing really well; most people run away when they encounter us."

Matthew smiled, still unsure but asked tentatively, "Can I see it? I mean the *Destiny Stone.* I presume that is what's underneath the flag?"

They all walked over to the plinth where the *Destiny Stone* was resting. As Mazu uncovered it, Matthew gasped. "Oh! Wow! That is spectacular! It's not quite what I expected. I thought it was made of sandstone. You know, the pictures look completely different."

The three messengers glanced at each other.

"Oh! right, I see, this is the *real* stone."

He kneeled down to examine the stone. It was black and smooth like marble. Iridescent metallic golden flecks sparkled beneath the surface.

He spoke quietly to himself: "It looks more like some kind of meteorite."

Micael offered more information: "Indeed, we call them *Thunderstones!*"

"You mean there's more than one? Can I ask a question?"

He was still holding the flag in his hands. "Why Scotland? We are such an insignificant little country.

Many of us have just about given up hope of ever being free."

Micael answered with great compassion. "The Creator has always had plans for your land. Even in the midst of suppression and difficulties, he has had his hand upon you. Think of the incredible inventions and innovations that have sprouted from your loins. And consider how this creative ability has been totally out of proportion to your tiny population!"

Intrigued, Matthew turned his attention to the *Destiny Stone* once again. There were a number of symbols or pictograms carved on each side, in-filled with solid gold and studded with precious stones.

On the side facing him, he could make out the head of an animal like a bull or an ox, along with some hieroglyphics he couldn't understand.

He examined the stone for some time but could not find what he was searching for.

Looking dubiously at the object, he asked: "What about the gemstone? These are all too small. And what does this have to do with the three gemstones?" Uzel touched his arm, "Don't fret. It will all make sense shortly."

"Is this what you are looking for?" Mazu opened his hand to reveal a large sparkling gem, similar in size to the one on Iona. This is the Agate. You will take it to Josh, and he will deliver it to the *Kosmocrator*.

Matthew stepped back in awe. "Before we do that, let us look upon the *Glass Book of the Ordination of Kings*. You must see what is written."

Micael approached Matthew carrying a crystal-like book, indicating to him to look within.

With great trepidation, Matthew glanced upon the list

of kings. His eyes travelled down the noble register.

"No! That's not possible! I'm not worthy!" he shouted.

Micael touched his shoulder. "No-one is worthy, but you have been found faithful."

Time seemed to swirl within a whirlwind. Matthew had no idea how long he remained in the cave. It could have been one night or a thousand.

The three mysterious beings carried out a beautiful ceremony associated with the coronation stone. Michel instructed him to lie down. "Come, Matthew, lay your head upon Jacob's pillow. As his head touched the royal stone, he was astonished to hear the *Thunderstone* emit a high pitch. The frequency – like music – touched his heart and made him weep.

All at once, he entered into a dream-like state and saw both the past and future unravel before his eyes. Instinctively, Matthew knew that this event, the location, and the revelations he had seen were to remain veiled until the appointed time.

He could have remained in that place, content, his mind, and heart, filled with peace that surpassed anything he had ever known.

As the dream began to fade, Matthew opened his eyes as a warm hand touched his forehead.

"Come now, dear friend, we must return to the others." Micael was standing over him, smiling and urging him to stand up. It was difficult to refocus after his encounter with the future world. Micael had to steady him. Everything was beginning to make sense.

For the first time in his life, he felt fully awake. Everything he had experienced before was like looking through a heavy veil in comparison. Although he had known about the great cosmic battle that had raged from ancient times until this hour, he'd never understood the important role that man would play in the last battle.

"Are you ready to go back and join with the others? They will be waiting for us." Matthew looked at Micael, slightly bemused. He still felt as if he was in an other-worldly dimension, which caused him some reluctance to leave. Micael gently directed him to the cave entrance. "Come, my friend, I have been charged to protect you. We must make our way to Oban."

Darkness still hugged the wild, weather-worn land as they trans-relocated by some mysterious method of flight to the city of Perth. Angus, Emma, and Uzel were waiting for them, ready to make the journey back to Oban. Neither felt inclined to ask questions about what had transpired overnight.

Chapter 28

The Island

Sarah knew that she had made a huge mistake minutes after they left the jetty.

"Where are you going? This is the wrong way," she objected. Even in the darkness, she could access her finely-honed internal compass; she'd always been good with maps.

The man steered the boat without answering her.

Sarah lunged forward and tried to turn the wheel, but the large, heavy-set man overpowered her and pushed her back into her seat. His menacing eyes held her captive. Panicking, she considered jumping overboard. She knew that they were in a narrow channel, and the water wasn't too deep, but she couldn't see any land under the swirling, ominous sky.

Breathing deeply, she closed her eyes and repeated to herself: *Stay calm and make a plan.* Her options were limited. *My only hope is to try and swim for the shore.*

Moments later, her heart raced as she heard her husband's voice calling her name. It sounded like he was just behind them.

Relieved, she called back to him. "I'm here, John!"

Strangely, the boatman didn't try to silence her.

The truth quickly dawned on her, "Oh no! It's a trap!"

It was obvious to Sarah that she had been used as a decoy to lure John away from the island.

Frantic, she called, "Stay back John," but it was too late as his boat drew alongside, and he jumped on-board.

"Oh, John, I'm so sorry, I think we've been hoodwinked." Sarah gasped. "They've used me to lure you here. I thought I was going to get ill again. Cain said I needed more medical input, and without it, I could be dead in a couple of days."

John held his trembling wife. She was sobbing deeply. John whispered softly, "Don't worry, I think this had to happen. I need to face that man: there's nowhere to run to."

Just then, the cabin door opened, and John shuddered as he heard a familiar voice behind him.

"Ah, what a lovely scene," the voice uttered. The sorrowful wife being comforted by her gallant husband who's come to rescue her from the big bad wolf. You know, I really don't deserve this bad press. You will find out that I am merely trying to save the world. Soon you will understand everything."

John closed his eyes. Standing up to this man was the last thing he needed, but it seemed he was ensnared again. Somehow, his life was enmeshed with Cain's. Perhaps this was his destiny.

This mysterious man was able to influence corporations, banks, even governments. He had an army of people behind him. John had even witnessed his ability to manipulate time and space.

Would it ever be possible to stop him with his crazy plan to take over the world? It was obvious that he was incredibly powerful, but John had experienced another power at work. He just hoped for all their sakes that he was now on the right side.

John slowly turned around, then sighed with deep

relief when he realised that he was facing a video screen.

"Ah, John! We need to have a fresh start, my boy. I'm so sorry that I've had to coax you away from those awful people, but we will make it up to you. Let's resume the previous plans we were making before we were so rudely interrupted. A flight has been arranged to take you to the island I told you about. We will resume Sarah's treatment and get you fixed up too. Of course, I will join you in due course. Better get some shuteye; you have a long journey ahead."

John made no attempt to respond, nor was it expected. Cain was merely informing them about his plans.

Fifteen minutes later, they stopped at a jetty and were transferred onto a larger boat. They both knew they were bound for Ireland and away from the *Safe land*.

They sailed into Belfast harbour in the early hours of the morning. A crew member indicated that they should disembark quickly. After speeding across the sleeping city with ease, they arrived within fifteen minutes at a small private airport. Having no luggage to check in, the stewardess waved them on to the departure lounge. Security officers, fully engrossed in their T.V. screen – ignored them.

As Sarah paid a visit to the restroom, a steward appeared in front of John, towering above him. His stature was extra-large and filled the room. John looked up and was about to speak, but Uzel caught him in time with a warning look, indicating that John should pretend not to recognise him.

"Good morning, just to let you know that our flight will be departing shortly. Ah! – here is our captain. We should be leaving in the next ten minutes."

Sarah came through the restroom door and gasped as Ruel walked by her, dressed in a smart pilot's uniform.

He winked mischievously. Relief flooded over her, and she could hardly control her excitement as she made her way back to John.

She spoke quietly. "That's Ruel, look! He's come to help us."

"Yes, and Uzel is our cabin steward. They must have a plan." John whispered. Both felt they could breathe more easily.

Right on time, Uzel came back to usher the passengers onto the waiting private jet. Unsurprisingly, they were waved through Passport Control without any checks.

The absent Cain once again demonstrating his power over government officials, John reckoned.

Although it looked small, the twelve-seater plane was deceptively roomy and luxurious inside. Two men boarded the plane and sat at the back. They nodded but did not enter into conversation.

Must be the guards. John assumed.

When the engine started, and the seat-belt sign came on, John and Sarah sighed with relief when they realised Cain was not joining them on the flight.

Once airborne, Uzel came into the cabin, offering food and drinks. Although he could see that they were exhausted, he suggested they stay awake as they were making a short flight to pick up two other passengers.

John was surprised when the mystery passengers boarded the plane at *London City Airport*. He recognised the couple straight away. Greta was carefully guided by David into her seat. Her appearance shocked John. Her frame looked like it was collapsing, and her skeleton appeared to have shrunk inside her tiny body.

John told Sarah that he knew them and wanted to speak with them, but told her to rest because she was exhausted.

Unbuckling his seatbelt, he made his way to the seat adjacent to the young couple.

"Remember me?" John said.

Greta turned to look at him.

John flinched as he noticed the skin of her face looked transparent like parchment paper.

"Oh, It's you, John. We met at the Galton! How is your wife doing? What is her name?"

"Sarah. She's with me now, but she's sleeping." John lied. What's happened? Is the treatment not working?" he asked, concerned.

David spoke. "There has been a bit of a problem. They think that her cells have been overexposed to the medicine and so they are going to change the rate of treatment. You know, slow things down for a while."

The three passengers spoke for another ten minutes. John looked over his shoulder towards Sarah and smiled, then asked them if they would mind not telling Sarah about Greta's deterioration because he didn't want to scare her. He could see the distress in Greta's eyes but knew she understood.

Sarah quizzed John as soon as he sat down. "Who are they? How do you know them?"

John breathed in sharply before answering. "Oh! It's just a young couple I met at the hospital while visiting you. The girl is pretty exhausted and is going for a sleep. I'll introduce you later."

Uzel came back with a couple of pillows and blankets. Perhaps you would like to have a sleep now. We have a long journey ahead of us.

Sarah needed no persuading and was fast asleep within a few minutes.

Midway through the flight, Ruel came and sat across from Sarah as she was stirring from sleep. "There's going to be a little turbulence. I'm just checking if you are strapped in."

Sarah looked at John; he was sound asleep. "Yes, I think we are both fine." She sat back, aware that Ruel was looking intently at her. His posture told her that something was wrong. Somehow, he spoke to her without words. His sparkling eyes conveyed a message of hope, but he also told her there would also be a time of pain and sorrow ahead.

Sarah nodded silently. She looked at John, still sleeping like a baby and oblivious to their looming family apocalypse. Thoughts filtered through her mind as she tried to make sense of Ruel's words. *It will be difficult for John to live without me.*

Reassuring her again, *The Messenger* told her not to worry and that John would only grow in strength.

"If you remain, John will not have the courage to stand up to Cain. He will do anything to help you get better." She heard him say: "You know that he will give in."

This time Sarah wanted to protest, but Ruel stopped her. "You will always want to protect John, but this is the time to fulfil his destiny."

She knew he was right, but still, it was difficult to accept. Ruel made a gesture to comfort Sarah. "You and I will go as one. I will take care of you. I have been assigned to guard you."

Sarah had no idea how she could hear Ruel, but she knew that the communication between them was on a frequency that only she could hear. It was comforting to know that he seemed to be tuned into her in some way.

For the next hour, Ruel told Sarah about events yet to happen. He also explained how her personal journey would be different than expected. Sensitively and with great compassion, he told her that there was no need to be afraid as it would feel like she was simply walking through a veil. The next seven days would be a transition time for her, and then everything would change in an instant.

She understood.

"I'd better get back and relieve the pilot," he added. We'll talk later."

Deep down, Sarah always knew that she wasn't going to make it, but it had been great to have extra time to see Josh again and to watch John flourish in the middle of their struggles with Cain. Ruel had made it all much easier to accept.

The remainder of the journey was uneventful. When the pilot announced they would soon be landing, John braced himself. He knew that they were entering into Cain's territory.

Looking out of the window, he could see the island shrouded in the late evening mist. It looked mysterious and perhaps forbidden to outsiders. John shuddered as he thought of his new role because he knew that it wouldn't be easy. Whatever it took, he would have to find a way of bringing Cain's kingdom down. There was no point in trying to work out how that would happen. He just hoped that Ruel and Uzel would know.

There was no airport to speak of – just a few wooden sheds and a massive aeroplane hanger. Two cars were waiting for them at the edge of the runway to transport them to the hospital; a one storey purpose-built building. Although it was a modern structure, John expected something larger and perhaps more impressive.

Surely this can't be Cain's headquarters.

He noticed Greta being taken into the hospital by wheelchair. Thankfully Sarah was on the other side of the car, so she was unaware of Greta's arrival. He didn't want them to meet just yet. *She has enough to cope with*, he reckoned.

They both walked into the building with a certain amount of trepidation, not sure what to expect. However, the staff were friendly enough and led them to a large room with a hospital bed on one side and some comfortable armchairs beside the picturesque alcoved window. Sitting quietly opposite one another, they drank in the scenery. Even with the mist hovering over the water, the view was stunning. Lost in their own thoughts, silently, they gazed upon the idyllic turquoise ocean.

It wasn't long before the door opened, and Doctor Savage was explaining the new procedure they had planned for Sarah.

John looked worried, but Sarah didn't flinch. Apparently, they wanted to re-engineer some of the modifications they had carried out as other patients showed some signs of tissue degeneration. The doctor advised them that a new round of treatment would be required to fine-tune the previous repairs. The geneticist explained that this would involve intensive treatment for a couple of days. John was horrified. The last thing he wanted was Sarah being exposed to treatments that probably wouldn't work. He demanded to know, "Is this absolutely necessary?"

"I wouldn't be recommending if it were not!" the doctor responded curtly.

He went on to explain why the new procedure was necessary.

"The *Nanotech* we set up inside your body isn't functioning as expected. There has been a slight miscalculation because your body is used to working at a less efficient rate. It's like we've been trying to put new wine into an old wineskin. Not that I am saying your body is too old. It's not age-related; this would happen to anyone. Ironically, it's just that the human body has a peculiar way of working. So we will have to recalibrate everything. We have to slow it all down to let the cells catch up.

It's nothing to worry about. Leave it to the experts."

Sarah sighed inside because she knew that he was lying. They had not perfected the treatment, and she was merely a human guinea pig.

"I have one request, doctor. I would like to wait until tomorrow before starting the treatment. I just need some time with John. Could we go to the beach house? It looked so beautiful. I just couldn't face anything happening tonight. We've had such a long flight, and I'm exhausted. Would that be possible?"

Doctor Savage faltered. ". . . I guess it would make sense. We won't be starting tests until the morning. I'll arrange for someone to drive you up to the house."

Sarah quickly responded: "Oh, I'd rather walk. I've been sitting for hours. I need to stretch." The doctor reluctantly agreed with the proviso that Sarah returns first thing in the morning.

The walk to the house was breathtaking. A white sandy beach curved around the bay. The house perched on the rocky cliff at the end of the road.

Sarah had insisted they walked to give them time and privacy to talk. After the experience with the tracking device, she was wary of being in areas where they could be overheard.

This might be the last time we can talk privately.

"John, we haven't got much time, and I need to tell you something."

He stopped, purposely turning towards her. "You're going to be fine, Sarah. They will adjust the treatment and – it will all work out."

Sarah stopped him. "No, John, I want you to listen. I need you to be strong for me because I'm not going to make it."

He tried to protest, but she tenderly put her finger on his lips. "I had a long conversation with Ruel while you were sleeping. He told me of some wonderful things that will happen soon."

John raised his eyebrows and was about to speak, but Sarah continued sombrely: "But there will be a difficult time for you." She repeated Ruel's words. "A time of sorrow."

John turned towards the glassy still sea. They sat down on a large nearby rock. It was one of those evenings just before sundown when the sea and sky merged on the misty horizon. *Like a Turner painting, of an ethereal seascape,* John thought.

He wrapped his arm around his wife.

"No tears, John. Let's not waste this precious time!"

They sat in quiet contemplation until John broke the silence. "What did Ruel tell you?"

"Wonderful things, John! Do you know that we are really light-beings wrapped up in a temporary body, and this place we are in now is just a temporary dimension? He spoke about the visible and invisible realms. Something about the electromagnetic spectrum being vast, and yet we are caught in a narrow rainbow of visible light. That's just how our bodies are designed to function while we are here. But this rainbow dimension is only a fractal of what truly exists, probably only one percent. We just can't see all of it yet. Ruel and the others – they come from the other ninety-nine."

John shook his head in wonder. "I've seen it, Sarah. That's what Cain showed me!"

"No, John! What he showed you must have been in the visible spectrum in the second realm. Ruel told me that

Peter doesn't have access to the third realm."

"You mean he is confined here?"

"Yes. A bit like us. Our physical bodies are designed to have limitations while we exist here. Unaware of the invisible realm or the greater dimensions. Ruel explained that scientists are aware of these extra dimensions of the unseen. Think about how they can harness the waves of ultraviolet, infrared, or radio waves.

Cain is also bound to this cosmos but knows that it's temporary. His great master plan is to alter the *DNA* structure of mankind to keep us here in his kingdom. Otherwise, he will have a kingdom with no subjects to rule over."

Sarah stood up. "I think you will have to ask Uzel about the *Firestones*. Something to do with prisms and gates and Cain trying to gain access into the unseen realms. Prisms need to be in place or something like that. He lost me there!

All I know is that Ruel is my guardian and has come to take me through to the other side. It's my time, John."

"What about me, Sarah? When will it be my time?"

Sarah responded with some optimism. "I don't think it will be too long because there is a big event expected and it's just over the horizon. There is going to be a great unveiling of the invisible light. Everyone will see it at the same time. Meantime, you have something important to do, and Uzel has been sent to help you!"

John took Sarah's hands. "You've always been the strong one; how will I cope?"

They spent the night cradled in each other's arms, believing that it would probably be their last time alone together. In the morning, they walked back along the same road. This time the mist had lifted, and the sun shone on the clear sapphire sea. Time drifted: no longer their enemy.

Chapter 29

The blue sinkhole

Sarah resigned herself that she might not be leaving the hospital by the door she had entered. Ruel had sensitively revealed how long she had left, but she measured time in days now.

Although apprehensive, she couldn't halt the bursts of excitement that swirled within her. Part of her wanted to stay to experience the *Great Awakening* with John, but her body was letting her down. She genuinely was no longer afraid of dying because Ruel had explained what would happen. He didn't tell her the finer details of exactly where or when, but she knew that it would be a bit unpleasant and that it would pass quickly, and she would soon forget.

A pain-free existence! She could feel it beckoning her.

She reckoned that a couple of days would be long enough to make sure John had access to the hospital and find Cain's strategy room. Apparently, this was located beneath the hospital in a huge cavernous area deep underground.

The morning was a treadmill of tests and probes. Sarah used this as a reason to send John away. She needed time alone.

Reluctantly, John left the hospital and walked back along the beach and sat on the rock he had shared with Sarah. It wasn't long before Uzel turned up. John could almost say that he felt excited, but his anxiety levels about Sarah hindered his enjoyment of being a spy in the enemy's camp.

Aware of John's discomfort, Uzel placed a hand on his shoulder until John felt a weightlessness in his body. "Well, look at you, human, you've gone all sparkly."

When he looked down, he jumped back. He had no substance. All he could see was pure white light.

"Oh my God! What's happening. Where am I?" He exclaimed.

"Oh boy, I'm going to enjoy this! They won't be able to see me! I'm invisible!

How did this happen? How is it possible?"

"Just as well, I can still see you, or we'd be in trouble," Uzel joked.

"Would you call this an unfair advantage, Uzel?"

The two *spies* shared a time of exuberant laughter and a sense of victory even before the battle started.

"I've something interesting to show you." *The Messenger* beckoned him to follow.

Immediately, they were transported to the north end of the island.

Standing on the hillside looking over the ocean, John was entranced by something in the water a few hundred metres from the shore.

Pointing to an anomaly in the midst of the ocean, Uzel shared excitedly. "That's where we need to go."

The crystal cerulean sea was interrupted by a perfect circle of deep ultramarine water. On closer inspection, John could see a very deep hole in the seabed.

"What is it? Surely you don't want me to go down there? No way."

"Well, that's where we are going, but perhaps it would be better to find another way in."

John responded with trepidation: "You mean you want me to go to the bottom of the ocean?"

"Yes, but I don't want to drown you on your first day of quantum travelling. We'll save that for another day – not the drowning – the breathing in water thing . . . ha-ha!"

John laughed nervously again as he inquired "Where are we, Uzel? I know that we must be somewhere in the southern hemisphere, but no-one told me where."

"Oh . . . we are on a small island near Bermuda. This area is rather appropriately called the Devil's Triangle. Don't you love the irony of it! There are many of these underwater blue sinkholes here as well as all over the world. You should see the one in Egypt. Now that is spectacular! The sinkholes generally open up to a large underwater cave, and many have miles of connecting tunnels."

"How strange. Are they manmade?" John asked.

In reply, Uzel merely raised his eyebrows.

"We'd better get going. Remember! No talking or you will spook them, so we'll have to telepath," Uzel laughed as he instructed him.

John responded excitedly. "I don't know how to do that!"

"Don't worry, it's easy. I'll teach you. We could have used it before, you know – the notepad thing – when we had to write everything down, but we have to take these spiritual dimensions slowly. It can be a bit much for your tiny human brains to take in too soon."

"Hey. My brain is doing okay. Albeit that it is pure light just now and no one can see it."

Uzel put his arm around his charge, and they were transported to the entrance of the hospital. They entered the building with ease; however, finding the entrance to the caves below was going to take a while. Although they were no longer solid matter, Uzel informed him that it would take time for John to learn how to walk through walls. For now, they had to find a doorway.

The hospital staff seemed to be busy doing routine medical business, and there was no obvious way that led downstairs. In fact, their search turned up fruitless. There was no physical evidence of Peter's headquarters anywhere within the hospital building.

John looked curiously at Uzel. "I thought you would know everything?"

Uzel frowned. "I'm not omnipresent, you know, I've got limitations just like you. Anyway, exploring is the fun part; it's like a huge adventure unfolding the mysteries of the universe. Don't you agree?"

He pointed outside, indicating that he would search the grounds, but just as John was about to follow him, a nurse wheeled Sarah towards them. Her eyes widened when she noticed them, and she was about to speak but stopped herself just in time.

"Have you found anything yet?"

John was startled: he's heard her speak telepathically. He hadn't expected that. There was no grid for all that was happening. It was like existing in a secret world.

"You can see me! No, there's no sign of an entrance." John silently replied.

"How are you doing this?" He was enthralled that she had heard him.

"Ruel taught me when you were asleep on the plane. Try the gymnasium. It's across the hall from my room and I've seen several people coming and going who don't look like medical staff.

"I love you! I can say those words now without even

having to move my lips. I know that wherever you are, I will be able to communicate with you, and you will hear me." John responded tenderly as he bent down and kissed her.

They lingered for a few moments before something caught Sarah's attention. She drew back, then nodded towards the end of the hallway. One of the bodyguards from the plane was about to enter the gymnasium. Although reluctant to leave Sarah, they knew that this was their chance to find the entrance. John squeezed her hand before he left with Uzel.

They effortlessly followed the man and watched him walk towards the small hydrotherapy pool. After pressing a lever, the pool slid over to one side, revealing a set of steps. They quickly went after him and found themselves in a narrow corridor that stretched as far as the eye could see. Eventually, the man made his way towards another door.

This time both John and Uzel were ecstatic. They had found the stairway into a massive cavern. It was impossible to calculate its size.

In the centre of the cave stood a massive circular machine with tube-like structures, resembling huge arms, protruding either side.

A large window to one side revealed that they were under the sea. It was like gazing into an oversized fish tank but with all sorts of sea-life swimming by and totally oblivious to this strange hidden world of men.

John whistled. "Phew, pretty impressive. It looks like the machine they have at *CERN*. It's a *Hadron collider*! But why would they have one here under the sea?"

Uzel shouted angrily. "It's all part of their plan to alter time and space, John. They need to harness a lot of energy to access other realms. If they succeed, there will be such devastation in this world. Everything will be shaken. Even the stars will move out of place. Entities that have been held back until now will gain full access into this realm."

"You mean the *Kosmocratoras?* Are there more of them?"

"Yes. They are raw powers, violent and ruthless. Humans won't stand a chance against them. And there are others, the Archai. They are the higher powers; they are the 'Princes' that reign over 'Palities' – you call them cities. Or the Exousia . . . you really don't want to meet them!"

"If they are anything like Cain – I'd rather not."

"Believe me, this is not good because they don't have mankind's best interest in their plans. This interface with physical and quantum worlds is the greatest existential threat to mankind since the last time they tried it.

John looked puzzled.

"You've heard of the Tower of Babel?"

John replied, "Yes, but I thought that was just a . . . myth! You mean this is what they were doing . . . did they have this kind of technology thousands of years ago?"

Uzel shook his head in disbelief. "You have all the evidence in front of your eyes, and yet humans persist in denying it. Think about the ancient sites at Sacsayhuman or the pyramids. Both structures are prime examples of technology far in advance of anything you can build today. Right?"

John nodded.

"You say they are going to change time and space. What do you mean?" John asked.

Uzel hesitated. "I'm trying to think of an easy way to explain this. Okay! You have to disregard the idea of time as a linear process. Imagine that there are many types of time. In fact, there are multiple, but let's keep it simple. The first type is the time that the earth revolves around the sun, and that is cyclical. Then your earth is part of a spiral galaxy, and here we have another type of timeframe. Then think about the time that it takes for your galaxy to traverse the universe. Do you understand so far?"

"I think you have just described three types of time," John answered.

"Now, to travel between galaxies in the conventional way in earth-time would be impossible because your material body would expire before you could ever reach another galaxy. Andromeda is the nearest, and that's two and a half million light-years away, so you see, you'd simply run out of time long before you reached there by conventional means.

So imagine that the *Kosmocratoras* have found a way to create pathways between these different timeframes. Beyond macro-physics, you have to break through the barrier and go into the quantum realms to create shortcuts."

"But if they manage to do this – and it sounds like it would cause catastrophic events – how will any of us survive? Wouldn't this shifting of *matter* disturb everything in the universe? How can we stop them?" John asked.

Uzel stopped and surveyed the *light-being* in front of him with a broad grin. "Look at you now, John! You are existing outside of the visible spectrum. Your body is vibrating at such high energy frequency that you cannot be seen. Perhaps that is your answer!"

John examined his translucent hands in awe.

Uzel continued. "Is every material thing going to be displaced? Absolutely! Everything is going to be changed, and so mankind will be perplexed. No-one will know what to do. Everyone will look for a saviour."

And, don't forget, your mother demonstrated to you how to persevere and fight."

"My mother was weak," John replied angrily.

"Don't ever say that again," Uzel rebuked him. "Your mother fought Peter every day of her life for over thirty years. She never wavered, even when Peter took her husband away. Even when her son didn't understand her, but she held on believing that this day would come. How long have you been in this battle?"

"But look at the way she died!" John responded sheepishly.

Uzel closed his eyes. His nostrils flared. "Living in this world takes its toll, John. She had a particularly difficult journey."

John hadn't quite appreciated what his Mother must have gone through to protect him from Cain's wrath. He'd misjudged her as a religious fanatic when all the while, she knew what was coming.

He felt ashamed. "I'm so sorry, I guess I didn't understand."

"It's okay, John, she knows," Uzel said tenderly.

John's eyes widened. "You mean you've seen her?"

"I was assigned to your mother long before I met you! And yes, she is fine and is very proud of you. Now come, follow me; we don't have time to waste." John felt suitably chastised, so he followed meekly behind his guardian.

John wasn't sure how everything worked in his *lightbody,* but he seemed to transport himself to a location simply by thinking about it.

The next moment they were on the cavern floor looking up at the massive *Collider.* It was truly impressive. Images he had seen did not capture the immense size nor the complexity of the machinery.

"What should we do now?" he communicated silently to Uzel.

Shrugging his shoulders, Uzel responded with an unexpected answer. "We wait."

It wasn't long before they heard a commanding voice followed by a team of people.

"When will we be ready for the test?" Cain asked the chief scientist, a dynamic, spirited lady called Rebecca Johnston.

"Everything is good to go at 7pm tonight."

"You will all be well rewarded when I come into my kingdom, my faithful servants." Cain joked with the team. Everyone laughed as if on cue.

He left the group, and Johnston followed meekly behind. Uzel and John followed them. They overheard her ask Cain about the *Firestones*. He reassured her that they were on their way. "Oh, don't worry, the boy will bring them to me."

Johnston asked how that would happen.

"It never ceases to amaze me. Loyalty and love; both are disastrous for humans, but they never learn. It's their great weakness, and fortunately for us, we can use this to our advantage.

Johnston squirmed slightly when Cain spoke dismissively about humans. Somehow it didn't occur to him that he was talking about her kind. She had waited patiently for many years for this time and assumed that she was somewhere near the top of the list for the *DNA* upgrades. She was a top level scientist so felt sure she would be in great demand in the new age. She wanted to believe that *The Chief Kosmocrator* would surely need her expertise. However, it perturbed her that she was not entirely convinced.

Cain continued speaking. "We will patch up the woman when we switch on tonight. Give her a jolt so to speak. The quantum energy will work for a few days so that we can take the parents to Geneva. The boy will feel obliged to put on his hero outfit and come rescue her."

Johnston looked slightly unnerved as Peter's manic laugh eerily filled the airwaves.

Incensed, John punched Peter again and again. Undeterred that his immaterial body was not delivering his furious punches, he pounded into his enemy.

Mystified, Peter looked startled and afraid! He could feel something like a strong wind pummelling his body. Looking all around, he shouted, "What's going on. Who is there?"

Johnston responded, mystified. "What do you mean, Cain. There's no-one else here."

Chapter 30

The Atomic Accelerator

John woke up on the beach still wrestling with the absent Cain. A few feet away, Uzel patiently watched the scene unfold.

"He is a beast! He is not human! We have to stop that psychopath from destroying everything!"

Uzel let John rant for a few more minutes before speaking softly. "We know what he is planning now."

John, still furious, shouted, "I'll kill him!"

Uzel shook his head. "Ah, ah, dear friend! That is definitely not your call. Be encouraged, we have a great plan, but many things must happen first that you will find difficult to understand. For now, my friend, I need you to trust me."

John wanted to know more. "Why doesn't *The Maker* just stop these wicked *Kosmocratoras*. Why does he allow all this sorrow and suffering?" he was sobbing now.

Uzel looked away in the distance, contemplative.

He turned back to look at John. "Even I find this difficult to understand. I have not lived as a human, but I see your great struggle. This world is full of obstacles and temptations, hatred, pain, and violence. Honestly – it's a wonder anyone makes it beyond their first birthday.

Believe me, the faithful *Watchers* and the *Messengers* are full of admiration for the ones that remain faithful in the midst of such hardship. But still, I would not like to live as a human, nor would I want to live as a human on your planet. You really are being forged in fire. The cost of your free will almost seem too high a price to pay, and what will be created in the end is yet a mystery to me. But I trust the Maker, and that is why I do what he asks of me."

"But why do you obey him?" John persisted.

"That's an easy answer, dear friend. You must understand, where I come from is a place of great harmony and beauty. If only you could see it. Although, in the fullness of time, it is what you will come into. For now, you are like a woman bearing a child. I think all the pain and suffering you experience here will be forgotten after the birth.

Look, go spend some time with Sarah? I'm going to do some investigating."

John jested: "Is that your way of saying I'm a liability, and you are better off without me?"

Uzel raised his eyebrows and cocked his head to one side.

Not surprisingly, John experienced a bit of a jolt as he came back into his physical body. It felt strangely claustrophobic as it took a while to readjust to his electromagnetic visible self. "Is this what it means when it says we are made from the dust of the earth? It sure feels like it. It's like being encased in cement."

Uzel jested, "Great new name – *Dustman*!"

Sarah reacted strangely when her husband walked into her room. She seemed distant, even detached. There was something wrong, but he dared not ask her. He looked at the camera in the corner of the room.

Surprisingly the nursing staff agreed that he could take her into the garden for a while, so long as she used a wheelchair. *I guess they are so liberal because they know there is no means of escape; we're trapped on this island.* John walked the wheelchair to the far end of the garden and sat on a bench under a large cedar tree. This offered some shade from the hot tropical sun.

"I've got to help that poor girl." Sarah poured out her concern.

"You mean Greta? But why? How?" John watched as one side of her face began to twitch. He knew that sign. Seldom one to let negative emotions spill out, she thought angry people were simply venting their frustration on the world around them.

"They are using her for experiments, John. You saw. Her body is done. Her poor husband doesn't want to let her go, so he's allowing the torture to continue."

John shook his head. He had no idea how to comfort her.

"I'm next! I think that's what they intend to do to me!"

John caught the fleeting shudder that rippled through her body. He put his arm around her.

"I won't let them!"

Sarah winced. She knew that he wouldn't be able to let her go. Affectionately, she took his hand. "Haven't you wondered why they brought us here? Judging by the flying time, I guess we must be somewhere in the Southern Hemisphere."

"Uzel told me we are somewhere near Bermuda."

"Oh, well! there must be something they can do here that they can't do anywhere else." She was smart, but he felt it would serve no purpose to tell her what they intended to do!

He also thought it best not to say too much about the plan to take them to Geneva. She had enough to worry about. Tactfully, he managed to change the subject. "What do you want to do about Greta?"

"I want to tell her about *The Messengers*. Do you think Uzel would speak to her?"

They seemed to be assigned to specific people, so he was dubious if they could intervene.

"Well, at least I could tell them about our helpers. Give them hope, you know."

John suggested that she should wait until they could speak to Uzel.

He was about to kiss her when a nurse called out to them to return back to the hospital building. It was time for another treatment.

"It's alright, John. Uzel explained that this is all part of our assignment, so don't worry, I'll be okay."

John hated leaving Sarah, but he had to trust that she was in Uzel's capable hands. However, at the moment he was nowhere to be seen, so John decided to walk back to the house.

It dawned on him that he hadn't eaten anything since they arrived on the island. He felt rather guilty to be thinking about food in the face of everything going on but hunger pangs were gnawing at his stomach. Without any more thought, he reached into the fridge and pulled out a ready-meal that needed a few minutes in the microwave.

"Let me just check that!" Uzel appeared out of thin air.

"No, don't eat it." He thoroughly examined the plate of food. "Oh, what's this?" He pulled out a small device no bigger than a grain of rice.

"It's okay, you can eat it now!"

John looked at the food in disgust. "I think I'll give it a miss."

"Don't worry my friend. I'll make you a wonderful meal you will never forget."

John scoffed when Uzel produced his masterpiece. "What! Beans on toast! I expected the food of paradise."

"I've never learned to cook – not really my thing!" Uzel shook his head and chuckled.

"Food of paradise! Beans on toast, wait until I tell the others."

John felt his shoulders unfurl. He liked Uzel and felt safe when he was around.

"So what did you find out? Do you know why they brought us to this place? Sarah reckons there must be some reason to bring us all this way to Bermuda."

Uzel nodded. "I believe it's something to do with the *Atomic Accelerator*. As we heard, they have plans to start it up at 7pm tonight. I've had a look around and found a small room that has been set up with beds for a couple of people. It looks like a hyperbaric chamber; you know . . . the kind they use for deep-sea divers. Only, it is somehow linked in with the *Accelerator*."

Uzel explained that the machine could only be switched on a few times a year and that the one in *CERN* was scheduled to be offline for another few days. Time was of the essence; hence, that is why they had been transported to this location. John agreed that it seemed the likely explanation but still wanted to know what they intended to do to Sarah.

The *Messenger* sat next to John and put his hand over his. "They are going to use highly charged light energy to revive her body, but you know that the treatment has been too aggressive for her body to cope with."

John looked down at his hands. "I feel so useless."

Uzel explained how they had over-engineered the *nano-meds,* and her body was now rejecting the implants. The plan was to use the *Accelerated Particles* to supercharge her body cells. This is simply a by-product of the acceleration programme, John. It's not the main purpose of their goals.

Uzel looked apprehensive, but he had to explain about Sarah's future.

"You have to prepare yourself now, my friend. This treatment will work but only work for a short time. Sarah understands this.

She is aware that her earth-time is almost complete."

John felt his knees buckle.

Uzel tried to comfort his charge. "Don't worry about her because I've given her a glimpse of her future. She is content. I know this will be difficult for you, but Sarah needs you to be strong! This isn't a time for sadness because you will only be apart for a short time. Do you understand, John?"

For the first time in his life, John did not feel alone. He was becoming more aware of the grand cosmic picture. "It's okay, Uzel . . . I don't like it, but I get it!"

They talked for another hour. *The Messenger* knew that John needed to understand. It was the unknown that caused his anxiety. John told Uzel that he had done some research about *CERN,* and although he didn't understand much of it, he had discovered that classical and quantum physics were like two completely different operating systems.

"It seems like they are two separate worlds, and yet in some way, they exist in the same space. From what I understand, everything has the potential to exist as a *moving wave of energy* or a *physical particle.* I can't quite wrap my head around that! How can these two dimensions exist in the same locality? And how come they are not aware of each other?" Is it really just another realm of existence?

He concluded: "It's like the physical world is undergirded by another kind of reality.

Is that what you would call the spirit world? Could that be the reason that Cain and his kind are trying to break through to the quantum world? But surely that barrier is there for a reason?"

Uzel leaned back. "Wow. That's a lot of questions, *Dustman*. Let me see how I can explain these things to you. I guess you are now grasping the reality of the great cosmic drama that is unfolding. You cannot see the whole picture at once, but the great mystery is opening up before your eyes."

"Yes, I can see," John replied.

"Cain and his followers have a simplistic view of creation. They are like fish swimming in the sea of the universe; they can see another world above the water but cannot enter it. They have no concept of how different it would be from living in their water-world. This interface with the physical and the spiritual is forbidden technology. They believe that removing the veil between the worlds will give them the power to overtake the current order of the universe. This is not possible."

"But, they believe it to be so?" John asked.

"Oh, Yes. They surely do! And Cain now has the knowledge to tear the veil, but sadly it will only bring destruction upon your world."

Outraged, John roared, "Then surely we must find a way to stop him!"

"Good man, John! We just need a group of humans who will work with us to scuttle his plans. Although, for a time, it will look like he has succeeded, and the barrier will have been breached – but don't be alarmed! Cain will truly believe that he has triumphed, but in the near future, his empire will suddenly collapse like a stack of cards."

Sombrely, John responded, "I really want to help, but I'm not like you, I don't have incredible powers and the ability to bi-locate at will. What can I do?

"Oh, dear human. If . . ." Uzel stood up, his voice filled the room. ". . . if you only knew who you truly are. The incredible position you hold in the creation.

Humans have settled for the life of a slave when in fact, you are the offspring of the Maker."

"What!" John swayed backwards.

The whole room swirled around as if time was reversing. He saw his mother's kitchen. Heard her voice again. "Don't you know that the whole of creation is waiting for you to come into your true position?"

He looked down; she had dressed him up in a warrior's outfit with a helmet and a sword and shield. She was saying: "One day, you will need armour just like this; you will need it to fight."

He had no idea how long he remained with his mother, but it was as if all the words she had spoken became alive, and for the first time in his life, he understood.

Moments later, he landed with a thud on the floor.

"What the . . . what just happened there?

It's not a religion. She was just telling me the truth.

It's about taking back what was stolen. It's a war!

Oh my God, all my life, I thought I was weak, abandoned, and worthless. Just scraping by. The Maker is my . . . Oh God! – I am like the prodigal!"

"Okay, *Dustman*, let's keep our feet on the ground for now because we have to prepare ourselves. I've found out that Ruel has flown back to Scotland this morning. He is now in place to bring Josh to Geneva, and I have orders to fly out tomorrow.

Despite the seriousness of the moment, John jested with Uzel. "Did Ruel fly the conventional way or you know . . . like Superman?"

"Oh no, he is still undercover, so he had to take the conventional route and took the plane with him."

They both laughed, trying to deflect the gravity of the task they had ahead of them. They were right in the epicentre of the war of all wars. Although, at the same time, they were acutely aware that this was not a conventional battleground using tanks and guns, they were fighting on a different frontier.

Uzel stood up. "Let's go find Sarah. We need to help her through the next few hours." They walked back to the hospital in silence.

John wanted to ask more questions but was already overwhelmed. Mentally, he was preparing himself to help Sarah go through whatever they had planned for her.

He found her snoozing in a chair. Reluctant to waken her, John took a seat next to her and held her hand, he wasn't sure how long he was there, but they both woke up when Dr. Savage entered the room.

"Good! You are both here. I want to tell you about a new treatment we are about to start for Sarah. As you know, there have been a few technical problems with calibrating the *nano-medicine,* so we will do a little radiation therapy to compensate. This will take about thirty minutes, and you will have another patient along with you in the room. Her name is Greta. The nursing staff will accompany you to the treatment room. Ah! Here they are, just in time. Let's get started. I'm afraid you will have to wait here, Mr. Kayin, but we won't be too long."

John paced the walls of the room. When the door opened, he was startled to see Cain again. *Please, not now!*

"Oh, John, I'm sensing that you are not pleased to see me. I have come as the bearer of good news. Sarah has

271

had her treatment and is doing well, so she will join us shortly. I just wanted to fill you in on a few details about our forthcoming trip. We are leaving in the morning to go to Geneva, and there is something I want you to do for me."

"What do you want me to do?" he asked with gritted teeth.

Cain explained that they would be meeting up with Josh to pick up something he needed. "I want you to tell your son to bring me the *Firestones*. He is gathering them as we speak, but I'm sure he will have them all by tomorrow."

John wasn't sure how to react. He didn't want to give anything away. Curious though, he couldn't help but ask, "Why do you need the *Firestones*?"

Cain threw his head back and laughed. "I thought you would like to know. You are already aware of our plans to alter humans, but my dear boy, we must create a new environment so that your people and mine can exist together. You know the *Maker* has plans to destroy this universe; we must stop him.

We already have nine *Firestones* and just need the other three to create the new realm that will enable us to do just that. You see, we need to alter the speed of light at specific points, and where the light goes faster, it will create passageways through slower space-time. And voila! We will expand our realm of dominion as we witness the birth of inter-dimensional time-travel."

John shuddered at the thought.

For the next thirty minutes or so, *The Immortal* continued to talk about his grand plans. "The *Particle Accelerator* is good to go. Let's not get caught up in the details but trust me – it's simply beautiful science. We are almost there now, and everything is just about in place. All the systems of this universe will be changed. It will commence tomorrow and will take us just a few years to complete." Cain couldn't stop himself bragging.

John's head was spinning as he tried to absorb this new information, but even so, he had to know. "Why should I ask Josh to do this?"

Cain walked towards the door, deliberately turning his head back over his shoulder, purposely not looking at John, but merely voiced this chilling statement: "It's a trade – his mother's life for the *Firestones*!" The door closed decisively behind him. He did not wait for an answer, certain that John had no option but to comply.

Frantically, John reached out for Uzel, but he did not respond.

Punching his fist into the other hand, he called out. "Come on, Uzel, don't disappear on me now . . . I need you!" Still, no reply. John was about to go down to the beach to find him when the door opened, and Sarah walked in.

"Oh my goodness, you're walking again." John didn't expect that.

Sarah melted into his arms and whispered, "The treatment has worked, and I feel great!"

She spoke silently again. "Uzel was with me the whole time, and he spoke to Greta. She heard him, John. She knows everything and wants to help us bring Peter down."

John spoke softly. "Let's ask if we can go back to the house. I don't want to leave you here on your own."

The charge nurse reluctantly contacted Dr. Savage at John's insistence. She responded dryly as she put the phone down. "Okay, you can go, but come back first thing in the morning for your meds."

As they walked back to the house, they could speak

freely, and as they had hoped, Uzel met them at the rock.

Sarah thanked him for staying with her and for helping Greta during the *Light Treatment.* They spent the next hour discussing plans for their flight to Geneva and what to do next.

Uzel assured Sarah that Greta would be fine and was, in fact, on the passenger list to travel with them.

The iridescent glow of the moon flooded the nigh time skies with light.

Holding hands as they measured and treasured every step of the walk back to the house, aware that time was closing in on them.

Chapters 31

Superluminal

The early morning flight was uneventful, mostly because the passenger list was the same as the inbound flight. To everyone's relief, Cain was not on-board. Although the two guards were there again, they remained at the rear of the plane without engaging with the other passengers.

Uzel was able to move about freely, mostly communicating telepathically with Sarah and John. "Everything is going well, so don't worry, our plan is working," he said, attempting to allay their fears.

"What's in store for us in Geneva?" Sarah looked at John, uneasy.

"We have to trust the *Messengers*," John responded.

David and Greta were seated in the row behind them. They were all amazed at how well Greta appeared compared to how she had looked a few days before. Her face was less strained, and her eyes much brighter.

"If only this treatment was permanent." Sarah telepathed to Greta. "Whatever they did to supercharge us won't last!" Both of them knew they would reach burnout soon.

"They've made a video of me talking about the marvellous treatment I've received. I'm going to be their poster girl for *nanotech*. Isn't that ironic!" Greta responded, her eyes misting over.

Sarah turned to speak to the girl. "Why don't you join me for a cuppa?" They both needed to draw courage from each other as they walked a similar path over the coming days.

They made their way over to the other side of the plane, sitting with their backs towards the guards. Over the next hour or so, the women were absorbed in two conversations. The one the guards could hear through their earphones and another in-depth but silent discussion about the future.

They talked about their mutual concern about what would become of their families. Greta was anxious about David and how he would cope on his own as he had invested every day of the past two years to help her.

"He has given up his friends and his job, and sadly we had no children or close family to speak of. Greta was struggling to hold back the tears.

Likewise, Sarah expressed her concern that John might do something reckless.

"Josh will be alright, though. He had a deep inner strength like his grandparents." She smiled.

As Uzel watched the two women, he saw that they were suffering and empathised with them somewhat. But he would never fully understand what they were going through because his kind had no direct experience of pain nor death.

Just then, he saw Sarah take Greta's hand, whispering softly. "Tomorrow is not promised to us."

The two women sat in silence for a while, immersed in deep sadness as they contemplated their futures.

Uzel gazed upon the poignant scene. They made no sound as tears gathered around their eyes, running down each of their faces – with nowhere to go.

He wanted to tell them that time on earth was just an illusion, a mere blink of an eye, but his eyes looked into the distance from an eternal perspective. Humans found this concept difficult to grasp.

This made it tough for him to resist the urge to comfort them, but he was fully aware that humans had a deep need to express their inner conflicts. Tears, he learned, were an emotional response to the stuff of life. Sometimes they expressed great feelings of joy. But here, in this interface with Sarah and Greta, as they faced their last days on earth, he knew he had to let them pour out their grief. There was no histrionic behaviour, but a quiet, dignified drama sadly played out – totally unnoticed by the others.

Around an hour away from touchdown, Uzel approached John and led him to a small bunk-room the crew used. They briefly exchanged glances, but neither of them spoke. As Uzel closed the door, an overhead screen opened up, startling John as he heard Cain make an announcement.

His presence still unnerved John, even if it was only a recorded image. The sound of his voice made him shudder. "It won't be long before the plane lands, so John, my dear boy, it's time for you to send your message to your son as we agreed. Just look straight ahead at the screen and read what is on the message board that the steward will now give to you. You'll be glad to know that their task has been completed."

John was aware that this was Cain's way of telling him that the *Firestones* had been found. Closing his eyes to contain his urge to lash out, he took a deep breath. A deep sense of injustice filled his belly with contempt for this man.

How dare this beast use my family to build his kingdom. Bowing his head, he tried to get a grip on his emotions.

The Messenger touched his shoulder reassuringly, then handed him a clipboard with a typed message attached. Then he nodded to John as a sign that he should comply. Reluctantly, and without emotion, John began to read the scripted message. "Josh, your mother and I are on a flight bound for Geneva today. I would like you to come to meet us there in the morning. Details of your travel arrangements will be posted after this message. You have to bring the *Firestones* with you, and then your mother will be good to travel back to Scotland with you tomorrow night."

"It's okay, John. Remember – we have a plan!" Uzel silently conveyed.

John returned to his seat, slightly shaken by the revelation that he would be remaining in Cain's territory alone. He just hoped that Uzel was smart enough to outwit his enemy.

Sarah asked if he was okay. Although he was aware that the colour had drained from his face, he nodded. "Yeah, I'm fine, just making some plans for our arrival."

There was no point in worrying her; she had enough to bear. The strange event in the staff room had unnerved him. Somehow, Cain had managed to normalise the situation by ordering him to convey the exchange to Josh in such a clinical way. There was no pleading, no emotional meltdown, or trying to entice Josh. But The immortal man had a creepy ability of encoding great threat in a simple message. If he didn't do what was expected, his family would not be allowed to return to Scotland or anywhere else for that matter.

Shortly after landing, they were whisked through a

private gate at Geneva airport. Even without passports or travel documents, customs control made no attempt to stop them.

John and Sarah exchanged glances, acutely aware that their captor held incredible influence in governmental spheres. There were no obvious barriers to stop him.

A convoy of cars left the airport, driving for around twenty minutes before reaching their destination. As they entered the gates of *CERN,* John shuddered as he beheld the logo. He motioned to Sarah.

She turned her head slightly, then read the infamous number – *666.*

Her eyes darted back to John as she telepathed to him. "Why would any organisation choose such a number that everyone knew was associated with the Anti-Christ?"

The car drew up alongside building 39, a hostel on Meyrin street. Cain was waiting for them, standing a few steps away from a statue that seemed totally out of place in a campus dedicated to science. Walking towards *The Immortal*, John and Sarah stopped in their tracks as he casually leaned against the supporting plinth.

"What kind of place is this?" Sarah communicated to John.

Cain sneered as he looked at their bewildered faces. "Ah, I see you are perplexed by our beautiful statue. Are you wondering why such an esteemed scientific facility would embrace such an icon? Some would say it was simply given as a gift from India and has no supernatural significance whatsoever. What do you think?"

Sarah responded dryly. "I can't imagine them accepting a gift representing any other spiritual symbol" – she hesitated but couldn't resist – "Such as an image of Christ. What do you think?"

He scowled at Sarah. Ignoring her question, he continued: "Shiva is, of course – the Hindu god of destruction. He is known as *The Conqueror of Death and Time*. How appropriate is that!" he scoffed.

"He is the perfect icon for our purposes. Don't you agree, Sarah?" He threw out this rhetorical question before walking away. As darkness descended, they became aware of the huge ominous shadow the statue cast on the wall behind it. Shiva was indeed dancing the great cosmic dance of death.

Sarah had hoped that Greta and David would be with them, but disappointingly she saw them being driven away in a separate car. They walked a few hundred yards further before entering into a non-descript warehouse building. Although they knew that Uzel was close by, they both felt that sinking feeling of dread.

"Come along," Cain urged. "We have much to do, and the clock is against us."

After they entered the building, their eyes adjusted to the low light then gazed upon an array of strange-looking machines, as far as the eye could see.

Awestruck, Sarah stopped to look around as she tried to grasp something about the power and knowledge of the people who'd built them. They looked technically superior to anything she had ever seen.

John noticed. *She thinks this is incredible, but she hasn't even seen the Accelerator yet.*

Cain offered an explanation. "Don't be too impressed with these old relics. They are all prototypes, and although this technology has helped us gain incredible knowledge through our experiments – they are obsolete. However, with our state-of-the-art machinery, we have totally mastered the science of manipulating matter. Come Sarah, John, I will show you technology that will totally blow your mind."

The Immortal was unaware that John had been present in the underground headquarters on the island and had overheard some of the secrets of how they planned to use the *Particle Accelerators* and *Colliders*.

As the elevator door opened some floors below, Sarah gasped when she saw the scale of the underground facilities. After boarding a small jeep that transported them through vast tunnels, they passed by machines that looked as though they belonged on a distant planet, millions of light-years away. As the jeep approached the *Collider*, Sarah shook her head. "Oh my goodness, it looks like some kind of star-gate or a portal to another world!

What is this? Who built it? Is this some kind of alien technology?"

Thrilled by Sarah's reaction, Cain took great pleasure in showing off his creation. "Oh Sarah, I can see that you are impressed, but this is just a fraction of what we have built." Boasting proudly, he continued unabated.

"Have you ever seen a machine like this? Of course, most people are unaware of its existence. And the ones who know about it haven't a clue what it is. It's one of those mysteries that's been hidden in plain sight," he scoffed.

"Seventy years, Sarah! That's how long it has taken to complete, and it's the largest machine ever to be built. It's 27 kilometres in circumference. Just long enough to accelerate particles in opposite directions at near the speed of light and collide them to create energy called antimatter. You see . . . if we could contain only one gram of this antimatter, it would produce energy that would be equivalent to a nuclear bomb. Just think about all the antimatter out there in the cosmos," he sneered as he pointed his hand towards the skies.

Cain was almost salivating as he continued. "We are on the edge of harnessing this power, and your son is on his way here with the technology to do just that!"

John had heard some of it before, but Sarah wanted to understand, so pressed him for more information. "What are you going to do with this antimatter? What happens when you put matter and anti-matter together? Won't that kind of power destroy the world?"

Cain answered enthusiastically. "Of course, if you put these two energies together, they will destroy each other, but currently, we have only managed to isolate small amounts of antimatter in Penning traps – suspended in magnetic fields. But as from tomorrow, we will have in our possession the ability to capture the infinite energy of antimatter using the *Firestones*."

Sarah and John glanced at each other, confused.

Ignoring their response, Cain continued to explain. "The *Firestones* emit a very special kind of power that will allow us to transcend the current restrictions of the light spectrum. We have big plans, indeed, massive plans to separate us from the unseen universe using energy that is greater than the speed of light. And that form of energy will sustain us forever.

At last, we will be totally independent from *The Maker*. We will be sovereign and rule over our own territories. No more rules or laws! We can do whatever we want! It will be wonderful. Don't you agree?"

Sarah shivered. Feeling uneasy talking to Cain about his plans for the future but sensing his vulnerability, she pressed on for more information. Strangely, she felt that he was somehow looking towards her for approval.

She continued to press: "Let me see if I understand Cain . . . you mean that with the *Firestones,* you will be able to create some kind of prismatic light that can block the electromagnetic energy that currently sustains everything?"

Smiling smugly, he continued to gloat. "Everything

282

will belong to me. Everyone will bow the knee to me. It's a perfect plan."

Although she was feeling squeamish at this remark, Sarah felt compelled to ask more questions.

"Hmm! Right, I see . . . you aim to switch the current energy source of the cosmos and exchange it to the new source powered by the *Firestones*. I guess it's like changing from oil to gas."

Cain responded eagerly: "Well, that's simplifying it somewhat but in essence – yes! We will create an energy field, and this will effectively put up a barrier around our cosmos."

Sarah responded sharply. "And keep *The Maker* out?"

Cain replied mockingly. "Oh my, dear girl, you are very clever!"

Pausing for a few moments as her brain was trying to unpack this information, she had an awakening moment. She asked directly, "So what is so special about the *Firestones*? I mean, what's unique about them?"

"Oh, Sarah, I would love to have you on my team. You have a beautiful brain, my dear." Sarah struggled not to be carried away with this flattery.

"Let me explain. Everything in this universe is set at a certain speed. Nothing can travel faster. You know this because we call it *The speed of light*. No matter how we accelerate particles, they simply become too heavy as they reach light-speed. There is no method of propulsion that can make us go further or faster. Do you understand?"

Fascinated, Sarah nodded.

Cain continued: "What we need is something that is intrinsically faster than light. We call that object *Superluminal*."

Sarah felt her knees buckling underneath her as her thoughts scrambled to understand the consequences of this *terrorist* acquiring such an object. Steadying herself, for she dared not show any sign of weakness, she looked at John, and they gasped simultaneously. They both realised why the prized gemstones were the keys to Cain's success. They were *Superluminal*! It was clear now that *The Immortal* was planning to enclose the cosmos with this new power!

Although she felt afraid, something was compelling her to challenge him.

"And will you be able to destroy what lies beyond our cosmos?"

Cain looked surprised. "There's no need to do that! We will be totally self-sufficient. As I said many times, everything is energy – and energy is everything. Without energy, there can be no life, and soon we will have an unlimited supply."

Sarah persisted. "Really! How do you know that? This has never been done before. Isn't it still experimental? If you have only been able to capture one gram in a magnetic field, then how can you be sure you will be able to contain large amounts of antimatter without causing the total annihilation of the material universe?"

Cain glared at Sarah. "You have no understanding of who I am – or how powerful I am. I have controlled the worlds for millennia. Humans are no match for me; it is so easy to manipulate them. I keep them busy with their petty little lives and pointless wars.

Fortunately for me, they abdicated their position, so *I* took up the role of *Landlord* of your solar system."

His mouth curved into an ironic smile.

"If only humans had been smart enough and joined forces, they could have taken back what I now possess."

John and Sarah balked at this disclosure.

"Don't pretend you didn't know this because it's all in the prophetic writings. You could have had dominion over all creation. But that will never happen because, quite frankly, it's too late. I've already won the battle. Humans are not only blinded by greed – you are incredibly stupid!"

Sarah rose from her chair. She knew that she had nothing to lose. Her body was deteriorating, and she could feel it fragmenting, so she breathed deeply and looked directly into her enemy's piercing brown eyes. When she spoke, it was like her tongue was a flaming sword ready to cut through his words.

"You may have more superior knowledge than humans, but what about the Creator. Wasn't he the one who made all of this? Surely, he also made the *Firestones*. Don't you think he will stop this?"

Enraged, Cain stood up as if to charge at Sarah, but he stumbled, knocking over a table as he fell. He tried to pull himself together, but his whole body shook in protest at Sarah's words. It was as if her words cut him to the core of his being. He tried to defend himself. His voice thundered throughout the building.

"The *Superluminals* will create a ring of fire around us."

Sarah looked down on the ancient man as he lay on the cold marble floor. She measured her next words carefully before declaring –

"That sounds like a vision of hell to me!"

Fuming; his nostrils flared in disgust and anger, Cain shouted, "Take her away, get her out of my sight." His body contorting in anguish.

Two guards came towards her as Cain shouted. "You

don't know who I am? I am the ruler of this galaxy! I am the supreme *Kosmocrator!* You will all bow down to me!"

Sarah smiled as she was forcibly removed – she had touched a raw nerve. It was incredibly satisfying to see *The Beast* squirm. She savoured her moment of victory.

The air was thick with fear as John tried to slide out unnoticed behind Sarah. But the *Kosmocrator* called out. "Don't think I'm finished with you, John Kayin, we have a contract! Remember?"

John stopped dead, terrified of the old man's wrath. Intensely aware that there was no point in resisting, he slowly turned back. Resigned to his fate, he sat down on a vacant seat, with shoulders slouched.

It was inevitable – they were slowly going to harvest his genetically modified *DNA*. He knew that the dwellers in Cain's new world would need the *Recombinant DNA* to survive in an immortal state. No-one had explained the process to him, but his imagination took him to the gates of hell.

Cain regained his composure then ordered John to listen to him.

"When Josh arrives here tomorrow, I want you to comply with my instruction. If you do, I will let your wife and son go back to Scotland. They will be protected there for a time, but if you do not do as I say, I will detain them here. It is up to you."

The ancient man stood menacingly over John until the hairs on the back of his neck stood up. He could feel his every breath on his skin. He saw his mouth form words that terrified him.

"Very soon, the world will call out for my help. No one will be able to survive without me!"

Unsure of what to say, John simply nodded as he had no desire to converse with him.

"Take him away," Cain called out to the guards.

Chapter 32

Locked horns

They spent the night in separate rooms, locked electronically, and at either end of the corridor. Sarah was elated that she had at least sown some doubt into Cain's mind, but John sat deflated for hours. Sleep would not shut down his persistent ruminating about a world dominated by *The Kosmocrator's* cruel hand. It seemed like he had just dozed off to sleep when someone shook him. "Wake up, John, we have to discuss our plan!"

Uzel stood at the end of his bed, looking like he'd just won a great battle. John hadn't really looked at him properly before. Somehow, they had always been caught up in the crisis of the moment.

This time he deliberately surveyed the strange being from head to toe. He had the body of a top-ranking athlete, lean and tall, and ready to outrun any opponent. He was exceptionally good-looking with translucent flawless skin most women would die for. His unfashionable long black hair gave him the appearance of a celebrity rock star from another era.

Uzel laughed heartily. "Remember, I can hear you!"

John turned a bright shade of crimson. "Oh, sorry, I forgot. Let's get down to business."

Uzel could not resist the urge to jest. "So how good

looking am I? Ha! A rock star."

Sarah woke up early; it was still dark as she became aware of muffled voices coming from next door. Although she couldn't quite make out what they were saying, she was sure that Uzel was with John. She breathed a sigh of relief when they appeared in her room a few moments later.

John, looking slightly dazed but pleased with himself, announced, "I did it, Sarah . . . I walked through solid matter!"

Uzel gently scolded him. "This is no time for congratulating yourself; they will be here shortly. We need to get ready."

John answered with a touch of sarcasm. "Hey, who was caught up in rating their good looks just five minutes ago!"

Uzel pulled a face at John behind his back that made Sarah laugh.

"Okay, boys, let's get down to business. What should we do?"

When the guards unlocked the doors, the couple were sitting in their respective rooms waiting to be released. They suspected nothing about the nocturnal visit. The guards roughly handled the couple as they were led to an antechamber and told them to sit on a low wooden bench. Holding hands tightly, they glanced at each other. There was no need for words. The situation was tense and uncomfortable, and their future uncertain. Thankfully, they both knew what the other was thinking.

They didn't wait long before being summoned into the grand hall. The room seemed out of place in the underground science facility. It had the appearance of a large chapel with beautiful cathedral ceilings held up by two ornately decorated round pillars rising from a pale ivory marbled floor. The room was filled with people, mostly strangers, who all turned to stare at the pair as they entered.

Cain sat regally at the far end of the hall on a large throne-like chair, watching their every step as they walked towards him. He seized the opportunity to mock them. "Ah, my little lambs, come and join me at the altar. Are you hungry?"

He looked around the room, making sure he had commanded attention before announcing. "In our new world, we will all have to make sacrifices."

John visibly shuddered, hoping that was not a literal statement.

A menacing voice beckoned them. "Come dear children, sit next to me while we wait for the arrival of your beloved son."

They sat down on two high-backed chairs next to Cain, feeling totally out of place. Various festivities were taking place around the room. The audience looked pleased and shouted praise as various acts came before them.

The couple felt traumatised as they watched the surreal gathering. Sarah felt she might lose consciousness when a group of dancers filed into the room.

"What the . . . John, what are they?"

They continued to stare as strange-looking creatures performed alongside humans.

John telepathed to his wife.

"They are hybrids, and if they succeed, that is what the next generation of our species will look like!"

Sarah froze. It hadn't occurred to her that the transformation of humans had already begun. Seeing the beasts shocked her to the core.

Had these poor animalistic creatures once been

human? Did they volunteer to give up their humanity? How did they feel locked inside a part-animal body?

She looked sideways at her husband, appealing to him. "We have to stop this, John!"

The bizarre entertainment took up most of the morning before the host stood up and requested that lunch be served. They all went next door and sat around grand tables covered with every type of food imaginable. The guests ate and drank heartily, but Sarah and John declined. A woman sitting next to them questioned the couple. "Not joining us?" Obviously not expecting an answer before turning away. They knew she was mocking them.

Cain approached them again. "Come, my friends, your son has arrived, and we have some business to attend to." His pretence at playing happy families angered the couple. They felt manipulated and mocked, but they had no choice. They were trapped, and so for now, they had to play along in his game.

Once again, they entered the cathedral hall, but this time without the other guests. Two men joined them, and John recognised them as part of the legal team from the Alpha Towers. Josh was waiting for them there, and to their surprise and relief, his grandfather was with him.

The three generations gathered, united, and facing a man that somehow bound them together since the beginning of time.

"This is so much better than I expected." Cain sat down, indicating to everyone to do likewise.

He gazed intensely at his descendants, sitting obediently before him in a semicircle. Never before had he felt such a powerful yearning to be part of something that looked like family.

Wavering momentarily, he felt that he could almost

abandon all of his plans if they would have him. His resolve was fracturing as he realised that he'd never ever trusted anyone. Not a single soul. Not even his allies. Everyone he knew was afraid of him, and until now he had always preferred it that way!

One of the legal team interrupted his thoughts. "Does the boy have the *Firestones*?" he asked abruptly.

Cain was transfixed, mesmerised by his three grandsons. The team was urging him to make a decision. "Yes, Yes! I'm just coming to that. Just give me a moment. It's not every day that I am face to face with family members," scowling as he replied impatiently.

The legal team glanced nervously at one another, and then the second man spoke up. "We need the *Firestones*. The trial run is arranged for this evening, and we haven't got much time."

Cain snapped out of the hypnotic state. "Of course, fetch them now," he ordered.

Josh felt compelled to question the *Immortal*. "How did you know we would find the *Firestones?*

"You think I don't know about the breastplate." Cain quipped with a hint of mocking humour. "I can read the prophecies too, young man. I simply followed the trail."

Josh reached into his haversack and pulled out a pristine piece of fine linen, then rolled out the cloth to reveal the three recovered gemstones. Cain's eyes widened, and any thoughts of a family reunion now melted like winter snow.

He grabbed the linen cloth from Josh's hands like a man possessed, examining the gems with jeweller's eyes and inspecting them thoroughly for any flaws. They looked perfect in every way.

The family gasped as unexpectedly, Cain fell to his knees and shouted. "How long I have waited!" His words reverberated menacingly around the vaulted ceiling creating an eerie echo that sent chills through them all. He turned to the Kayin family and repeated. "Do you know how long I have waited for this moment?"

He held the jewels up to his mouth and kissed them. With glee, he selected the purple stone and gazed upon it intently. "*The Achlama*; oh how I have sought this royal stone."

He so wanted his descendants to be fully aware of the significance of this moment. It was important that he could share this moment of victory. It was time to explain why. "This is the last foundation stone of the *New City*. This treasure has been hidden for millennia. At last! I have in my possession – the greatest weapon in the universe – it's like a cosmic sword that will divide my kingdom from his! This is my time! These *Firestones* are the keys to my kingdom."

Sarah beheld the scene with fascination. She couldn't help it. In front of her, she was observing four generations of a family bound together by genetics. But ideologically, the three younger men were totally polarised from their forefather.

She watched Cain, fuelled with hubristic pride as he paraded before his descendants with conceit and arrogance. His audience watched him circumspectly, unsure of his next move.

He continued to obsess about his achievements. His narcissistic behaviour was obvious to everyone but himself. In contrast, the three men sat quietly. Not so much in submission but rather protectively guarding each other. They did not wish to rile their enemy while he was so highly charged with his perceived success.

Cain stopped in his tracks, turned, and walked over to the older man. "Come on, Matthew, you must have something to say! You've waited all these years to challenge me so here is your chance. What would you like to ask me? I'll grant you one question."

Slowly and deliberately, Matthew looked down at his hands for a few moments, then looked up and faced his enemy. "Yes, I have a question. All of this, everything you have been striving for. What would make you give it all up?"

His arch-enemy laughed in Matthew's face. Cain walked around to the back of his chair, leaned over Matthew's head, and spat words venomously into his ear.

"Nothing would entice me to give up my power. There is nothing I desire more than this. My kingdom will rise, and everyone will submit to me. My laws! My rules! *Do what thy wilt*, I say." He laughed maniacally as he leaned down again and faced Matthew nose to nose.

Then in a menacing voice, he prophesied.

"You will all be begging me to help you. Just wait and see!"

Ignoring Cain's threatening proximity, Matthew kept his composure as he replied: "All I know is that this won't bring you happiness."

His adversary replied coldly: "Who is in need of happiness . . . only fools!"

The battle went on for another half-hour with neither member of the Kayin clan willing to compromise their position. Fascinated, John was reminded of a time in Scotland when he watched two stags fight for superiority during the rutting season. One of them had to win the prize. Matthew was satisfied he'd sown seeds of doubt; otherwise, Cain would have dismissed him first-hand. During this time, Josh and John remained silent, deferring to the seniority of the two men embroiled in their fiercely contested debate.

Cain, obviously frustrated, paced in front of the three men. Suddenly, he stopped just a few feet away from them. He looked at them intently, as if he were trying to capture their very souls. The connection was palpable. At that moment, they all knew that their genetic relative longed for them to join him! The four men were locked in a battle of wills. No-one could tell how long they were there.

Time hovered outside of them.

Brows knit together in utter frustration, Cain hissed audibly, then without another word, turned and left.

They all looked at each other – astounded!

Sarah, who had remained out of sight as the two men had locked horns, came forward from the shadows. "We need a plan to escape from this place, so how do we get out of here?" There were no chains nor any guards, but they knew they were prisoners. It was not going to be easy to leave the facility.

John pointed out that it didn't really matter where they went because The *Kosmocrator* now possessed the *Firestones*.

Josh sniggered before whispering to the others. "They are not the real stones. Well! One of them isn't. The other two are genuine."

Three pairs of astonished eyes bored through his scull, simultaneously shouting, "What do you mean?"

Josh mischievously answered his dumbfounded family, "You don't think I freely handed over the most powerful nuclear weapon that the world has ever known to a crazy man!"

John interrupted, "You know that he will kill us all when he runs the trial tonight and it doesn't work!"

Josh went on to explain that he had seen this time when he was with Ruel in the other dimension, so he knew what to do. "It's okay, folks. First of all, we are too valuable for him to kill us, and secondly – Cain will think that his experiment has worked. He will not be aware that it will only have a temporary effect.

When the sky begins to alter, and the earth begins to rock and roll . . . it will be abundantly evident to everyone on the planet that the world as we know it is coming to an end.

It will also be a time of great separation. Everyone will have to choose either to go with Cain into his crazy new world or believe that *The Maker* has a rescue plan and this is the time of restoration . . . and the end of *The Kosmocratoras* reign."

John stood up, determined to lead his family to safety, then ordered them to follow him. No-one questioned his authority and fell into a single line behind him. He seemed to be sure about where he was going. Five minutes later, they all piled into a lift, hoping the guards were gone.

Instead, Uzel and Ruel were waiting for them when the lift doors opened, then Uzel looked at John and winked: "What has kept you all? We've been waiting here for hours?"

Chapter 33

The Achlama Stone

They all held hands and immediately found themselves on an airport tarmac looking up the stairs of a small jet plane. Within minutes they were seated and ready for take-off.

"Isn't this Cain's plane?" Matthew asked.

The Messenger winked roguishly. "Oh yes, we've just borrowed it. We need to get you all back to the *safe land*."

"What about Greta? We can't leave her behind." Sarah looked at the *Messenger* with pleading eyes.

Uzel crouched down, looking with compassion upon her troubled face.

"I'm sorry, Sarah, but they won't be joining us," he spoke kindly. "David did not choose to come, and Greta would not leave him."

Sarah started to protest, but he took hold of her hands and looked sternly at her.

"I want you to listen to me! Every human has been given incredible power, Sarah. They have been given the right to choose their destiny. David and Greta have made their choice. This is their will. You must respect that."

With a heavy heart, Sarah sighed a deep audible breath, then turned to look out the window.

Moments after they boarded the plane, Ruel began to taxi the runway, cheerfully ignoring the protests of Air Traffic Control as he ascended quickly into the waiting clouds.

The Kayin family cheered as Ruel announced over the Tannoy that they had crossed the Swiss border and were now flying over France. "We will reach our destination in around three hours, so settle back and enjoy the flight."

After savouring an in-flight ready-meal, everyone was exhausted. They all dozed off, but John could not sleep as he gazed out at the thick clouds, now obscuring everything beneath them.

Uzel sat next to him. John wanted to know more about their destination. "Why Scotland, and why do you call it the *safe land*?"

The Messenger frowned. "Don't you understand your history, John?"

Puzzled, John responded: "I only just found out that I was born in Scotland, so why would I know anything about the history?"

"Yes. I guess that's true. You see – Cain did not want you to know about your birthright. That was kept hidden from you. He forbade your parents to tell you."

The Messenger was pleased to explain Scotland's special purpose to John. "We know this territory well. Where I come from, we call it *The Prophetic Land*. A place where you will still find some people with a deep-seated understanding of the sacred writings.

You just have to look at the famous Scottish flag greatly honouring the martyr Andrew. You made him a symbol of your country. Now that is a compelling message to identify the character of your people.

This strength and commitment were demonstrated powerfully in a generation of people from long ago. History records that when all others submitted to the

Kosmocratoras call to obey their ways, a very brave remnant would not swear the King's *Oath of Abjuration* that would force them to sign away their free will.

Tens of thousands resisted the King's command to follow him rather than *The Maker*. Instead, they signed a national covenant in the year 1638 in the capital city of Edinburgh. It was a courageous move. However, that incredible act of bravery was likened to signing their own death warrant. One day you should visit Greyfriar's Prison and graveyard in Edinburgh. The people were incarcerated there with little food or shelter in the middle of winter. In the end, twenty thousand *Covenanters* gave their lives to keep the truth alive."

John couldn't understand Uzel's reasoning.

"But that happened hundreds of years ago. What's it got to do with us now?"

The answer surprised him. "Every action creates the need for a response, my friend, and there were many executions in those days.

The blood of these Martyrs was spilled, and the land cries out for a response. You see, *Time* is a peculiar thing, most would believe that historical events cease to exist, but *The Maker* does not forget.

To this day, the land is considered sacred because of these precious ones. Consequently, in the last few years, there has been a great awakening; many have become aware of this kind of loyalty towards *The Maker* and have effectively signed a covenant against Cain and his kind."

Remaining quiet for some time, John was reluctant to make any hollow statements. After much internal debate, he turned to Uzel and spoke.

"There is no escaping it; really, we will all have to make a choice."

His companion nodded. "And this is the cost of free will, my friend!"

Matthew sat across the aisle from them, listening with his eyes tightly closed and his heart wide open.

It seemed like it would never happen, but this was the day he had longed for. The day when his son would wake up and discern the reality of the *Powers and Rulers* who worked by stealth to destroy humanity. Content to let John explore the facts, he continued to listen as Uzel revealed the truth about the *Dark Powers* to his son.

John sat quietly for some time, trying to absorb everything he had seen and heard in the last week. His mind churning with questions. He glanced again at Uzel.

"Can I ask you something?" John was slightly wary, not even sure if he wanted to hear the answer.

"It's about something Cain said. He was adamant that the world would need him. He said that everyone would turn to him for help. Is that true?"

Uzel looked at the Kayin family gathered before him, partly with sadness and partly with frustration.

He responded without reservation. "Yes! What Cain says is true.

You see, the world is so polluted that the ability for humans to continue to live here is nearing the point of no return."

Taking a deep breath, John braced himself. He could see anger rising within Uzel, like an iron fist.

"Of course, you already know this, but let me give you a summary of the choices you humans have made and what effect this has had, not only to your planet but right into the depth of your galaxy and beyond."

I've hit a raw nerve. John realised.

"The earth is increasingly exposed to radioactive toxins, and the sea is polluted beyond repair. Marine life is dying, if not by choking on micro-plastics, then by entanglements in rubbish. Even the air you breathe is changing. If that's not enough evidence of man's self-destructive ways, then consider the millions of innocent lives destroyed in the cruellest way every day. They suffer pain and agony as they are literally torn out of the safety of a mother's sacred womb."

Uzel could not contain his anger or disgust. He roared!

"And we are the ones who have to deal with the aftermath of this holocaust. The great sacrifice of the innocents to *Molech*!"

Terrified of Uzel's reaction, John shrank back. He dared not ask who this *Molech* was.

Uzel quickly contained his anger. He now looked despondent.

"We watch, we weep, and we wait.

It seems like there is little hope. Few cry out! It's as if everyone has abdicated responsibility and yet . . . if you only knew who you were truly created to be." He closed his eyes and shook his head in disbelief.

Everyone was paying attention now. They all looked stunned by Uzel's outpouring of indignation and sadness. It was impossible to ignore his expression of injustice towards his Master. His eyes were ablaze.

"Our Watchers have been observing this madness for years.

You think you were smart when you learned to split the atom, unleashing lethal doses of radioactive energy that will remain active for generations to come."

The family looked at one another in shock.

"You mean you think there is no long term effect from the nuclear age? Do you know that they can use radiocarbon testing to forensically measure the increased amount of carbon–14 in human tissue of every person on earth since the 'bomb-pulse' of 1945? Nuclear fallout lives happily in every cell of your body!"

They all squirmed uncomfortably at this revelation.

There was no stopping Uzel.

"What about Chernobyl?

It will take around 20,000 years before humans can live there safely again. You've all buried your heads in the sand. You are like children playing with grenades without any adult supervision.

Not content with atomic fireworks on planet earth, your next trick will be on a cosmic level. Machines that are smashing particles to create lethal energy with the potential to rip apart the very fabric of the universe.

Don't you see that the physical world is being torn apart, atom by atom, cell by cell? And on top of all that, you want to alter the very blueprint of human life by restructuring *DNA*.

That particular route will set humanity on a trajectory guaranteeing that you will be extinct within one generation!"

No-one dared move.

"Cain is hell-bent on altering everything about humanity. His plan to *transform* you all is well underway Have you checked out what they are teaching your children in schools? They are all being programmed. No one pays attention to their plan. He brings them in covertly while you are busy looking elsewhere. Truthfully, unless *The Maker* intervenes, there will be nothing left of Creation. Would you like me to continue?" he bellowed.

Everyone was now on the edge of their seat; horrified to hear Uzel's summary of humanity's attempt at governing the earth. It was shocking to listen to another species describe the crazy world they lived in.

"With the world on the road to destruction, Cain will take the opportunity to step in as the saviour of mankind. Very soon, there will be apocalyptic signs of the end, and people will begin to polarise. In the end, many will call out to *The Maker*, finally realising that they need his help and that self-rule has always been a bad idea.

Others will look to Cain. He will promise to fix the mess, although ironically, he created the chaos in the first place! Does that answer your question, John?"

John bowed his head. Hearing the truth summarised like that – made him feel uncomfortable.

"Cain knows that *The Maker* will come again in the New City that is coming down upon the earth. This is where the new earth will be governed from. The twelve foundation stones will link up with the earth and bring order once again. You must understand that his plan is to divert the city using *The Firestones*. You know that he has eleven and one replica."

John tentatively asked. "What is so special about that particular stone? Why hold that one back?"

"Ah! *The Achlama Stone*. It is a type of amethyst. Purple in hue, a symbol of royalty. It is known by other names. Some call it *The God Stone*. Others call it *The Dream Stone*.

It is also known as the final foundation stone of the *New City*."

Curious, John wanted to know more. "You mean that it is some kind of connector stone? Oh, I'm getting it. He wants to connect the *Achlama* to his city – his place of government!"

"Exactly!" Uzel replied.

John exclaimed. "But that would be –"

Uzel interrupted. "Let me finish that sentence . . . catastrophic for mankind."

"But why hasn't *The Maker* intervened . . ."

Uzel's face looked like thunder.

"What, you mean . . . he has already?" John was beginning to understand the backstory. It happened two thousand years ago, but it seemed obvious now!

"This has all been recorded in the prophecies, but you chose to ignore at your peril. And yes! He already sent the *Special Messenger* to warn you and open up your eyes.

Don't you remember what he said?

"I have come to tell you the truth, to set you free and let you out of your prisons."

He did everything he could to warn you, and look what your kind did to him."

"That's what my mother was trying to tell me, he didn't come to start another religion?"

Obviously frustrated, Uzel responded: "What do you think!" then walked away.

John tried to follow him, but the plane hit a pocket of turbulence knocking him off-balance, and he ended up back in his seat.

An hour later, after giving John and the others time to digest what he had told them, Uzel returned to give them an update on the flight.

Feeling somewhat responsible, John asked him. "Is there anything we can do to change the outcome?"

The reply. "Of course, you all can play a part in restoring the damage."

"Yes, but what should I do?" John enquired.

Uzel answered without hesitation: "You know that we want you to go back, John. I mean to Geneva."

John half-smiled. "I guessed that if I don't, Cain will never leave us alone. But I made a covenant with him. It was the wrong covenant. *The Maker* will never forgive me."

Uzel disagreed. "Oh John, he already has forgiven you, but you can be more useful in the enemy's camp. But still, he won't force you. You can choose to stay here. He will find another way."

With great compassion, Uzel looked down on Sarah as she slept; his eyes could not hide his sadness. "Don't worry – you have some time to think it over."

John looked over at his sleeping wife and understood. "You're giving me this time with her."

The Messenger always found this type of news difficult to deliver. He touched John's hand. "Enjoy these last few days with her. Make it special."

John spent the remainder of the flight next to his beloved wife, his heart pouring out tears of liquid sorrow.

They landed in the early evening at Oban airport. Grey skies and torrential rain greeted the Kayin family as they walked across the tarmac to the terminal building. The weather seemed to suit their solemn mood.

Ruel spoke to the group as they stood at the entrance to the building. They would have to do a time-shift once more as none of them had passports, nor did they have Cain's influence over custom officers.

Sarah called out, trying to lighten their mood. "Someone is going to have to do a lot of explaining about who landed that jet!"

Everyone laughed as they turned to look back at the abandoned plane.

They stood together, holding hands, and immediately transferred to the other side of the building where Samu was waiting in the camper van. The last ferry had departed an hour before, so they found accommodation for the night. No-one really knew why they were returning to Iona, but it seemed like the obvious place to go. At least they could meet with the others and make some plans.

Then I saw the New Jerusalem descending out of the heavenly realm . . .the city wall was made of Jasper. The twelve foundations of the city walls were decorated with every kind of precious stone – jasper, sapphire, agate, emerald, onyx, carnelian, chrysolite, beryl, topaz, chrysoprase, turquoise, and the twelfth – amethyst. Revelation 21v19 NIV

Chapter 34

The Awakening

They reached Iona by midday and met with the islanders who'd gathered at the cathedral to hear the news. The air was thick with questions, causing a buzz to reverberate around the ancient sleepy building.

Some wanted to know about what happened in Geneva and about the *Firestones,* but everyone wanted to ask the pressing question about the future. How would they manage to overcome their enemy? Sarah had been sitting patiently at the back of the hall.

The crowd started to quieten as she walked slowly forward. Everyone hushed as they could see that she was weak.

Refusing to sit down, determined, she held onto the table in front of her. "Whatever the *Kosmocratoras* offer you – and believe me, they will offer you an incredible future – let my passing be a warning to you all."

Whispers spread through the building, charging the atmosphere with fear. Was Sarah dying?

She interrupted their murmurings. "Please, everyone, settle down and listen." She waited for silence. "Cain offered to restore my body to full health and told me that I'd live forever, and naively I believed him. You see, he knew exactly what he was doing. It's no fun being sick, and so he cast his line, and I swallowed the hook. It sounded so wonderful – but the truth is, the treatment didn't work."

"Unfortunately, the claims of *Nanotechnology* being able to solve just about every medical problem doesn't quite line up with reality. We humans just don't realise the advanced technologies they are using now, but I need to warn you that it is still in the research process, and little is known about the long-term effects.

It is just a matter of time before they offer everyone the elixir of eternal life. I was simply part of a grand attempt to or alter – or should I say recreate – our *DNA*.

Please listen to me. The consequence of accepting these new technologies are far-reaching." She deliberately paused and looked around the room.

"I want you to understand this. If you choose this way – your adapted bodies will no longer be human. In effect, you will be an eternal non-human entity.

Are you getting this?"

Everyone affirmed that they understood. "You've all heard of *Transhumanism,* and probably you think it's *pseudoscience*. It's not!"

Sarah continued to inform the group, hoping that she was getting through to them. She looked down at her hands, her knuckles had turned white with the strain of holding on, but she was bent on finishing her story.

"Regrettably – by default – we are all being sucked into this new world every day. They are marching us towards a soulless, post-human existence."

She stopped for a moment to catch her breath.

"Be aware, this is not far into the future. It is happening now!

You may think that what I'm telling you sounds unbelievable, like science fiction, but believe me – I was living in a nightmare. I stopped listening to the truth and let that *Beast* tempt me with his utopian new world! Sure! Of course, the treatment bought me a little bit of extra time, but now I am dying." Sarah could feel the unrest spread through the group, but still, she pressed on. "Believe me, they will find a way to tempt you and use any little weakness to draw you in. I am warning you. Resist with all of your being!"

They had to know what was happening, and so she continued to explain. "I regret what I have done and I can't change that now, but I can expose the plans of the *Kosmocratoras*. They have devised a two-stage upgrade. Firstly, to repair any damaged cells and secondly to change your mortal *DNA* to immortal. You see, my body needed to be repaired before they transplanted the *immortal DNA,* but the repair didn't work, so I will no longer be eligible for the upgrade. In the little time I have left, I can only tell you what they are planning to do! But I'm just a little fish, and in reality, I was bait to catch John. He is their prize possession now." Sarah paused to look at her husband and her son, clearly upset, but this moment was too important for tears.

She pleaded, "Please don't be fooled by Peter Kayin. He is a master when it comes to manipulation."

John stepped forward, his eyes looking around at many startled faces. They all gave him their full attention as he spoke.

"Please listen. Cain knew exactly how to appeal to my needs, and unfortunately . . . I'm a greedy man. I'm ashamed to admit that I listened to his smooth talk. My life was so difficult at the time, so – to tell you the truth, I knew deep down what I was doing was wrong, but I didn't care about the consequences. I just wanted someone to fix everything.

At first, I convinced myself that my motives were pure. You see, he promised me that he could make Sarah well. That may sound altruistic on my part, but I have to tell you that I was overwhelmingly seduced by the promise of great wealth and immortality.

He will use a time in the near future when mankind is vulnerable. It will be a time when we will all be looking for *A Saviour*. But you don't want to be trapped in his web of deceit. You've heard our stories of how we both fell into Cain's trap, but it was Josh who put us right."

He cast his eyes around the room to find his son.

Josh was standing at the back of the hall, his face greyish. He hadn't faced the reality of his mother's imminent demise. It was shocking to hear her say it publicly. As a family, they hadn't had a chance to face this together in private.

He hardly heard his father as he explained to the group about his entanglement with Cain.

"You see, my friends, nothing comes free, and the cost of immortality was pretty high. My body would have been used as a perpetual donor and picked clean of my modified *DNA*. And! I totally ignored the fact that his wealthy friends would be the recipients of superior gene editing and the rest of you . . . well, you can imagine!

Be warned! There is a great price to be paid!"

Rhona spoke up. "Hasn't this been their plan throughout history – to create a two-tier slave and master race? Only this way would be catastrophic. There would be no escape for the slaves. Ever! What do you think?"

John let the silence answer. He then spent the next few hours detailing he *Kosmocratoras* plans for the future.

At this point, Duncan spoke up. "We've been reading the prophecies for so many years. This has all been written down for us, but it's hard to believe we are now living in the days foretold so many years ago. What can we do?"

This time Sarah responded without hesitation. "You have to go and warn as many people as possible!"

Matthew had listened carefully to everyone. Usually, it wasn't in his nature to make any decision in haste, but he was fully aware that Cain's plan would be implemented soon, now that he had the *Firestones*. He took his position next to John.

The excited crowd began to quieten down as one by one they noticed their leader waiting to speak. He gazed at the people for a few minutes, knowing what he had to say required their full attention.

"What Sarah said is true. We must tell people about what they are planning to do, and so we will need a well-coordinated plan to reach as many people as possible."

Struggling, Matthew closed his eyes. "As individuals, we will find it difficult to resist the *Kosmocratoras,* but collectively we can stand against this assault on everything it means to be human. Let it be our quest to expose the real cost of this so-called upgrade."

Matthew was so angry that he could hardly speak. He'd been kept imprisoned for so long with little power to fight back. With the revelation about the *Kosmocratoras,* he was determined to fight Cain and his kind with every fibre of his being. He gave an impassioned plea to everyone in the room.

"We need to be fully aware of the consequences of what they are planning to do." Everyone hushed, transfixed. Waiting on tenterhooks to find out how to navigate the future.

"They are guiding us into the event horizon – none of us are truly grasping this great delusion." John's voice quivered as he made this announcement.

"If they succeed, we will enter into a totally artificial evolution of mankind!"

Matthew reached out to support his son, encircling his arms around him.

"We've seen them, Dad. We've seen the Chimeras. They are half-man, half beasts. The transformation has already begun." He sobbed into his father's chest.

Matthew could hardly contain his wrath against *The Beast* they called Cain. Searching the faces of his people, he announced. "Now, we are the ones who have been given the knowledge of how to stop this madness. We have a great task to complete."

The mood was sombre. Everyone seemed reluctant to speak until Duncan made a comment.

"Best not to use the internet. They will probably block or alter anything we post. We really need to do it the old fashioned way."

People began to shout out suggestions. Relieved that people were grasping their positions, Matthew responded.

"Yes, you are right, Duncan, everyone, yes, we need to go to all the corners of Scotland first. Then! As we gather momentum, we can go further afield, hopefully with more help as others hear about their plans. There are so few of us that are physically up to the challenge."

Someone shouted. "We only need a few dedicated people. It's been done before. The one known as the Celtic Dove left this island to reach the people of Scotland. St Columba went with only twelve others." The mood lightened, and they all cheered.

Josh reminded Matthew about the Messenger he had met at Dunadd. The man had entreated him to bring Matthew to the fort. After a couple of hours of debating, they reached a consensus. They would all go to Dunadd to meet the enigmatic *Messenger*. It was a short journey from Oban, and they all agreed that the sacred staff the man had wanted to give to Matthew could be crucial for their journey ahead. They planned to make their way there and then travel throughout the country, working in small groups of two or three. It was comforting to know they already had a healthy network of people throughout the land they knew they could rely on for accommodation and support.

As it was getting late in the day, and as the last ferry had sailed, they decided to leave early the next morning.

No-one objected when John requested to stay behind on the island with Sarah. Josh waited until the group dispersed, but there were no words to express their family's sadness. They needed some time together.

Matthew stood in the doorway and looked back at his newfound family, sensing that he hadn't quite earned that level of intimacy they needed right now. With deep sadness, he left them, giving them space to mourn together.

Early the next day, they gathered in the hall to plan their journey. It wasn't long before they realised that their main problem would be transport as the island was a car-free zone, so few people owned vehicles. They had access to the camper van, the transit, and a car.

Robert, a local bus driver on Mull, offered his services. He joked, "The tourists will have a long way to walk today!"

Matthew replied, "Great! that solves our problem about us all getting to Dunadd.

Emma, Robert's daughter, pointed out: "But dad, you might lose your job! You can't just take a public service bus without anyone noticing."

Without hesitation, Robert replied, "This is our time, lass. The whole world is about to come under the deception of the *Kosmocratoras*. We all need to be ready to make sacrifices to stop them. You know this, Emma. You've seen the visions."

She wavered, then replied, "I'm sorry, Dad, I'm just a bit . . . scared."

Robert put his arm around his daughter. "We all are lass. But this is our time; it's our destiny."

Matthew spoke again. "We'll have to get in touch with all the people we know in Oban and ask if we can borrow their cars. Morag has been busy overnight, making lists of the groups we should contact. If this works, each team will send out more people so that every area will be covered."

Angus spoke up, "Do you think they will believe us?"

Matthew didn't flinch, although he was thinking the same thing. "I certainly hope so!" After this, he paused for a few moments, deep in thought. "I guess humanity will divide. Some who choose the way of Cain and the one's who know of the prophecies and have been waiting for this day."

The ferry landed in Oban around noon. Matthew had contacted the local group to tell them about their plans and to drum up some support. Fortunately, he had known James for many years, so it didn't take long to persuade him to arrange to meet others who would be willing to help.

He was keen to be involved and was pretty sure that he would have more than a dozen willing helpers. James was also keen for his people to accompany them to Dunadd, so he put out an urgent call. Within an hour, the hall was full of locals ready to join the islanders.

Matthew told the gathering of all that had transpired. If the support they received was anything to go by, he was hopeful for a similar countrywide response. There was an overwhelming offer of cars, food, and accommodation. Everyone wanted to help.

No one seemed surprised by the revelation as many of them had been given dreams and visions of these times and were eager to be involved. James looked pleased as he turned to Matthew.

"We've been waiting for a very long time. It's a privilege to come with you!"

Everyone was relieved when they arrived at the Hill-fort to find it deserted, so the enthusiastic group wasted no time as they clambered up the rocky mound. The less able-bodied were pushed and pulled up to the terraces as the hill was tricky to negotiate at some parts.

The group was surprised to see the place of the coronation stone had been dug up and the genuine stone exposed and ready to receive its next leader. Someone must have known they were coming and had carefully removed the replica stone. The true stone lay about a foot under the surrounding turf. Now the engravings of the boar and the mystical *Ogam Writings* were clearly visible, and the sacred footprint had waited patiently for well over a thousand years to welcome the new leader. Matthew noticed that they matched the etchings on the true *Stone of Destiny*.

No-one wanted to miss this moment. They had seen it before in their dreams and knew it was coming.

Half an hour passed, and the excitement grew as they waited in anticipation for the *Messenger* Josh had spoken of. "Look out there!" he shouted.

A steady stream of cars could be seen travelling along the distant road, then turned into the single-track road heading towards them.

Just then, a voice called down to them from the upper terrace.

"This is the day spoken of old. The gathering of sons and daughters. We must wait for them!"

Over the next few hours, the hill and surrounding fields were bathed in light as hundreds of people held up candles and torches.

Matthew stood in awe of all that was happening, then he looked up at the incredible being standing proud with the staff in his hand. Then Matthew shouted. "Who are you?" A mighty voice echoed all around the moors in response, "I am The Spirit of Scotland come to anoint the leader!"

The land shook as a roar went up from the crowds.

It was an incredible sight to behold as the *Spirit Being* – who looked in every way like a man – seemed to emanate blue-white light as he descended the narrow path to the coronation stone.

People were laughing; some were crying as they witnessed the sacred scene. The able-bodied climbed to the upper terrace to secure a better view. Many, determined to be right up-close to everything, clung precariously to the edge of the hill.

When everyone was in place, the man spoke out with a loud booming voice so that everyone could hear.

"Ah Josh, we have met before. You have brought me the faithful one. He has waited three and thirty years and has been proven worthy. Behold the one who will lead the *Great Awakening!*"

He held up the staff and pointed at Matthew. The crowd cheered jubilantly.

The one known as the *Spirit of Scotland* beckoned Matthew to approach the sacred coronation stone. Dressed in the highland attire of kilt and sash, the ancient being was a formidable sight. He opened up a beautiful reliquary box, the colour of the deepest ultramarine, and the lid made of the finest gold, fashioned in an intricate filigree design.

His hand drew out a brilliant sparkling gemstone, then handed it to Matthew, announcing: "This is the *Achlama*. Matthew looked upon the royal, purple *Firestone* and cried out.

Again the *Spirit Being* spoke out: "Now place the stone upon this staff." Matthew followed the instructions – although his heart was racing, he obeyed. He had led such a quiet restrained life until that day, but he knew this was his time to take up his position. He strengthened himself, stood tall, and received the staff – it was now the time to fight back.

"Are you ready, Matthew Kayin?" the ancient-looking man asked in a loud voice for all to hear.

Without hesitation, Matthew answered, "I am!"

"Now place your foot into the stone and say after me:

'I make a covenant with this land to be as a husband as he marries his wife. To be married to the land and to the people of this land as their leader.'

Will you bear this responsibility?"

Matthew took hold of the staff as a symbol of his pledge. "Gladly. I will."

The *Firestone* lit up, and a beam of light shone from one end of the valley to the other.

In the fields below, great celebrations began. The crowd was enthralled. Musicians played the Celtic sound of drums and the lowland pipes, causing spontaneous dancing to break out amongst the people.

No-one knew how long into the evening the celebrations lasted but victory was achieved that night. Everyone went home knowing exactly what they should do. Every inhabitant and every square inch of land would know that this was the land of the prophetic people. The years of waiting were over.

Chapter 35

The Resistance

As the celebrations were taking place at Dunadd, a poignant drama played out in Sarah's bedroom in Iona. As John held her tightly in his arms, he looked outside the window and saw a lonely figure waiting on a hillside not far from the house. Sarah turned, then looked back at John. Her eyes a mixture of sorrow and relief.

They both knew. Their time together was drawing to an end.

Sarah tried to comfort her husband. "It's alright, John, I'm ready!"

John burrowed his head in the crook of her neck as he tried to hold back the tears.

"Remember, you can speak to me any time, and I will hear you. Our spirits are joined forever. It's only going to be a short time, then we will be together again." She whispered softly as she ran her fingers through his hair, then stroked his cheek as she kissed him.

John tried to speak through the strained rise and fall of his chest as he struggled to breathe. He spoke between great sobs of grief and sorrow. "It's me who should be comforting you, my love. I . . . I, just don't know –"

Just then, Ruel came towards them, his eyes fixed on Sarah.

"I promise you, Sarah, I'll defeat Cain. No matter what it takes!" John whispered as he let go of her hand.

He had expected that Sarah would close her eyes and take her last breath, but to his surprise, Ruel held out his hand to her.

The grieving couple's eyes met briefly. There were no words.

She slipped out of his arms and walked out the door with Ruel in bodily form then, vanished.

John threw himself on the bed where Sarah had lain and wept bitterly.

He fell into a deep sleep – upon wakening, he was startled to see Uzel lying across the end of the bed. The compassionate *Messenger* saw John's tear-stained face and looked at him with great concern.

John noticed a single tear fall from Uzel's large brown eyes and flow down his cheek, gathering at the corner of his mouth.

Surprised, he uttered. "You're crying, Uzel!"

"Yes, my friend, it makes me very sad each time I see you separated from someone you love. It feels like it is also happening to me!" John felt overwhelmed by the love Uzel was expressing.

"I had no idea that you . . ."

"Ah! You thought I had no emotions, John? If only you could understand. I have been with you since the day you were born. Don't you know that I am intertwined with your life?"

Utterly bereft, John blurted out: "I don't know why you stay. I've failed everyone. And on top of losing Sarah, I now have to go alone back to Cain's headquarters. I don't know if I can handle that! Why can't the *Maker* just stop him? Why doesn't he just destroy them all?"

Uzel sighed deeply. "If only it were that simple. He can't do that because Cain is immortal.

The Omega Point is almost upon us. The prophets have spoken of this since the beginning of time. Everyone gets to choose their destination, and everyone chooses who will be their King. Don't you think that is fair?"

John agreed.

"Come with me. I have something for you." Uzel handed John a small item wrapped up in a deep ultramarine blue cloth with a fine-linen lining.

"Open it, John. Inside you will find a white stone. It was foretold that such a gift would be given to the ones who will overcome the *Kosmocratoras*. This stone is a prophecy unfolding. Look here, there is a message written within that will give you great courage."

John tentatively unwrapped the stone. The moment he held it in his hand, it started to glow and change colour; it took on the appearance of a large blueish-white diamond.

"This stone has electrical properties. Think of this as your personal walk-talkie." Uzel jested.

"You know I can only manifest in this world at certain times, but you can use this to speak to us. Only you will be able to see it, and only you can read it."

Immediately John strengthened. He gazed deeply into the stone until the pupils of his eyes dilated. He shook his head in disbelief, then he looked up.

"It's okay, Uzel. I know what to do. I'm ready to go back."

Within an hour, they were standing on the airport tarmac. The plane was still parked on the runway where they left it, as if time had been standing still for the last two days.

Uzel placed both hands on John's shoulders. Looking with great compassion upon his charge, he pulled him in close to his chest. "After we have completed the time of the *Great Awakening*, we will move into a new era.

Your father, Matthew – truly a great man – has taken his place over Scotland to lead his people, and will give instruction to many. Cain's kingdom will completely collapse over the territory of the Scots – it has already begun.

Many now understand the prophecies regarding this peculiar people. Surely, it is their destiny to defeat the enemy. It will start here and be like a fire spreading across the world. *The Destiny Stone* was brought here as a deposit thousands of years ago. It still cries out! Nothing is by chance. The cry has also risen from the spilled blood of the people of *The Covenant*. These seeds have been lying dormant in the land, waiting for the right time to germinate. Now is that time!

We must return to Geneva for a short time, and then on to Jerusalem. We have to return the *Destiny Stone* to its rightful place.*"*

"Jerusalem!" John shuddered. "Is that where Cain will set up his temple?

"Oh, John, it's much worse than that." The *Messenger* sighed deeply before adding, "Don't you realise that it's not a temple made of stones and mortar that he plans to rule from. It's the temple of your body that he seeks to inhabit!"

Feeling bereft and utterly alone, John's chest heaved in a wail as he cried out for his family.

Uzel tried to comfort him. "Don't be afraid, John. Sarah has no more pain, and I promise you, you will meet again; sooner than you think. You are all in position now.

Matthew has found his position as ruler over Scotland after many years of waiting and holding on; he knows what to do. Josh, your brave son, will be commissioned to go south, and you, my charge, will be a great light – in fact, our treasure, right in the midst of Cain's kingdom.

"I'm so aware that I just don't deserve this position," John said between sobs.

Uzel laughed gently. "*The Maker* doesn't always choose the perfect ones or even the brave ones. It's good enough that he sees the desire of your heart to defeat His enemy. You now understand their agenda like no-one else on this planet!"

Uzel lifted John up and roared like a lion. "Come, my friend. This is not the end. It's just the beginning. This is our destiny. We shall do this together!"

And he shall think to change the times and the law: and they shall be given unto his hand until a time and times and the dividing of time. Daniel 7:25 KJV

About the author
The author lives with her husband in Scotland; loves reading science fiction, thrillers, and mystery genres. She shares a common interest with her husband, visiting art galleries when they can and taking up a paintbrush to dabble in art projects together. She has always been fascinated with the concept of *Time*.

About this book
My journey to write this book has been somewhat unusual and had the unlikely origin in a café near the Jaffa Gate in Jerusalem.
Seven years ago when visiting the Holy Land, my friend and I were approached by a stranger. He told us incredibly detailed information about our lives; we were amazed at the accuracy of his words. As he was about to leave the café, he turned and looked directly at me with piercing eyes then told me about a future event. He said, "You will write about the Book of Revelation." Hence, the idea of writing this book was not my own.

After a period of wrestling with the idea, two years later, the quest to write my first book began. The title of the final book in the New Testament is derived from the Koine Greek text: apokalypsis or "the unveiling." Therefore, the book is written in the style of a modern-day parable, based on the book of Revelation. The story takes us on a speculative journey, uncovering possible events we could face in the near future.

The storyline ploughs into the ethical and moral decisions we will have to make as new technologies and medical procedures will allow us to alter our DNA. This technology is currently being tried and tested worldwide using *CRISPR* Cas 9 gene editing and Nanotechnology.

Every new advancement in science and technology has the potential for good, but history tells us that technology can also work against mankind. Are we on the cusp of the greatest existential threat to what it means to be human? Is there anything we can do about it? You decide.

Coming soon. A book series based on the mystical idea of Oneness.

The Blueprint of Heaven. Echad.

Website: lindakerr.com
Email: lindakerr.author@gmail.com